BREAKING THE CYCLE
OF VIOLENCE

BREAKING THE CYCLE OF VIOLENCE

Interventions for Bullying and Victimization

Richard J. Hazler, Ph.D.

Ohio University
Athens, Ohio

ACCELERATED DEVELOPMENT
A member of the Taylor & Francis Group

USA	Publishing Office:	ACCELERATED DEVELOPMENT
		A member of the Taylor & Francis Group
		1101 Vermont Avenue, N.W., Suite 200
		Washington, DC 20005-3521
		Tel: (202) 289-2174
		Fax: (202) 289-3665
	Distribution Center:	ACCELERATED DEVELOPMENT
		A member of the Taylor & Francis Group
		1900 Frost Road, Suite 101
		Bristol, PA 19007-1598
		Tel: (215) 785-5800
		Fax: (215) 785-5515
UK		Taylor & Francis Ltd.
		1 Gunpowder Square
		London EC4A 3DE
		Tel: 171 583 0490
		Fax: 171 583 0581

BREAKING THE CYCLE OF VIOLENCE: Interventions for Bullying and Victimization

1 2 3 4 5 6 7 8 9 0   B R B R   9 8 7 6

This book was set in Times Roman by Sandra F. Watts. The editors were Judith L. Aymond and Holly Seltzer. Technical development by Cynthia Long. Cover design by Michelle Fleitz. Printing and binding by Braun-Brumfield, Inc.

A CIP catalog record for this book is available from the British Library.
∞ The paper in this publication meets the requirements of the ANSI Standard Z39.48-1984 (Permanence of Paper)

Library of Congress Cataloging-in-Publication Data

Hazler, Richard J.
    Breaking the cycle of violence: interventions for bullying and victimization/Richard J. Hazler.
        p.   cm.
    Includes bibliographical references and index.

    1. Bullying.   2. Violence.   3. Aggressiveness (Psychology).
    4. Children and violence.   5. Victims—Psychological aspects.
    I. Title
    BF637.B85H37   1996
    371.5'8—dc20
                                                            96-21385
                                                            CIP
ISBN 1-56032-508-9 (cloth)
ISBN 1-56032-509-7 (paper)

TABLE OF CONTENTS

Section I
YOUNG PEOPLE IN TROUBLE

CHAPTER 1
CYCLE OF VIOLENCE   3

CHAPTER 2
DOMINATING BULLIES   21

Section II
PROMOTING ISSUES IN COMMON:
A MODEL FOR THERAPY

Section III
DIRECT ACTIONS FOR INDIVIDUALS AND GROUPS

LIST OF FIGURES

FOREWORD:
The Pain Doesn't Stop at Age 18

A Personal Subject

I know now, at age 50, that I (Richard Hazler) led a safe and secure life as a child. It was not so clear then because I had fewer life experiences with which to compare my day-to-day existence. My mother, father, and teachers were loving, friendly, caring and never raised a hand to me although they somehow convinced me to adhere to basic standards of behavior. I had plenty of friends. I was a good athlete. I walked to and from school, as did everyone within eight or so blocks of school. There was virtually none of the violence that many children see all around them today in their neighborhoods or on television. The stability and safety of that world is something I wish I could have given to my own children.

My childhood world never seemed as safe and secure as I now know it was. Bringing home one of many poor report cards, needing my mother to sign a disciplinary assignment, explaining rips in clothes, or hiding cuts that I got doing stupid things felt more like major life failures than normal childhood mishaps. During those periods of time when I would be teased or threatened by stronger or more verbal kids, I felt only inadequacy and failure no matter how minor or time-limited the maltreatment. No, my world did not *feel* safe. Perceived failures and dangers would cause me to ruminate about plans for running away or for having an accident where I would be badly hurt so that expectations of me would be lowered. I even considered the where, when, and hows of committing suicide.

I became an adult, thinking I had left my childhood fears behind. I pushed them further back as my teaching and counseling experiences put me in touch with children whose lives made mine look like a fairy tale. It was humbling even to consider that I could have complaints about my life when I compared it to the troubled lives of so many others. But those fears were not kept so easily out of my adult life. The fears came back in dreams and thoughts of failure and interpersonal inadequacy. I was doing fine and had no right to complain, so I hid my dreams and anxieties rather than admitting to them.

My experiences over time as a counselor, a parent, and a researcher slowly brought me to the recognition that a child's fears and anxieties are not tied closely to the adult's view of reality. The nature and extent of children's fears are associated more closely with the limited life experiences that they have had. Ideas such as "Things will work out" and "It will not last forever" have little meaning to a child whose only reality is yesterday, today, and tomorrow. Children live in an experientially limited world that magnifies their problems many fold.

If I have lingering repercussions from growing up in a safe, secure, stable, white, middle-class, male environment, then what are the continuing effects on those not so fortunate? I have worked with and known many people less fortunate than myself. Several years ago I began a professional relationship with one of those individuals, Tom Brown, who had both suffered greatly *and* undertaken a life of realistic actions to help others. His story is a sample of those that bring to mind my own childhood fears and also help me put my fears in their proper perspective. Tom gives me hope for all of us. People with Tom's courage have helped me grow in my understanding of children and how childhood impacts adulthood. Tom agreed to provide some of his story to help you understand the need for this book.

You Never Really Get Over It, by Tom Brown

I would get home from junior high school at about 3:30 in the afternoon, immediately retiring to my bedroom where I either would listen to music or lie down and read. I couldn't concentrate on the reading. Fear does that to you. There was nothing to be afraid of in my house, but I already was thinking about what would happen to me the next day at school.

I never told my parents about the bullying I was receiving in school. I was afraid that, being the caring parents they are, they would go to school and raise all kinds of hell, and then I really would be in trouble with the antagonists. I'm pretty sure that, after their butts were chewed out by the principal, they would know exactly who told and I'd be dead meat before the end of the day. It would be unrealistic to think that they could get warned to leave Tom Brown alone without knowing full well that Tom Brown and his parents shot their mouths off in the first place.

There was another reason I wouldn't tell. I was a boy. Although I was not "Joe-Jock" or "Mr. Macho" who could fight any battle, I was still a boy, and I needed to keep at least some small sense of pride. To admit that other boys were making fun of me or pounding the crap out of me daily would be admitting that I was a little baby unable and unwilling to defend or take care of himself. I couldn't do that; I wouldn't do that. So, I just took it-the hits, the punches, the slaps, the shoves, the names, the put-downs. You name it, I got it; I just took it.

One thing that I am proud of is the fact that at no time did I ever cry in front of these guys. I held it in, and believe me when I tell you from the depths of my soul that it isn't easy to hold in tears after some kid has just slugged you in the stomach or led an entire group of kids in a chorus of "Tom Brown is a lard-ass."

Gym class was a nightmare. Personally, I think that schools should do away with the notion that gym should be required in any grade. For all those skinny or athletically inclined kids it's just fine, but what about for those shy, overweight, or physically or emotionally challenged children? They don't want to be there, but they have no choice.

Gym is that time when all the "jocks" really shine, but the other kids basically get to look and feel like scum for an excruciatingly long hour. I would screw up in volleyball: Did they stop and show me how to set up better or handle the ball? No! Instead, it was, "you fat asshole" or "retard" or whatever clever little name they could hand me. I would strike out in baseball, just like the "jocks" would do as well on occasion. Did the majority of the kids put the "jocks" down when they struck out? No! However, when I or one of "my kind" struck out, we would be greeted either with a little insult or, if the coach wasn't looking, a hit or a pinch.

Taking showers after gym was even worse. Most 12-year-old boys are a little squeamish about undressing in front of other boys, especially if they are, like myself, overweight. It wouldn't have been so bad, I guess, if you could've stripped, showered, gotten out, dried off, and dressed quickly. But it wasn't that way. Some kids would make fun of you if you weren't an "ape" in certain regions or if you weren't as well endowed as they were. That wasn't the biggest problem though, because most of the boys parading around in the buff in that locker room weren't very well developed or hairy in all the right places, which did much for calming my nerves and sense of self-worth. In fact, I was more developed than a lot of the boys in that room, but I couldn't make an issue of it. I mean, how can you show pride with your developmental stage when your butt looks like 50 pounds of chewed bubble gum?

I remember one particular kid who thought he was an adolescent Adonis—slender, athletic, and the kind of cute that girls go nuts over. He made life absolute hell for me in that shower. It was not uncommon for him to shove me away from his favorite spot in the shower, spit on me, or grab one of my breasts and exclaim loudly for every person to hear that I genuinely needed a bra. (To this day, I absolutely cringe when I hear someone, usually a kid, tell another child that he needs a bra.) At other times, usually when there were just a few kids or maybe no one else at all around, he could be just plain sadistic. One instance that immediately comes to mind is when this fellow 12-year-old took one of my nipples and twisted it until it nearly broke off. I'm standing there naked and shivering in this shower, holding on to a bloody and torn nipple, and trying hard not to cry.

In my bed at night, I would lie there and think just what I could have done in my life to deserve this kind of treatment. I didn't hurt anyone. I was quiet. I was a nice kid. I wasn't a perfect kid. I could have been more help around the house, more willing to do things to help my mom and stepdad. I could have spent more time outside instead of being cooped up in my room. I could try to be more sociable or more interested in the things that boys are supposed to like, but the fact was, I hated myself for being such a loser and a baby when it came to fighting back. I just wanted to hide out alone. I prayed hard that somehow this would all end and, one late morning, it certainly appeared that God heard my prayer.

Our gym teacher announced that anyone who would rather not take gym but instead go "work out" in the dungeon was welcome to. I was flabbergasted. There were four of us who chose to do this—all victims of bullying, all either overweight or painfully thin, all totally inept at sports, and all eternally grateful for this salvation. We would have a separate time to change into our gym clothes and a separate time to take showers and get ready for our next class. Most of the time, there would be nobody but us in the shower or locker room once returning from the dungeon. It was incredible—a feeling of safety and security that I had not felt for a long time. I was absolutely giddy from the overwhelming sense of relief.

The dungeon was a cool place, literally. It was one of those abandoned fallout shelters and was located far back and underneath the nearby elementary school. You would walk quite a distance through those sparsely lighted tunnels, and then suddenly you would enter this well-lit room filled with weight lifting equipment. We didn't lift weights all that much at first. There was no supervision, so we didn't have to. Instead we would sit huddled together in one of the corners of that cool room and just talk and laugh. It was pure magic and a contrast that is impossible to describe from what we had endured during regular gym class, and it ended all too soon.

Someone got the idea to send over an older student with us, and the guy they picked was a ninth-grader. He was a total psycho, although nobody who mattered knew it. He was terrifying, and nobody had the guts or insanity ever to tell on him. He didn't look like the "bully from hell" that he was. He was tall, conservatively dressed, and wore dark-rimmed glasses. He looked like Robert Young of "Father Knows Best."

At first, it wasn't too bad. He would just pick one of us out and maybe slap us or knock the wind out of us or something. It wasn't a constant thing either. Even the "bully from hell" gets tired every once in a while and wants to rest. What was scary was never knowing when the ninth-grader suddenly would switch gears and pretend we were all punching bags. He convinced us we would be killed if we told. Now I went to bed at night out of my mind with the overwhelming fear that one of the other four would tell. The bully would be nailed—possibly suspended or expelled—and then someday, somewhere, he would get us.

No one told, but it got worse. Now the bully was inviting his friends to toy with us in the dungeon. They were even older and all kicked out of school for one crime or another. We would huddle together while they would circle, hit, and kick us in the stomach, legs, and back, but never in the face (that would leave marks). When they got bored, they would turn out the lights and stalk us, picking out one victim at a time.

I thought about killing myself a couple of times but didn't have the guts to do that either. I couldn't do that to my mom and stepdad and other people who loved me. One thought of them weeping at my funeral put any thoughts of suicide out of my mind. I was completely and totally helpless, and the situation seemed utterly hopeless.

One day the gym teacher told us that the administration decided not to allow anyone over in the dungeon, and that was it. The nightmare was over. As sick as it sounds, I was relieved to return to the name-calling, the put-downs, having my clothes thrown into the shower, and taking the occasional punch.

The following are things kids heard during my school days and the same things kids hear today:

"Being bullied is a part of growing up."
"You need to take up for yourself."
"Beat the shit outta someone who is picking on you."
"You need to toughen up, be a man."
"They tease you because they like you. They're just jealous."

Kids hear these things from people whom they love and respect. They hear these things from people who mean well. The respect kids have for these people makes the statements and the situation even harder to accept. For many years, I tried to create a tool to help with this problem. I wanted to make a film that would address the issue realistically and graphically by speaking directly to children. I wanted to touch the hearts of victims, bullies, and those children who are neither the victim nor the bully but who nevertheless choose to do absolutely nothing about it, contributing to this problem far more than they realize.

Between 1981 and 1990, this task was all trial and error, with each video becoming a little better than the last. The work began to take over my life but, with the exception of a few class presentations, the films sat on a shelf and collected dust. Schools weren't all that concerned, but I could see the kids' reactions and I knew it was important. Few authorities seemed to care, and some people actually ridiculed me for my obsession. One school principal actually told me he was "turned off" by my enthusiasm for the subject and hung up on me.

I almost had given up when a fifth-grade boy in a Child-Assault Prevention class I was teaching threw his arms around me and cried his heart out, soaking my flannel shirt. The boy had been told earlier in the day that he would be beaten up on the bus that afternoon. He told the principal but left feeling he was on his own. He told his teacher, but she was too busy. He somehow knew I would understand, so he told me.

I have never seen anyone cry that hard or shake that intensely. His fears and tears haunted me for days. He was terrified in school, and he felt completely alone with this problem. He was a victim of bullying. His childhood slowly was being ruined. His security was all but destroyed.

I felt hate for that principal and that teacher, but then I realized it wasn't just their apathy that was responsible. It was the bullies, the bystanders, and the entire system that needed to be reached. A few months later, I created *Broken*

Toy. This 27-minute video was my last-ditch effort to create a useful tool to help the many schools and individuals facing this problem. Over 2,000 schools in the U.S. and England are now using *Broken Toy,* and orders are coming in daily. It feels good but not good enough.

Recently, I was the subject of a syndicated program called *Life Choices.* The producers wanted to return to my school and that gym to interview me about how it feels to be back in that once nightmarish place. I wasn't expecting much of an emotional reaction since I was now a pretty secure adult. After all, I'm a 40-year-old movie critic for three publications and a somewhat successful educational and experimental video producer. I created a video that is actually helping children, I've appeared on the nationally televised "LEEZA" show several times, and kids even ask me to sign autographs after viewing the film in class. Surely I'd left my problems behind in childhood.

On that late-winter afternoon, however, in my old school for the first time in 19 years, I realized how close to me those problems had stayed. As I sat on that wooden bench in that gymnasium, with the camera in front of me, and that friendly producer standing nearby with a smile on her face, suddenly it all came back—that musty smell of sweat, the cold from sitting there in those thin blue shorts and the white T-shirt, that feeling of impending doom, that churning sick feeling, the fear of what would happen during and after gym class, in the locker room, in the shower, in the halls, in the lunchroom, on the playground, on the bus . . .

"lard-ass, retard, fat boy, momma's boy, fat-ass, big-tits . . ."
sticks and stones . . .
slap . . . punch . . . shove. . . .

I guess there are some things you never forget. The things that happened to me have affected me all my life whether I was thinking about them or not. You try to put thoughts and feelings away in a forgotten place, but they come back at times and in ways you don't expect. I hope Richard's book will help adults understand and deal better with their problems and the problems of their children. Most of all, I hope it will lead to safer and more secure childhoods for young people, that lead them to better quality lives as adults.

Tom Brown lives in Zanesville, OH where his work continues. Information on the film *Broken Toy* can be obtained by contacting Summerhill Productions, c/o Tom Brown, 846-1/2 McIntire Avenue, Zanesville, OH 43701 (phone: 614-455-2035).

ACKNOWLEDGEMENTS

The one person who has been a part of this project from its origins in my practice to final publication is my wife, Kitty Steen Hazler. For more than 25 years, Kitty has seen me through the traumas resulting from my continually pushing clients, students, friends, and family as well as ourselves to get the most from our abilities. She has been my wife, friend, cheerleader, editor, and critic while at the same time building her own life and managing our family. The freedom I have had to pursue what I felt were the "right things to do" even when they were financially and socially problematic is in large part attributable to her belief in me and the support she provides as my partner.

JoLynn Carney was instrumental in improving both the content and quality of this book. As a graduate assistant, she was totally reliable, required minimal supervision, found resources and materials well beyond my expectations, and always could be counted on to help me move forward when I was struggling to find the right words or ideas. JoLynn has evolved from working as my assistant to being a trusted friend and colleague with whom I look forward to many more years of a productive and enjoyable relationship.

The essence of this book comes from the young people, parents, professional colleagues, and friends who have knowingly or unknowingly communicated to me important aspects of their lives. Some shared their experiences through professional conversations, others in personal dialogues, and many were just there for me to observe during the struggles we all have in our quest for better ways of handling life's gifts and problems. Each of you has made your personal contribution to the thoughts, feelings, style, and content of this book that is greatly appreciated by myself and everyone who may benefit from it.

SECTION I
YOUNG PEOPLE
IN TROUBLE

Talking about my work with bullies and victims often brings responses I would not expect. Three types of comments stick out in my mind as being ones I would not have thought of years ago, but also being ones that help make sense of the problems on a larger scale.

One of my closest and brightest friends suggests my ideas are way off: "All societies use a form of bullying in order for the strongest to win out and promote the species. It is true for animals, prehistoric man, and modern man. Someone has to be on top and someone on the bottom. That is the way the world runs."

I always am thrown by his message because he is also a very peaceful person who is fair and reasonable with people. He is neither abusive nor particularly competitive and he is good at negotiations during conflicts. Yet his ideas on this subject are close to the most competitive people I know. Observing the societies of animals and humans also would tend to give substance to his argument.

Another friend who is more active in a variety of formal peace movements than anyone I ever have known shocked me one day with the following comment: "You know, I really do appreciate your work with bullies and victims. Helping kids is great, and I'm glad to see that someone cares about peaceful

1

people. I'm especially glad that someone is looking out for victims. It is about time victims get the chance to stick it to bullies."

I find that even among the most peaceful of people there is often a demand for revenge as this friend wanted. As much as most people want peace, caring, and nonviolence to be the way the world works, they frequently choose violence as a form of revenge when they or a loved one has been hurt badly. Human beings may be able to overcome violence in themselves, but it also would appear that violence is not overcome automatically.

Every time I am on a radio talk show, someone will call in and make a statement something like the following: "Aw, that's just kids. It happened to me and I turned out all right. Kids will grow up soft if they don't learn to deal with this kind of stuff."

Each of these statements speaks of people in conflict being a natural event and particularly for children. Seeking ways to control your own life and how to do that with as little abuse of another is something children must learn. Experimenting with bullying and experiencing mild forms of victimization are probably samples of the ways they learn about these aspects of themselves and relationship development.

Bullying in some form is probably an important childhood behavior where children gain knowledge and skills about how to deal with other people. Those who do not learn sufficiently, or who learn the wrong things, will suffer both as children and as adults. The majority eventually will learn how to get their own needs met without hurting others for the most part. The lessons are there for children to learn, but it is up to adults to set up the proper learning process and to follow through on the daily lessons of how to deal with people.

Violence among teenagers is rising rapidly and that seems at least partly attributable to the lessons they did or did not learn at younger ages. This section provides information on that increasing violence and its relationship to the development of bullying and victimization behaviors. Learning who victims and bullies are and the impact of being in those situations are the primary goals. This information provides the basis for future chapters that speak more directly to what needs to be done and how to do it in ways that will benefit all children and our society in the future.

Chapter 1

CYCLE OF VIOLENCE

Tom

Tom lived on Third Street, just down the block from the corner grocery store. He took different routes to the store when he thought he saw Bill or Cal in the distance. They were two of his worst tormentors. It wasn't much of a difference to go around the block to the store, Tom told himself, and it certainly made life easier when he could avoid trouble.

Bill and Cal didn't like Tom and took every opportunity to demonstrate their feelings. They would see Tom in the distance and go out of their way to get him. Tom could see the excitement in their eyes as they prepared to get him. Just the thought of that look turned Tom's stomach over, made him feel weak, and brought on an overwhelming sense of dread and personal inadequacy.

Then they were in front of him. "Hey fag, going to the store for your momma; going to meet a boyfriend? Will you be kissing him? Huh? Huh? Why don't you answer?"

They pushed, poked, and pinched Tom all the while they were talking to him. No matter what Tom said, they would use his own words against him as an excuse to hurt him physically and verbally even more. If he said nothing, they used that too. It was a no-win situation for Tom. Even when he finally got by them, he would feel no joy. Instead, there would be feelings of anger that must be suppressed for the moment because he did not know what to do with them. But he would dream of eventual revenge. Only his feelings of weakness,

3

embarrassment, and inadequacy remained as he went on his way hoping mostly to forget and make sure no one had seen him.

It is an ongoing story for Tom. On the way to the store, at school, or on the bus, he knows they will be trying to get him. It hurts when they do get him. It hurts when he worries about "it" coming. It even hurts in bed when he is just thinking about himself, his life, and the days to come. The worry just doesn't go away.

Mary

Mary quietly slunk out to the hallway as the class dismissed. She didn't want to do anything that would make the "in group" pay attention to her. Every time they got close to her, they embarrassed her to tears. They said the worst things about her: "Get away Pig! We don't want to catch what you've got. Where do you get your clothes? They're trash."

What hurt just as bad was the way they ignored her at other times. It was as if she wasn't even there. She could be sitting at the end of a crowded lunch table and no one would even look at her. She didn't know whether to be glad (i.e., at least no one is picking on her) or mad (i.e., no one seems to like her). She ate as fast as possible so she could go off quickly in a corner alone to read. Hiding out alone, she could avoid her tormentors for a while. She avoided everyone for that matter. It was a lonely and embarrassing place, but it also felt safe, if only for a little while.

No matter what Mary did, she felt awful. Even the rest of the kids who didn't pick on her, stayed away. They didn't want to be seen with her for fear that they would be picked on just like Mary. No one was proud of the way they acted, but personal, social, and physical fears, not pride, were their main concerns.

Carlos

Carlos just died in the hospital from gunshot wounds. Everyone in the neighborhood is saddened and scared. They know that this gang shooting will only escalate the violence that has been increasing among teenagers. Carlos was the 16-year-old leader of a gang that controlled the neighborhood.

How did this friendly first-grade child turn into this violent teenager whose life is now suddenly ended? When did harsh words and occasional fist fights turn into battles with guns and knives? Why have bloody noses been replaced by dead young people? How did a quiet and safe neighborhood turn into a violent battlefield? These are the questions adults in the community are asking themselves as they seek to understand how things got so bad. Except for those who would chalk all of this up to fate, everyone else realizes that these behaviors started somewhere. Perhaps more important, they realize that things could have been done or not done to reverse the progress of sickness that led to this trauma.

Sam

Sam came home with a ripped shirt, a bruised cheek, and scrapes on his arms. His mom was scared and furious at the same time. She sent her son off to a safe school and this is not what she expected to come home from such a place.

"Are you all right? How did this happen? Who did it? I'll get the kid who did this, whoever he is!"

Sam explained that an older kid punched him, "for no reason, Mom. I was just minding my own business on the playground when he ran into me going after some ball. Then he blamed me and I told him it wasn't my fault. He said I did it on purpose and then he hit me, threw me down, and stood over me. When my friends helped me up, he went back to his friends."

"Who is this bully? I'll see to it that he doesn't pick on anyone. He'll be punished for what he did to my little boy," Mom said with a bright red face and tears welling in her eyes.

Sam was not at all happy with his Mom's idea to get involved. "Mom, please don't do anything. Gene only bothered me one time before today. Sometimes we even have talked about stuff a little. Maybe it was just a bad day. I'm worried about what will happen tomorrow in school. But before you do anything, let me see how things work out. I don't want you to make things worse."

WHAT IS BULLYING?

Tom, Mary, Carlos, and Sam each have been hurt by other children, but probably they have not all been bullied. These youth, their parents, their friends, and the school will have different things to worry about depending upon whether these events were examples of bullying, the common mistakes of childhood, or other forms of violence.

Bullying can be commonly defined as repeatedly (not just once or twice) harming others. This can be done by physical attack or by hurting others' feelings through words, actions, or social exclusion. Bullying may be done by one person or by a group. It is an unfair match since the bully is either physically, verbally, and/or socially stronger than the victim.

The death of Carlos provides the most striking difference in the examples. Whether or not it was an example of bullying, a victim fighting back, or some other form of violence is not clear based on the information available. We have no sense of fault or history to guide us in understanding why this occurred. But such an occurrence is so obviously devastating and wrong that it will be condemned by virtually everyone regardless of its causes. Most bullying and victimization, however, is not this extreme or this obvious. The result is that bullying often goes on without peers and adults demonstrating the outrage and indignation they are likely to show in the case of Carlos. We become outraged over disasters but rarely over the events that lead up to the disasters.

When a group of people continually harms others, it often is called *mobbing.* Mary is clearly a victim of mobbing by a group of girls who are more socially powerful. That power comes in part by being a member of a group that allows select people in and demands that others stay out. This membership offers a form of status that is not available as individuals. It also allows members to avoid a degree of responsibility for negative behaviors by giving that responsibility to the group or to specialized individuals in the group rather than accepting responsibility for their personal involvement.

M. Scott Peck, in his acclaimed book *People of the Lie: The Hope for Healing Human Evil* (1983), emphasized the role of groups in the evil behaviors of individuals. He made the case for how easily individuals can abdicate moral responsibility to other specialized parts of the group. Allowing the leader of the group to decide rather than making one's own choice of behavior is one example. Often there also will be more aggressive or abusive group members who will be forgiven their behaviors and often even supported because "that is just the way they are." In each case, the choice can be made to abdicate one's own moral responsibility to the nature and needs of the group.

The mob uses its power to discredit Mary and reduce the weight of her potential accomplishments. The result is that Mary is put down, which in turn allows the mob of girls to feel they are better than Mary. They have managed to raise their own self-image by lowering another's. This is a common aspect of all bullying circumstances where one person or group devalues another to make themselves seem superior.

Another major difference between the examples is the fact that Sam was only attacked once or twice. The rarity of the attacks does not diminish the hurt Sam feels right now. He still will need support from family and friends, but the impact of being abused once or twice is not the same as being abused continually. Sam's rare victim experiences tell him he can be hopeful that tomorrow will bring a brighter day. Tom and Mary see much less hope for improvement in their situations because of how regularly those situations occur. Their discouragement is based on more consistent and long-term experiences that produce a bleak picture of the days to follow. They most likely will seek to avoid further contacts with anyone attached to their pain rather than believing in the possibility of finding a more positive solution to the problem.

WHEN IS SOMEONE A VICTIM?

Victims of all abusive acts, whether those acts are bullying or not, have common experiences that require assistance. Each of the previous examples carry physical and emotional pain and the individuals need help from others to get over that pain and its repercussions. Those who inflicted the pain were at least thoughtless about the welfare of their victim and at worst gleeful that they could inflict the pain. The common element for all victims of abuse is that they are harmed by others who verbally, socially, or physically attacked them.

All victims need support whether they were victims of bullying, another type of abusive act, or even victims of accidents. The experiencing of these traumas on a regular basis and by consistent perpetrators is what differentiates the victims of bullying from other victims. This repetition produces a negative outlook on their world and their place in it. The development of such a pessimistic outlook in an impressionable young person can produce a variety of long-term consequences that go beyond the psychological hurt that victims of isolated traumatic incidents experience.

Sam is not a classic victim of a bully because he only was attacked one time. He needed to know his friends were still with him and their actions proved they were there for him. He had to tell his mother about the incident because the results were obvious from his torn clothes and bruised body. Her support and willingness to comfort him were confirming for him although her level of anger and readiness to intervene on her own were not appreciated. Sam needed her comforting but not her intervention because he saw this as a single incident that he probably could rectify rather than the continuing act of a bully that true victims likely would feel unable to control.

Victims of bullies come in many different varieties. Some *innocent victims* have little to do with the causes of the bullying but still have choices to make on how best to deal with the situations. Other *provocative victims* may have very specific behaviors that encourage or aggravate the bullying. Most victims fall somewhere in between these extremes because they behave in some ways that either encourage the bully or at least reduce the normal hesitancy a bully might have to pick on a specific individual.

An example of a primarily innocent victim might be Tom who got along well in his old school before he moved to his new neighborhood. He was well-liked by his old schoolmates and came to the new school with a positive attitude even though he was anxious as almost any child would be. Unfortunately, a mixed group of boys and girls recently had been punished for problems they caused in school and their anger sought a safe target. Tom was a convenient and easy victim because he had no friends yet and didn't know his way around the school. Picking on him served no real purpose other than for the mob to regain some sense of power by putting down another person.

Tom did not understand what was going on and his first days at school were miserable. All he knew was that he was tormented continually by one group, a few others chose to pick on him from time to time individually, and all the other kids shied away from him. This was not the way it had been before and was not the way it was supposed to be. Tom had not been a victim of bullies previously and maintained a primarily positive outlook throughout his painful experiences. He was looking continuously for ways to improve things by gaining understanding of the motivations of others in the school and relating to them based on this increasing knowledge base.

Maintaining his positive attitude and going about his daily life in a regular manner helped Tom eventually make some friends. The more friends he gained and the more he learned about informal rules of the new school, the less useful he became as a scapegoat for the mob. They eventually lost interest and went on to other more vulnerable targets. He had maintained many of his best inter-personal behaviors, learned some new ways of acting, and created part of a support system that would make him less likely to be a victim. Only a couple of boys remained as tormentors and their actions were only successful when they could get Tom alone, which was less and less as Tom's friendships increased. Tom may not have found perfection, but at least he can see his world as both liveable and improving, which promotes faith that an even better future is possible.

A provocative victim provides a different picture. A victim being provocative does not excuse tormentors' abusive actions in any way; however, it does explain partly where their motivations originated. Ann was picked on consistently by two girls in a variety of ways. The worst of their tactics was cornering Ann in the bathroom where they would abuse her verbally abuse, mark on and tear at her clothes, and pull at her hair. Ann would complain immediately to the teacher and, after school, to her mother.

Ann was very friendly with the adults in school and was always ready to answer questions and do favors for the teachers. She also was ready to take favors from teachers and to make sure peers knew she got these favors that others didn't. Ann, her favorite teachers, and her parents were quick to point out to the bullies that Ann was the kind of girl they should be like. It was made clear by Ann that she was better than the bullies and that she had ways of putting them down and getting them in trouble that she would use whenever she wanted.

The bullies would get in trouble regularly for their actions, and Ann would be happy to tell them, as well as any other who would listen, how it was she who got them in trouble. Ann did get revenge and the bullies both resented it and appreciated having it as an excuse to strike again. The resentment served to fuel the bullies desire to get back at Ann even harder. A vicious cycle was forming that is common in relationships between bullies and provocative victims. Provocative victims, hurt by bullies, use their provocative ways to get back at the bully, but their success only causes additional acts of vengeance toward the victim, retaliation from the provocative victim, and so forth. It is a cycle not easily broken when all sides are feeling devalued, hurt, and able to hurt the other side back. It can be the cycle of bullying and victimization for youth and the cycle of war for adults.

Whether Ann's actions were right or wrong was less important to her continually being bullied than was the fact that she added to the bullies feeling of being put down. What she did provided additional excuses for the bullies to continue their actions. Ann was helping to maintain a competition between herself and her bullies that encouraged them to fight back. None of the girls would accept responsibility for their own part in the interactions and therefore the situation continued.

WHEN IS SOMEONE A BULLY?

Bullies behave differently from others who get into occasional physical, social, or verbal hassles. Conflict between human beings is normal and it should be expected that children will not be as good at handling it as adults should be, not that adults are particularly good at it either. Young people do not have the life-time of experiences with interpersonal relationships that adults do. Successful adults were not always good at relationships. They were the ones however, who were able to learn from their mistakes. Many of the abusive behaviors in children are those mistakes that hopefully will be used to develop more acceptable ways of relating to others.

Normal verbal, social, or physical conflicts among children tend to be occasional happenings in which either or neither side may come out victorious. Conflicts involving bullies are different in that they continue over time in a pattern where only victims with a weakness that the bully can exploit easily are chosen. Bullies will continue to abuse specific victims who have less verbal, social, or physical prowess than themselves, but they do not attempt to pick on those who might have as much or more of the bully's qualities. This behavior is not a testing of the bully's power and skills; instead, it is the use of the bully's obvious prowess in a given area to hold down another individual, thereby demonstrating their power over the victim.

Carlos had become a bully, but he had not been that way always. Many bullies start out as victims either at home or at school. The frustrations from being hurt, humiliated, and controlled by another often produce deep feelings of anger and a desire for revenge. Victims often have imaginary scenarios where they maim or kill their tormentors to their great satisfaction. Usually they recognize that even thinking in this way is unacceptable behavior so they tell few people of such thoughts; however, when a gain in physical, verbal, or social power offers the chance to seek revenge, they are likely to take the opportunity in some form. Victims who gain power can turn into bullies easily.

Small size and being slow in school were Carlos' burdens as a young child. His chance for power came when he realized that he had the ability to befriend and direct many of the outcasts of the system. Here was a group of angry young men who saw no real hope for themselves within the system that seemed to be stacked against them and was unwilling to recognize their needs. They wanted little more than to show people how important they really could be and Carlos recognized how to do just that: *intimidation.*

Carlos and his friends became a gang when they recognized they could intimidate weaker individuals with little immediate risk to themselves. Intimidating a few caused many others to stay out of their way. The result was that Carlos' gang gained substantial influence even though they had never really had to test themselves against a relatively equal opponent. This new found power allowed them to thumb their noses at the school and community that disapproved of their actions.

What would stop bullies? Once bullies know they cannot demonstrate their power over another at will, they begin to look for another potential victim. Traditional literary themes depict a young hero, who always is being picked on, developing into a strong, self-assured individual. These changes cause the bully to give up trying to overpower the hero after several failed attempts. Similar literary themes follow the socially inept girl as her appearance and social skills grow to a point where she eventually wins over her tormentors and they all become close friends. These themes arise from real-life events that demonstrate that bullies cannot continue successfully to pick on people who have the self-confidence and persistence to maintain their strengths and improve on their weaknesses.

WHEN IS SOMEONE A BYSTANDER?

Bystanders are probably the most overlooked group when attention finally is given to a bullying problem. These are the people who stand on the sidelines and do not get involved. Professionals, parents, and friends understand that they need to pay attention to the victims because they see them as receiving the brunt of a hurtful situation. The bully or criminal gets attention because our society demands punishment of those who harm others wrongfully. Less often, some will recognize that bullies need therapeutic interventions as well to provide them with more appropriate ways of interacting with others for the betterment of everyone. Bystanders, on the other hand, do not get much attention even though the impact of the events on them can be great.

It is hard on a person's self-respect and self-confidence to see someone get hurt and know that he or she has done nothing to stop it. Bystanders generally remain on the sidelines because they don't know what it is they should do. They are fearful of becoming the brunt of the bullies' attacks or that they might do the wrong thing that causes even more problems. Entering the middle of a conflict situation where who is right, who is wrong, and whether you can gain the upper hand will raise any normal person's level of fear. The emotionally safest route generally looks like the avoidance of getting involved and it is by far the most common route taken.

The desired result of avoiding involvement is that any clear or obvious direct confrontation and potential failure are avoided. The negative consequence is to give bystanders a feeling of powerlessness, similar in some ways to that of victims. Victims know everyone is watching and that a loss of everyone's respect is a real possibility because the actions are so obvious. The negative consequences for bystanders are more subtle. Their own loss of self-respect and the fear that others might recognize their failure to act is not as obvious as being involved directly. Keeping out of the situation is a way that bystanders can control their potential for failure in the eyes of others, but they still forfeit a significant part of their own self-respect.

HOW EXTENSIVE IS THE PROBLEM
OF BULLYING?

People such as Tom, Mary, Carlos, and Sam are not the exception in today's society. They are the majority. Research tells us that bullying is a much larger problem than many adults, including professionals, realize. Much bullying goes undetected by adults even though the effects have significant impact on individuals, groups, and the total environment of schools and communities (Cole, 1977).

Appearing on the national talk show "Leeza," I was asked, "Everyone in the audience has had experiences like this. How widespread is the problem?" Leeza and her audience had answered the question for themselves. You cannot get a room full of teenagers or adults together without virtually all of them recognizing that they have been touched in some way by an episode of bullying, and the research collected to date would confirm these informal observations.

Violence and abuse against other humans are problems for all communities. They are obviously apparent in the most dangerous communities that make news headlines every day. But they are also apparent in those places traditionally identified as the safest places to live, to work, and to send children to school. Justice Department statistics for 1989 show that rural, suburban, and city students report very similar rates of being victims of violence or fearing violence (7% to 8% in each type of location) (Gutscher, 1993). It is not a problem confined to only one area or one group of people.

Neither is bullying a problem that is confined to one generation. A family gathering of teenagers, parents, grandparents, and great grandparents would find everyone with experiences and opinions on bullies, victims, and what to do about the problem. Each person would have stories about what they experienced, what they saw, and how they or others handled the problem. There would be no lack of opinions on the prevalence of the issues or how to deal with them.

The great common knowledge about bullying and victimization is in stark contrast to the small amount of actual research done. The fact is that, in comparison to other areas of research, relatively few studies help demonstrate the extent, nature, and impact of the problem. Until recently, very little research was available on the topic in the United States (Hoover & Hazler, 1991) or in much of the rest of the world for that matter (Besag, 1989). Only the Scandinavian countries, Japan, and Australia have shown consistent interest in evaluating and dealing with the problem in an organized way.

Casual discussions of widespread, common experiences with bullying and victimization seem to be confirmed by research with middle and high school students. Studies from even the safest, small-town environments find that more than three out of four students report being bullied (81% of males and 72% of females) (Hazler, Hoover, & Oliver, 1991). These numbers are even more startling when you consider that they only deal with reports of being bullied on or around school grounds, which should be one of the safest places in a child's life.

The problem of bullying is not likely to stand on its own. The greater probability is that bullying reflects the increasing visibility of violence in our society. The years 1980 to 1990, for example, showed a 79% increase in the number of young people (ages 15 to 24) committing murders. The same period showed a 50% increase in assault arrests by youth. The changing situation is particularly relevant to the United States where the homicide rate has been estimated to be as much as 11 times greater than the other industrialized nations (U.S. = 22 per 100,000 and all others = 2 per 100,000) (Fingerhut & Kleinman, 1990).

Violent juvenile gangs are on the increase in most parts of the country and particularly in the inner cities. A national survey of school crime (Bastian & Taylor, 1991) reported that 15% of students felt their schools had gangs, and others concluded that gang activity is emerging in almost every U.S. community both large and small. Los Angeles County alone reported 771 gang-related murders in 1991 (Drass, 1992).

Families are supposed to be ultimate safe havens for young people. This too does not seem to be the case for increasing numbers of youth. The number of single-parent households has increased by 200% since 1970 so that one out of five children has only one adult at home for support on a daily basis. Families also have less income on which to rear their children, and this is particularly true for the most common single-mother families situation (Center for the Study of Social Policy and Annie E. Casey Foundation, 1991). Perhaps these serve as examples of the potential reasons for why, according to the President of the Children's Defense Fund, Marian Wright Edelman, there are three times as many reports of child neglect and physical or sexual abuse of children since 1980 (Edelman, 1994). Perhaps they also convey why we should be less than surprised that an estimated 70% of juvenile offenders come from single-parent families (Federal Bureau of Investigation, 1992). The family and home of today clearly has less social and financial stability and fewer opportunities for communication, support, and supervision than have been available to children in the past.

The problem of violence in schools finally has forced itself into the consciousness of our society. Each month over a quarter of a million students report being physically attacked. One in five high school students avoid the school rest room out of anxiety about safety (Learning Publications Inc., 1988). Clearly, Tom, Mary, Carlos, and Sam are not exceptions. Situations similar to theirs with equal or greater consequences can be found again and again in schools across the country.

Teachers and schools recognize the changing levels of violence though they are less clear on how to stem it. One poll showed that 44% of teachers believe that disruptive school behaviors are getting worse. A poll in 1940 showed that the top disciplinary problems were the following:

talking out of turn,
chewing gum,
making noise,
running in the halls,
cutting in line, and
dress code violations.

How far is that world from the same poll taken in 1990? In 1990, the top disciplinary problems reflected a much more troublesome environment for our children and those who care for them:

assault,
robbery,

drug abuse,
pregnancy, and
suicide (Toch, 1993).

The problem of bullying in schools is extensive and one that follows other trends in our modern society. There is more abuse of people in general and clearly much more abuse among youth in our society than there ever has been. How these various problems are related is still open to scientific questioning. What is not in question are the many troubling patterns evolving that make school, home, and community a more physically and psychologically danger-ous place to live. Bullying and victimization in schools is one of the develop-mentally earliest places to see and interact with these patterns of abuse and it makes sense that we should do all we can to attack these problems at this time.

WHAT IS THE IMPACT OF BULLYING
ON CHILDREN?

The fact that everyone has experiences with bullying may be a part of the reason that many people will see it as a normal aspect of life. That school bul-lying is common is true; however, any implication that bullying has little im-pact on individuals because it is normal is clearly false. The reality is that it appears to have a great deal of impact on children, their later lives, the school, and probably even the society as a whole.

Sarah was a student who attended a newly constructed, consolidated mid-dle school that was much larger than either of her previous two schools. She was secure in her old school where she had learned how to get along by adapt-ing to the special circumstances of the friends, activities, and teachers who were there. Her old ways didn't work in the new school and there quickly developed a group of girls who picked on her daily. Teachers saw it as teasing. Sarah attempted suicide.

Young people who report being bullied overwhelmingly (90%) believed it caused them problems (Hazler, Hoover, & Oliver, 1992). Twenty percent of these students felt that the problems it caused were severe. The kinds of prob-lems caused by being victims were varied, but social and emotional problems were the most common. The loss of friendships and the feelings of isolation were regular themes for these young people. They felt inadequate and unable to handle their own lives. These feelings are among the most common themes reflected in people who give up on life at any age. What may seem like only child's play has the potential for much greater consequences.

Students giving up on their lives is reflected in school dropout rates, which remain high, and in an increasing number of informal dropouts who give up on education but stay in school. The social and emotional problems reported by victims of bullying may have been the most reported, but a significant number (17%) of students also reported academic problems along with them. These troubling findings now finally are being recognized even at the highest levels of government. One particular example of this recognition is that one of only six national education goals for the year 2000 included in *The National Education Goals Report* (National Education Goals Panel, 1993) dealt specifically with the problem of violence in schools:

> Goal 6: Safe, Disciplined, and Drug-Free Schools
> By the year 2000, every school in America will be free of drugs and violence and will offer a disciplined environment conducive to learning. (p. 147)

One of three primary objectives in Goal 6 stated that "Parents, businesses, and community organizations will work together to ensure that schools are a safe haven for all children" (National Education Goals Panel, 1993, p. 147).

The concern for safety goes beyond the students' immediate situation to influence both juvenile development and adulthood. Chronic victims as well as bullies are more likely to be truant and drop out of school with all the negative implications that go with these actions (Floyd, 1987). Psychosocial problems (Hartup, 1979) and psychosexual problems (Gilmartin, 1987) are examples of the difficulties found to follow chronic victims into adulthood. Bullies are likely to maintain their aggressive behaviors throughout school (Olweus, 1994) and these behaviors can continue into later life where having a school bully background is associated with an increased likelihood of having a criminal record as an adult (Eron, Huesmann, Dubow, Romanoff, & Yarmel, 1987).

World wars, bombings, mass suicides, mass starvation, gang shootings, and increases in child abuse deaths get our attention quickly and move our society to action. These are clearly among the most troubling and life-threatening examples of inhuman treatment of one person to another. School bullying and victimization seems to pale in the adult vision of importance when compared to these other events. But children clearly are troubled by bullying and victimization to a greater extent than adults generally recognize. The effects of bullying and victimization can make their young lives a horrible existence and has the potential to limit their potential for happiness and success as adults.

HOW EFFECTIVELY ARE WE RESPONDING?

Perhaps the most positive part of the answer to how well we are respond-ing is that attention to the issues of bullying, victimization, and violence is in-creasing. Domestic violence, child abuse, date rape, and sexual harassment are just a few examples of problems that are now receiving widespread attention after largely being ignored both socially and scientifically for decades. For de-cades and even centuries these problems generally were seen as insignificant or inappropriate for public discussion and formal action. Avoiding such discus-sions was probably a major reason why people didn't worry about them. "If you don't talk about it, then it must not be important." We may know the state-ment is not true, but we seem to act as though it were in many cases. Bullying fits into a similar category of problem behaviors where people choose to avoid important discussions and taking direct actions.

Research on these problems as well as programs and materials to deal with these problems are beginning to surface. It is critical that they do because two out of three children report that schools handle the problem of bullying poorly. Only 6% felt these issues were handled well by the schools. Many students believed that their teachers weren't even aware of these problems occurring in the school (Hazler et al., 1992). Our children perceive the problem in ways that adults do not and they seem to recognize that adults are not acting on the prob-lems to the degree they could. Increasing research and the development of new techniques and programs may be bringing the adult world more in line with what students want and need in this area. Perhaps we are coming closer to-gether on the issues in order to increase the chances for making a school a safer and more productive place to live and learn.

WHEN DOES BULLYING OCCUR MOST?

The onset of adolescence, with all its accompanying hormonal and social changes, is a turbulent and difficult time of life. The physical and social adap-tations that these young people need to make reduce self-confidence and send students seeking any way possible to secure their acceptance in their rapidly changing world. Patterns of bullying and victimization also appear to be af-fected by these changes and become most common at this age.

Students report being bullied at all ages in schools, but the worst times are clearly at early adolescence from the sixth to ninth grades (Hazler et al., 1991).

The ability to define people as in or out of a given group and then to enforce those decisions through bullying behaviors fits into the pattern of human developmental needs at this age. By focusing attention on the inadequacies of others, bullying behaviors can convey the idea that "I must be adequate because those people are not." This "put others down to make myself feel adequate" model creates an unrealistic picture of one's self-worth since it emphasizes other people's characteristics and ignores one's own true strengths. Unfortunately, the more doubt people have in their own ability, the more inviting becomes the potential to raise oneself by demeaning others. We should not be surprised that these difficult developmental times for young people are also the times that bullying and victimization are likely to be most common.

WHAT DOES THE FUTURE HOLD?

Increasing research and attention to the problems of bullying and violence among young people provides hopeful signs in the midst of all the negative information pointing to the growth of these problems throughout society. The rest of this book is designed to help people better recognize these problems where they occur and also provides a model for dealing with everyone involved.

Recognizing problems as they occur and understanding the people involved is the first critical step for someone who wants to help. Section I describes bullies and victims as the key participants. Who they are, what they are like, how they evolve into these roles, and the implications for their future are highlighted. Factors that impact this development are evaluated including personality, physical characteristics, family, schools, and society.

A model for productive intervention in bully-victim problems is presented in Section II. The basic factors that effect successful change in individuals and groups are offered to lay a groundwork for the why's and how's of working with these problems. Promoting Issues in Common (PIC) provides a step-by-step model for successful intervention with the individuals and groups. It emphasizes therapeutic work with everyone who is either directly or indirectly involved in the problem. The model can be used to deal with a wide variety of circumstances. It can be used in a specific bully-victim event including where the bully and victim are clear and can be dealt with directly and immediately. The model also can be used to deal with more complex situations and even as a general model for prevention on a school or community level.

In Section III, specific techniques are provided that can be integrated at points in the PIC model. Techniques are provided specifically for individuals such as counselors, teachers, administrators, bullies, victims, bystanders, and parents. Separate chapters also provide techniques for groups of people including families, schools, and the community.

Chapter 2

DOMINATING BULLIES

Juan

Juan finds a strange comfort in an alley several blocks from the apartment where his family of seven is crammed into four rooms. It is 2:00 a.m. and gang members have gone their own ways for the night. He feels both a strange peace and also anxiety when he is alone like this. Here, for a short while, he doesn't need to prove himself continually, but he also knows that to hold his self-respect and position in his world he will have to start proving himself all over again tomorrow.

Juan appears relaxed and in control going to school the next day. People know he can mean trouble if they are on his wrong side so they either stay out of his way or try to show him how much they like him. The regular small group forms around him. June and Del are his closest friends at school and also run with him at night. They are together most of the day. A few other boys are not really close to Juan, June, and Del at all, but they stay with the group as much as is allowed in order to capture some of the group status.

An unwritten rule for Juan is that he must maintain his respected status by being the most feared in school. Accomplishing this requires regular demonstrations of why and how other students should fear him. Everyone knows that some students or even teachers will be singled out as examples today by Juan and his gang. Juan has a good idea of who are most afraid, and they are likely to be the unfortunate chosen ones. These are singled out as the easiest targets. Each day some of them will have to be shown their place in the pecking order in no uncertain terms. A punch here, a threat there, the taking of someone's lunch money, or the ripping up of some smart kid's homework are all effective tactics. Only seldom will Juan and his friends have to resort to a sound beating of a weaker student or two to convince people of their power. Maintaining their reputation and demonstrating their power usually can be done with less physical energy than outsiders would think; however, the social and emotional energy needed to maintain this status comes at a much higher cost.

Gail

Gail always had been bigger and stronger than other girls. She could not keep up academically and had fewer nice clothes than most, but she could stop their teasing and take part in their activities simply by physical force. At least that was how things went until her freshman year of high school. Gail began to recognize that she had lost some control over other girls during the seventh and eighth grades. By becoming more aggressive with them, she still managed to keep much of her status even though she did get into more trouble at school. High school was going to be much more of a problem.

"Why couldn't everyone be like Jill?" Gail would think. "She does what I want so I don't have to fight with her, not like that jerk Sally who always is saying something behind my back. I'd like to clobber her like I used to in third grade, but now everyone gets on her side if I even look cross-eyed at her. I really don't get why the older kids get with her to gang up on me too."

Gail looked for Jill at their usual meeting place, but she was not there. Gail was not pleased when she finally found Jill talking with the "in crowd." Angry and frustrated, Gail barged into the girls by pushing, shoving, and cursing as she told bad jokes much too loudly. The girls quickly moved off, but Gail hung onto Jill's arm to make her stay. Jill was embarrassed and would rather have left also.

"What a bunch of whimps. Let's skip class and go have a smoke," Gail said with a grin that said "you'd better go" as much as "I'm pleased."

Jill looked for an excuse: "I really can't go now. My mom is mad at me for missing too many classes, and she will not let me go to the dance this week if I get in trouble again."

"You're getting to be a whimp just like that bitch Sally and her friends. I'm gonna kick her ass after school so you better not be with her or you'll get it too. So just go back to your asshole friends and be a good little girl in class."

Jill was worried about what Gail might do to her, but she also knew that Sally seemed to have lots of friends who protect her. Jill decided to try to smooth things over with Gail and hopefully also hide the time that she spent with Gail from the others. "Look, I don't really like Sally and her friends. I would hang around with you, but you're not in any of my classes and they are, so I have to put up with them. Let's go out and have a quick smoke at lunch when no one will miss us."

It was not all that Gail wanted, but this was one of the few offers of friendship she was getting these days. "Okay, we'll go at lunch, but you'd better watch out or you'll turn into a goody-goody just like the others."

Jill later told Sally what Gail said in hopes of getting closer to her and her friends: "You know Gail says she is going to get you after school today. I just wanted you to know because I didn't want you to get hurt. She's making me see her at lunch and I'll tell you if I find something else out."

Sally

Sally took the message calmly. "That big butt is nothing to worry about. My friends are juniors, and they'll take care of her. All I have to do is let them know Gail is hassling me. They hate her too, so they'll love to kick her ass."

Sally wanted more than protection, however, so she told Jill to have lunch with her and her older friends. When Gail showed up, Sally made sure that Jill was the center of attention at their table and everyone was laughing and happy, including her older friends. They also had a table in clear sight of the monitors. This table was the loudest and most visible in the room. Gail realized that she could not win in this situation. She knew she had been had. The only option she saw was to pretend she didn't care, so she turned her back and left school for the rest of the day.

POWER AND CONTROL

Bullies like Juan, Gail, and Sally are common, and history shows that their stories are not new ones. Geoffrey Walford of Aston University in England has presented evidence to show how gross and sadistic bullying has been a part of public schools in England since their inception. Such practices were probably a part of a corporal punishment system that allowed older students to haze younger students in order to help administration keep control of the overall student population.

Bullying behaviors in humans also have comparable behaviors that can be seen in animals. Bullying behaviors are an accepted part of the animal kingdom where status and dominance appear to be integral parts of how animal societies function. Posturing, scolding, and actual fighting are used regularly by animals to get what they want, confirm leadership, and maintain control of a group. Human societies have civilized many of these practices by regulating them into the games we play. Boxing, wrestling, football, basketball, and track and field are just a few examples of the organized sports in which acquiring dominance over individuals or groups is a sanctioned activity where prizes traditionally are awarded to the most dominant. Also, mental contests such as board games, spelling bees, and quiz shows are held where the whole purpose is to identify the one person or group that is better than all others and then reward the winner. Monetary games (sometimes called board games and sometimes called business) appeal to adults where the major task is to get more money or things than anyone else.

All of these activities to evaluate dominance among people are supposed to happen in controlled ways so that the losers do not get hurt badly. Unfortunately, controlled games can be followed by less controlled actions where only the most dominant make up the rules and choose the players. Being in charge of rules and participants thus assures the continuance of their dominance. The problem of bullying falls into this last category. It is not officially sanctioned, and the strong play only by rules that will keep them dominant. When Juan, Gail, and Sally manage to control the rules and the players, they can dominate, and that is exactly what they mean to do.

Juan is a different person when he is alone late at night than at school during the day. He can relax when alone because there is nothing to prove at that time, but during school he must demonstrate his power over others or see himself as a failure. Everyone wants to feel capable of influencing people and will find whatever ways necessary to demonstrate these abilities to themselves (Mendler, 1992). At school, Juan has found a few basic ways to control people through physical and verbal threats and actions. These are the only means he has found yet to demonstrate the importance of himself as a person in this situation.

Gail provides a good example of a bully whose intimidation methods of controlling others were at one time successful; however, over time these have become inadequate. Physical intimidation got virtually all the students to do as she wished as long as she was significantly stronger and they did not possess other skills that might offset her strength. Once the others became closer in size and better at verbal and social skills, Gail lost her ability to control them. Sally, on the other hand, developed the social organization skills that Gail lacked and now can use them to control other students in ways that Gail cannot.

Gaining and holding power and control over others are ways bullies compensate for underlying fears of inadequacy (Roberts, 1988). Most people have fears of inadequacy, but overcome them primarily by facing them directly. Bullies, on the other hand, choose to demonstrate their personal adequacy by dominating less able others, which allows bullies to avoid challenging their personal fears. Juan avoids most activities where he would be pitted against others based on rules he cannot control (e.g., academics, sports, games, etc.) because he is not confident that he would come out looking competent. Instead, he dominates others with the very few ways in which he is confident that the outcome will lead to some form of success. The means that he uses to gain power and control are limited and the success he gains is not great, but his behaviors at least serve to soothe his fears of inadequacy for the time being.

SUCCESS IDENTITY

Gail gives up in her attempt to control students in the lunchroom and runs from school because her limited tools for gaining success would not work there. Sally had created a situation where physical threat could not succeed in the cafeteria and Gail saw no other alternative but to run. The strengths in Gail's self-concept revolve around being physical, which is the only means to success that she can imagine for herself.

Gail, Juan, and Sally all have very few aspects of themselves in which they can feel confident. Their actions and reactions are designed to preserve their dignity and self-image and to avoid thinking about their perceived weaknesses. *Bullies often cannot even think of a friendly response that can preserve their dignity and self-image so they see no alternatives to aggression* (Greenbaum, 1989). Juan sees himself as physical, dominating, and a leader of a small group and is continuously aggressive in order to maintain that image. Gail can see herself as successful only by being physical and dominating while Sally ignores this aspect of herself to focus on keeping others in a social status subservient to her. Each of them pushes attention away from their areas of personal doubt in order to pretend they do not exist.

People often do not have a self-concept that is accurate for many of the same reasons as Gail, Juan, and Sally. We don't like bad news so we create an imaginary and incomplete picture that is acceptable, no matter what the cost is to us. One part of that cost is a feeling of insecurity because we are afraid that someone will find out about the real person inside. Insecure people are generally not able to chance the risks involved in reaching out to others for help or to learn new ways of reacting to the world. This insecurity is confirmed even more by not reaching out because little progress then is made in the problem areas. Bullying behaviors commonly are found as symptoms of children caught in this cycle of insecurities, fears, and difficulty in reaching out to others for help (Robinson, Rotter, Fey, & Vogel, 1992).

Bullies tend to have a poor self-concept and a limited success identity brought on by internal feelings of being unloved, unimportant, and inferior. These feelings hurt so much that bullies are not likely to admit to these feelings. *Bullies find that the best way to deal with their fears is indirectly, by projecting those same feelings onto their victims* (Mendler, 1992). Projection is a rather common means people use to say to themselves, "I know I don't have this weakness because you do and you are less than I am."

Juan doubts whether he is actually an acceptable person but does not know how to attack that fear within himself or in the outside world where he is afraid to express it. He has found that he can cover up these feelings by making others feel inadequate. It doesn't eliminate his fears but, at least for a little while, it lets him feel better in comparison to some other unlucky people. He actually has achieved no more success for himself by hurting others, but at least he feels in control as long as he maintains this one-up position. The only times he feels successful are when he is controlling others. Recognizing few other ways to gain good feelings about himself, he must use this one method almost continuously or risk admitting to his feared inadequacies. Bullying thus becomes a way of life rather than a more normal occasional means to an end.

LEARNED BEHAVIORS

Ron was new in school and watched the lunch scene between Sally and Gail with interest. Talking to Jill later in the day he commented, "That Sally really can be a nasty bitch. Is she always like that?"

Jill looked surprised, but after she thought about it she said, "Actually, it was only really this year that Sally has been like that. She used to be quiet and just followed the crowd as much as anybody. Then she started hanging out with some of those older kids. Next thing you knew, she was different, and she sure gets her way a lot more than she used to. Yeah, she is really tough now."

People change in part because they learn the specific behaviors that appear to work for them. Everyone understands this principle and we employ it every day of our lives. We reward people when they do what we want with the expectation that the reward will encourage them to do the same again. We punish behaviors we do not like as a means to try to stop them. The same principle plays a key role in the making or changing of bullies.

Albert Bandura (1973) confirmed for us that aggression can be learned through watching aggressive people we see as models. Children don't have to look beyond television cartoons to see plenty of violence. Violent cartoons increased from one and one-half hours per week on major television channels to 43 hours per week in just the five years from 1981 to 1986. That same year of 1986 saw 11 of the top 20 selling toys at holiday time based on cartoons of a violent nature. Also, the growing number of sensational news shows, police action shows, and other shows emphasize violent acts, which offer additional views of how people get along in the world.

Models for aggressive ways of getting what you want at the expense of others are available throughout society and most youngsters have seen plenty of examples. Those who grow up in the inner cities, like Juan, where violence among the young is particularly prevalent, are likely to see such behaviors as the norm. It used to be that only the villains were regularly violent people, but no more. Children now are exposed to heros, villains, and those in between who all use violence to get what they want. An unlimited number of reasons seem to exist that now justify the use of violence. Everyone Juan knows has had experiences with violence so it is a common part of his existence. He also has seen that many of those who act violently can avoid the negatives that are supposed to follow. The fact that violence has become commonplace and the negatives that should follow violence can be avoided serves to reduce his fear of what might happen to him when he acts like the models he emulates.

Sally recognized that some of the younger girls became more powerful by getting on the good side of the older girls. With relatively little thinking or planning, she found herself doing the same thing. At first, she was worried that teachers, parents, and friends would get down on her for what she was doing. She found instead that they did not criticize her. There were no hassles; instead, they seemed to treat her with more respect and attention. She was being rewarded for modeling bullying behaviors much more often than being criticized for hurting others, so she continued.

Sally's and Juan's cases are more the rule than the exception when people are reinforced in similar ways. Children who are continuously aggressive and not very selective about whom they attack receive plenty of condemnation for their actions. They are continually in trouble. *Bullies are different from the basic aggressive child because they pick their targets more selectively.* The fact that bullies only pick on selected victims who generally have little influence with others gets them less condemnation from peers and adults. The rewards they receive are not as likely to be offset by the negatives (Hoover & Hazler, 1991).

The rewards and punishments for Gail are changing and these changes increase her potential to develop in either positive or negative ways. No longer is Gail able to avoid social condemnation for her physical bullying. Peers have found ways to get back at her and adults are less accepting of physical bullying, particularly by girls, as people get older. The number of rewards are diminishing and the negative consequences are increasing. Gail will try hard to continue those behaviors that have worked in the past. It is normal human nature to keep doing what has worked before even when it stops working. Eventually, however, the disadvantages of her actions will be so great that she will recognize the need to do something different.

The lunchroom example saw Gail decide to back away, which is one of those new behaviors for her that she has not had to use in the past. She might start using this new behavior in the nonproductive way of isolating herself from others. This would help her avoid condemnation but would not offer much hope of increasing her social abilities and her desire to influence others; however, she also has the positive possibility of using the backing away technique to observe, learn better ways of interacting, and consider how to use these better interaction methods in the future. Which direction she chooses and whether or not she maintains that direction will be at least partly dependent on whether she feels rewarded or punished for her new efforts.

VERBAL AND RELATIONSHIP SKILLS

Sally always has been small and weaker than many of the other girls her age. The social and relationship demands of adolescence finally have served to minimize these weaknesses for Sally and allowed her to emphasize her verbal and relationship skills. It is a common situation that changes the degree of influence drastically for many children at this time in their lives.

Girls, in comparison to boys, approach relationships as ways to become closer or to affiliate with others. Boys tend to see relationships more as a means of obtaining social power within a group and are less concerned about closeness (Roland & Munthe, 1989). The result is that girls place more emphasis on getting emotionally closer to people, which results in fewer but stronger relationships than boys. Boys, on the other hand, likely will have more casual friendships and fewer close relationships than girls (Shapiro, 1967). Developing the more intense verbal and relationship skills needed to achieve greater affiliation that girls desire with others increases the likelihood that bullying by girls will take the form of verbal and social attacks (Hazler et al., 1991).

One seemingly common denominator among bullies is that they are more likely to see hostile intent in the actions of potential victims than non-bullies (Dodge, Murphy, & Buchsbaum, 1984). When Gabe, who is smaller and a better student, does not see Juan signal for him to come over, Juan takes it as a personal challenge rather than as an accident. It feels to Juan like a direct challenge to his manhood and status that cannot go unpunished. So he hits Gabe, throws him down, scatters his books, and threatens him with worse, "if you ever ignore me again." Juan's reactions reflects the common paranoid thinking of bullies and how that paranoia can drive them to act in ways all out of proportion to the actions of others.

Bullies also tend to have little empathy for their victims (Besag, 1989) so that remorse is seldom an issue as it might be for most people. The fact that bullies are quicker to anger and use force to get their way sooner than others (Edmondson, 1988) results in an individual who is more likely to hurt someone without regrets. This is particularly true if the bully acts immediately rather than taking time to think about the situation (Dodge & Newman, 1981). Juan probably has little understanding of the physical and emotional pain Gabe feels and so has no reason to feel sorry for him. He only sees the event and its results from his own perspective.

Gail, Juan, and Sally each have developed their own specialized hostile responses for use with victims. They may be physical, verbal, or social, but they have the common denominator of being hurtful responses. This is standard among bullies who tend to be less likely to recognize prosocial responses to threatening situations than other people (Dodge et al., 1984). Bullies either do not have as great a variety of positive social responses to threat as non-bullies or, what is more likely, the positive social responses they do have are not the ones selected when the bully feels under pressure.

Problems with relationship development skills are likely to be a part of the reason for the many social problems bullies can expect to experience. For example, based on teacher ratings of antisocial behavior, negative playground habits, and the number of discipline contacts with the principal; future arrest records can be predicted with about 80% accuracy (Walker, 1993). Should Juan, Gail, and Sally not have their antisocial bullying behaviors effectively modified, they will be likely to carry their picture of a violent world, where only aggressive actions prove successful, into their adult lives. Such a direction would not bode well for either the bullies or society.

Leadership is another characteristic that depends heavily on the quality of relationship development skills. Gail presents the most traditional example of how aggressive people such as bullies relate to leadership. Even in kindergarten, it was obvious that Gail did not fit into play groups like others. Her way to express leadership was, and for the most part still is, to demand that people do things her way. When they did not give in to her demands, she would attempt to get what she wanted physically and, when this failed, she would go off by herself. She was not good at following others, asking for help, or suggesting changes that might help the situation along. These characteristics of always demanding acquiescence and, when they do not get their way, isolating themselves, are common among youngsters who become identified as bullies (Trawick-Smith, 1988). They also do not prove very effective as interpersonal skills, which probably explains why the popularity of overly aggressive youngsters tends to decrease as they get older (Besag, 1989).

PHYSICAL CHARACTERISTICS

Everyone recognized that Gail was stronger and older than her victims. She came from big parents, started school one year late, and was held back a year after kindergarten. Size and age differences are the most common differences people tend to think of in bullies and victims. While it is true that bullies tend to have greater than average strength (Greenbaum, 1989), are more energetic, and are generally older than their victims (Olweus, 1978); everyone recognizes that there are many exceptions. The actual physical differences are probably not as important as how they are perceived by others. For example, Gail is still stronger and older than the other girls, but she no longer incites the fear that she did before. On the other hand, Juan is not necessarily larger than boys his age, but he clearly conveys an image that he is more powerful.

Physical image as opposed to the realities of physical differences is important in understanding the makeup and impact that a bully has. Juan conveys the traditional dominant male model in his bullying. Everyone has seen this model on television, in print, and in movies and knows that it should be feared. People have become convinced that Juan is tougher and can endure more pain than they can, so they make the logical choice not to challenge him. He is not involved in athletics but everyone assumes he is athletic, energetic, and active from the way he carries himself. The feeling they have is that he could be an athlete if he decided to put his presumed superior energy and ability into these activities.

How accurate these perceived differences between Juan and the other students are and how much is just the image he has developed remains unclear. What is clear is that Juan gets his way because the others believe he has these advantages. He will control by maintaining this image until such time that the realities are tested effectively by other students.

Most research on bullies and aggressive students has been on males, but Sally demonstrates how some of the same concepts might be applied to females. She is small in size and not physically strong or particularly coordinated. But the bullying she does is of a verbal and social nature, which is more common among females (Hazler et al., 1992). Socially and verbally Sally is very big and very coordinated. In fact, few others her age or younger can approach her strength and toughness in the social and relationship areas. They have learned to avoid any actions or talk that Sally might take as a challenge because they fear the social and emotional consequences they believe she can bring about. Like Juan, she will be able to push people around until the realities and limitations of differences in her social and verbal abilities are tested effectively and challenged in public.

SCHOOL AND ACADEMICS

Gail never has been good at schoolwork, and Juan has had his ups and downs over the years. Sally always has been a good student, though teachers always have said she is not living up to her potential. These three are typical of the variety of academic expectations we might have for bullies. School is generally an important place for them to be, because school is where they can find their victims most easily and demonstrate influence over their victims. It is hard to reap rewards from being a bully if there are no readily accessible victims. Unfortunately, the motivation for being in school and the critical tasks bullies set for themselves do not make great matches with the traditional tasks and goals of the school. The result tends to show bullies performing enough appropriate school behaviors to maintain some level of acceptance mixed with a series of problems that arise from bullying activities.

Bullies tend to have a less positive attitude towards schoolwork even though they have average intellectual abilities (Lagerspetz, Bjorquist, Berts, & King, 1982). Like Sally, their time is taken up planning and carrying out their controlling activities. Bullies are not unlike the sheep herder who, in order to control his herd of sheep, must watch over them continuously, stop potential intruders from getting close, attempt to keep the herd from straying, and bring back to the fold any that do begin to drift. Continual alertness and attention to controlling the flock is needed so that little time and energy is left for intellectual pursuits. Bullies are generally no slower or unmotivated than other children. They just do not have enough thinking, emotional, and work time left to meet academic needs after they have taken care of the rest of their life.

Bullies do have differing levels of need to be judged as acceptable in school. Gail, for example, has never been a good student and no one really expects it of her. The reasons for her lack of ability are partly intellectual (i.e., slightly below-average intelligence) and partly environmental because of low interest and expectations from family and friends. She manages to do enough to get herself passed from one grade to the next and that seems acceptable enough to everyone. There is little social pressure to do better.

Sally, on the other hand, has parents, teachers, and friends who expect good grades from her and put pressure on her to do that level of work. She has identified the level of success it takes to keep everyone off her back most of the time and that level determines how hard she works. Her teachers are right. That level is not what she is able to do but only what she is willing to do. She has other priorities that take up more of her time and energy.

Juan has had the most varied academic career. He was a good student in the early grades, but then his accomplishments began to drop. The trend towards lower achievement and grades came at the same time his bullying behaviors were increasing. Run-ins with the principal, his parents being brought to school, and a brush with being expelled brought him to the realization that being thrown out of school was not something he wanted. His work and politeness to teachers improved greatly for a period of time only to drop off later to a point of marginal acceptability. Juan is bright and can do enough to get by fairly easily. His up and down pattern demonstrates how a person often will do just enough of what is needed in one situation to allow time for the things that motivate them most.

MATURATION

Children do not come into the world with the knowledge, values, and skills necessary to deal effectively with power, control, influence, and acts of violence. Childhood is the time to make mistakes, learn, and develop in these areas in a relatively safe environment (Carlsson-Paige & Levin, 1988). This growth process is full of the natural problems and mistakes that follow anyone trying out new behavior and thinking patterns, experiencing their results, and hopefully choosing progressively better ways to act as they learn. They must try out many behaviors as they begin recognizing their needs, how to get them met, and the complexities of influencing people. Neither the knowledge, the skills, nor the behaviors come automatically with birth and the challenge to acquire them with the least amount of trouble is a great one.

Some bullying behaviors are a part of standard childhood experimentation with new behaviors. Normal maturational experimenting with using power to influence others is visible in the occasional or one-time bully who learns that these methods do not get needs met satisfactorily or have unacceptable negative consequences. All people have had experiences with this if they are honest with themselves and look objectively at their life.

One of my own attempts at physical aggression with someone weaker may serve as an example of experimentation and learning as a part of growing up. I was big and strong enough to stand up to most kids but I actively avoided fights. I felt inadequate in these situations and I also knew my mom considered it wrong, although I cannot ever remember any preaching from her on the subject. One day after school in the woods across the street from my home I began arguing with Gene who was an older but smaller boy. There was no one else around and I began gesturing, threatening, pushing, and eventually started a fight. There was a feeling of confidence in this situation that I had not experienced before and it felt good. We wrestled and threw a couple of punches, but I was stronger and, at least in my own mind, I clearly won. The victory made me feel proud including the symbolic bite mark Gene left on my arm.

Fighting was discouraged at my home so there would be no bragging, but I still wanted someone to know of my victory. My encounter with Gene still felt good when I sat down at the dinner table that night. I wondered if the fact that the other kid was older might make this acceptable with my parents? Mom noticed the mark on my arm and asked where I got it. I briefly tested the waters by saying briefly, "I was in a fight with an older boy." Surely the fact that it was an older boy would make the fight acceptable and they would be proud of this great victory.

Mom was consistent in her beliefs and in her understanding of me. She said in a calm and clear voice: "The boy wouldn't have bitten you if he were as big or as strong as you. [Dad shook his head in agreement.] I hope you are not proud of fighting with someone weaker than you."

Mom was right of course. I didn't deserve any real approval. There were no other harsh words or punishments, but the bullying had lost its value. My attempt at physical violence with someone less able was a part of normal maturational trial and error learning (at least that is the way I would like to think of it). What I learned was that it did not get me the influence and respect I wanted. The benefits for continuing the bullying actions were eliminated and the disapproval of my parents was there as well. The combination of no benefits and calm disapproval of the significant people in my life was a powerful force in shaping my future development.

The learning process does not always offer the neat outcomes for the straightforward reasons my own example might demonstrate. What if my mother and father had not been as sensitive and simply seen this fight as the victory I desired? What if they showed me they were encouraged by my standing up for myself in a fight no matter what the circumstances? What if my friends had told me how proud they were of me? Chronic bullies tend to have more selective recall of events (Dodge & Newman, 1981). So what if I only remembered what it felt good to remember? There are many factors that determine the directions a person takes in life, the behaviors they choose to keep, and those they choose to discard. It is important to remember that bullying behaviors will be tried by most children at times as a part of the normal maturational process. How others react to those test situations can have a great impact on the eventual development of that person.

The outlook in later life for chronic bullies is not good. We need to be concerned about Juan, Gail, and Sally particularly because they have been acting as bullies for extended periods of time. Those who remain chronic bullies during school age are much more likely to have a variety of violence and crime-related problems as adults (Oliver, Hoover, & Hazler, 1994), so the time to change their behavior is when they are young. However, we also must keep in mind that they still are maturing as human beings and the process is not nearly complete. Maturation could result in much more socially acceptable behaviors than they are currently demonstrating if the right conditions can be provided.

FAMILY

The family is a powerful force in determining whether or not a person will develop into a chronic bully because humans are most vulnerable to learning inappropriate behaviors when they are very young. The vast majority of what they see and hear at this age is from their family. Young children have little opportunity to compare what they experience to other people and ways of life so it is generally accepted as the way things must be. This picture of "my family is the way things must be" becomes very hard to change even when they make friends and enter school. These circumstances are positive if the family is healthy and helpful in the young person's development into a social being. On the other hand, the more problems a family has and the more negative are their ways of dealing with their children, the greater will be the likelihood that the children will develop problems of their own. In fact, families of bullies have three times the number of family problems than do the families of non-bullies (Mitchel & O'Morre, 1988).

Juan, Gail, and Sally all have problems in their family that increased the chances that they would become bullies. Juan lives with his mother, two younger sisters, one younger brother, and an older sister and her young child in a small, four-room apartment. Juan's father, who is also the father to one of his sisters, left the family when Juan was one year old. The father seldom comes to see the family even though he lives in town. When he does come, he usually is complaining about one or more of the family members and, as often as not, he is drunk. Things never go well. Juan feels a mixture of wanting to avoid any contact with his father and also hoping that maybe things will get better the next time.

Juan's mother, Rita, is a strong women and has done whatever is necessary to make sure the children have the food, clothes, and school materials they need. She works to make ends meet and gets home just in time to make sure everyone is ready for bed. Rita is a busy woman and Juan knows it, so he tries to stay out of the way. He also wants to avoid the hollering that is the common mode of discussion when someone gets frustrated at home and, because someone is almost always angry, there is a lot of noise. One way he stays out of the way that also provides escape from the overcrowded and tense conditions at home is to be away from home as much as possible. He stays on the streets as long and as late as he can.

Rita frequently does not know where Juan is, but she has little time to dwell on it because of all her other responsibilities. Not knowing the whereabouts of a child is a common problem with parents of bullies (Greenbaum, 1989). This lack of awareness may be caused by an overextension, as in Rita's case, or it can be from simple neglect where there is ample time and ability to pay attention but it is just not done.

The role models that Juan sees in his family are significant factors in his life. For all intents and purposes, he is the senior male in the house, which can carry significant weight, particularly in Hispanic homes. Unfortunately, his father provides little in the way of a positive role model. Juan desperately would like to see his father in a different light, but his hopes are dashed each time his father comes around. He, like many other bullies, will not find a good model of how to get along with others or how to solve problems in the person with whom he would most like to identify—his father (Greenbaum, 1989). Where will he learn more accepted ways of interacting if not at home?

Sally's family would be recognized by most people as pretty much middle class. Mom and dad both work to keep up payments on a nice home and three cars. Sally's older brother is a high school student and gets to drive the third car. There is a younger brother whom Sally takes care of when no one else is home, which is often. What outsiders would not necessarily see are the other factors working in the family that are not so traditional and much more detrimental.

Sally's parents have been together for 18 years, but their marriage has not been a smooth road. There have been splits and reconciliations over a variety of problems from excessive drinking to physical abuse to extramarital affairs. The events that affected Sally more than any others, however, were the occasional brow beatings her mom would give her over some small infraction and the one time that she was sexually abused by her father. Everyone was embarrassed, angry, and sorry at the same time after each trauma. Every problematic event was followed by a pattern of yelling, demeaning, hitting, and eventually avoiding any more discussion of the subject. The family seemed to feel that, if they were sorry and did not talk about it, there would be no lasting effects. Things just do not work that way after traumatic events.

Verbal, physical, and emotional abuse are common in families of overly aggressive children and adults. We know that four out of five violent children are victims of abuse at home, so it is important to recognize that bullies at school could well be victims at home (Hunt, 1993). The forms of abuse and violence used against children in the home demonstrate to them that these are effective ways to get what they want. "If they work at home against me, why wouldn't they work for me against weaker kids?"

Another dimension of Sally's abuse that probably plays a role in her development into a bully is the random timing and nature of punishments. Many bullies, like Sally, have one or more parents who are likely to punish harshly over a minor infraction at one time but ignore many other worse behaviors altogether. Harsh punishment is more likely to come because the parent is in a bad mood than because of the child's behavior (Edmondson, 1988). This inconsistency teaches only that "you never know when you are going to get it." It becomes difficult for the child to make any connection between doing something wrong and being punished. The only idea that is conveyed fully is, "I can abuse you when I want because I am more powerful!"

Gail gets very few hassles at home in comparison to Juan and Sally. As a matter of fact, she gets almost no attention whatsoever except for an occasional grounding for some minor offense. The grounding is no real problem though because her parents do not enforce it. Her parents pay little attention to her or what she is doing. Organized discipline is virtually nonexistent for Gail because no one really knows or even seems to care what she may have done either good or bad. Gail's home life is like many bullies where she gets little attention, does most things at home by herself, has no one keeping track of her, and receives inconsistent discipline.

The families of Juan, Sally, and Gail are very different in many ways, but they do have commonalties that can be found in many families of bullies. One thing that can be seen in these and other families of bullies is a lack of empathy displayed within the family (Olweus, 1978). Family members of bullies do little to try to understand the other person's point of view and even less to express that understanding. Rita has no time to do this with Juan. Sally's family does everything in their power to avoid thinking about the trauma they go through and how they affect the feelings and emotions of each other. Gail's family simply doesn't communicate about anything. Each of these cases results in the children not getting enough practice at attending to the feelings, thoughts, and emotions of other people. An even stronger lesson they are being taught is "Don't try to understand. It is not a good thing to know the feelings of the people you might hurt!"

Families who show little empathy for each other, spend little time engaged with each other, and who communicate infrequently often are referred to as disengaged families. These disengaged families offer comparatively little support, direction, or feedback to their children on how to get along with people in the world. Many bullies come out of such families probably because they have not been provided with an effective model for how to learn about dealing sensitively with other people (Oliver, Oaks, & Hoover, 1994). The insensitive and self-centered behaviors that accompany bullying may be the only personal relationship skills they see in use on a regular basis at home.

Scientific research confirms what attentive observation teaches most of us: Aggression is transmitted from family to child and flows through generations (Hunt, 1993). Parents who are abusive, inconsistent, poor problem-solvers, and who do not demonstrate understanding of others' feelings have a good possibility of raising children with similar characteristics. Parents with fewer of these problems or those who get help to improve themselves in these areas tend to raise children who are less likely to become bullies.

SOCIETY

Many aspects of our modern society as well as the people in it are under enormous strain. Thousands of articles, books, televisions shows, and movies have chronicled the multitude of factors that increasingly put people at risk. These are the factors that raise anxiety levels, incite hostility of one group toward another, and demonstrate society's failures. The disintegration of the traditional family unit, increasing differences between the have's and have not's, higher rates of violence, and cut-throat competitiveness where cheating and lying can become valued are just some of the everyday topics of conversation in the media. For many people, this is a fear-laden world that seems to care little about the humane aspects of people's lives. It should not be a surprise then that some choose to fight, not with logical and caring methods, but with methods that seem to match the violence, deceit, and fear being reported. It should not be a surprise to anyone then that bullying tactics gain great visibility for both children and adults.

There are endless facts, figures, and opinions that could be reported here to emphasize how our society fosters bullying behaviors in children and adults. I am sure you have already seen or heard most of them and, if not, it will be easy to find the information in any number of books or magazines. Perhaps we should spend some time with Juan, Gail, and Sally as they watch the evening news and see what they might be learning.

The lead-in to the newscast prepares us to see that many crimes are being committed, many people get away with their crimes, and that the criminals get a lot of visibility for their behaviors. One feature will be the now common report of a hostile business takeover that was pulled off by one of the most ruthless corporate bosses. Numerous businessmen and laborers had their lives destroyed by the new boss just as others were destroyed by the old boss. The overall message may be that this is nothing new, and it is all legal, so such ruthlessness must be acceptable for certain people. Few people would state it this directly, but many would understand it in this manner.

Another feature shows a well-dressed politician walking in an inner city housing project and promising to fix things. This is followed by a segment on how the United States Congress decided to cut spending on inner-city projects and reduce taxes for the wealthy. How much of the care and concern stated by the politician will be believed? Is it genuine or only a way politicians get what they want for themselves and their friends?

"Youth gang violence increases across the country" is the next headline, as if it has not been increasing for years. The segment touts the tremendous increase in youth gang violence and the often random killing that goes along with it. There is an interview with gang members who brag about how they do whatever they want and with the police who do not have effective ways of handling the problem. A mother comes on to say how one son is dead and she is afraid for the other child who is now in a gang. She wants help and wonders why the police have officers to protect the white communities but not hers.

Sports headlines are next. Surely this will be encouraging of caring and comradery among people. A batter is hit by a pitch and there is a bench-clearing brawl. A star pitcher signed a contract for more than most of us would earn in two lifetimes. This signing was right after his release from jail due to a fourth conviction for driving drunk. Finally, there is a new heavyweight boxing champion who, though bloodied, just made $10,000,000 by destroying the former champion who is now recuperating in the hospital. The new champ boasts, "I told him to fear me and now he knows why. He says he wants a rematch. I'd kill him!"

Individuals, families, and schools are parts of society that both help shape it and are shaped by it. Classism, racism, sexism, political correctness, poverty, the changing family, employment opportunities, and the increasing trend to use impersonal means (legal and violent) to solve personal and interpersonal problems are examples of the many sociological problems that can and should be faced directly. Only then will we see major improvement in a current environment that fosters bullying and victimization. Any honest effort to understand and deal with bullies must not forget that these people and their families do not operate in isolation. People must live within society, understand the impact society has, and take responsibility for improving the nature of that society so that a next generation will have a more helpful environment in which to develop.

Figure 2.1 lists characteristics of bullies, issues relative to each characteristic, and resources where more information on each characteristic can be found.

Characteristics	Issues	Cites
1. Power and control	Power needs—must demonstrate power or be seen as failure Compensate for underlying fears of inadequacy	(Mendler, 1992) (Roberts, 1988)
2. Success identity	See no alternatives to aggression in order to preserve dignity and self-image Caught in cycle of insecurities, fears, and difficulty in reaching out to others for help Feelings of being unloved, unimportant, and inferior—project those feelings onto their victims	(Greenbaum, 1989) (Robinson et al., 1992) (Mendler, 1992)
3. Learned behavior	Pick targets selectively with little influence; therefore, rewards not as likely set off by negative consequences Aggression can be learned through modeling Chronic—repeated behavior	(Hoover & Hazler, 1991) (Bandura, 1973) (Sharpe & Smith, 1994)
4. Verbal and relationship skills	Bullying by girls takes form of verbal and social attacks Paranoid thinking—more likely to see hostile intent in actions of potential victims than non-bullies Less likely to recognize prosocial responses to threatening situations than others Quicker to anger and sooner to use force than others Demand acquiescence, when fails, isolate self	(Hazler et al., 1992) (Dodge et al., 1984) (Dodge et al., 1984) (Edmondson, 1988) (Trawick-Smith, 1988)
5. Physical characteristics	Greater than average strength More energetic Generally older than their victims Physical image important	(Greenbaum, 1989) (Olweus, 1978) (Elliott, 1991) (Olweus, 1978)
6. School and academics	Less positive attitude toward schoolwork, even though have average intellectual abilities	(Lagerspetz, 1982)
7. Maturation	Chronic bullies have more selective recall of events Chronic bullies during school age more likely to have variety of violence and crime-related problems as adults	(Dodge & Newman, 1981) (Oliver, Hoover, & Hazler, 1994)
8. Family	Bullies have three times more family problems than non-bullies Parents not knowing whereabouts of child No good role models for (1) how to get along with others and (2) how to solve problems Physical and emotional abuse—four out of five violent kids are victims at home Inconsistent discipline—harsh punishment more to do with parents' mood than child's behavior Disengaged families Lack of empathy displayed in families Aggression transmitted from family to child through generations	(Mitchel & O'Morre, 1988) (Greenbaum, 1989) (Greenbaum, 1989) (Hunt, 1993) (Edmondson, 1988) (Oliver, Oaks & Hoover, 1994) (Olweus, 1978) (Hunt, 1993)

Figure 2.1. Characteristics of bullies.

Chapter **3**

SURVIVING VICTIMS

Tom

Tom tells his mother that he is feeling sick again and doesn't want to go to school. His mother knows he has been claiming sickness much too often this year and that it is happening more frequently recently. The doctor has found nothing wrong, and Tom usually feels better shortly after lunch. His mother worries a lot about him; therefore, she takes care of him, makes him a favorite food, gets his homework from school, and helps him do it at home so that he can keep up with his classes. The attention seems to get him back on his feet and help him be productive while at home.

Reading, playing computer games, and spending time with his mom and dad are the best parts of Tom's life. The worst parts are when he runs into Juan and Del anywhere and particularly at school. He would give or do just about anything to eliminate those two from his life. Not only do they pick on him every chance they get, but when they are done, other kids start in on him. It is a cycle that he sees no hope of breaking.

Juan confronts Tom on the sidewalk outside the school the next morning: "Hey, fat boy, how much money did mommy give you today?"

Tom says nothing and tries to walk by him as quickly as possible. He keeps his head down and hopes no one else sees him. The embarrassment is as bad as the actual confrontation.

Juan gets in Tom's face and grabs him by the arm, "Let's go over here and talk about sharing lunch money today."

Around the corner Juan pounds Tom in the stomach leaving him doubled over and gasping for breath. There is no resistance to Juan's hand in Tom's pants pocket taking out the money. They have been through this before. It is not an everyday occurrence, but it happens often enough that Tom worries every day about whether this will be the day.

"Thanks for helping me out with the money, pal," Juan sneers as he walks away. "Just remember that you lost it somewhere. Skipping lunch will do you good anyhow."

Tom knows most of the other kids are pretending they didn't see, but a few smile as if it was funny. These are the ones who will make faces at him, bump him in the hall, hide his books, or tease him throughout the day. He considers telling the nurse he feels sick and needs to go home. No, that will not work. He knows the nurse and the principal don't believe him anymore. They'll just tell him to go back to class. It just will have to be another long day of making himself as inconspicuous as possible and getting home as fast as he can.

It is next to impossible to think about schoolwork during the day when Tom has so many other things on his mind. Trying to stay invisible so that no one will bother you takes a lot of planning and even some success doesn't make you feel hopeful. Then there are the other things to think about—such as the many ways to hurt, maim, and, if lucky, kill Juan and his sick friends. Ah! Sweet revenge!

"What did you say Mr. Jones? I'm sorry I didn't hear you."

"Tom, where are you?" Mr. Jones replies after finally getting Tom's attention. "You're sure not here with us in this room and you haven't been for some time. What's going on?"

Mary

Mary makes her usual request: "Could I please stay in at lunch to do homework and read?"

"It's a beautiful day outside," her teacher says. "You need to get some fresh air and spend time with the other kids."

Spending time with the other kids is the last thing Mary wants. Now that her only real friend Deanna has left, there is no one she can talk with at school.

Only two kinds of kids will be on the playground as far as Mary is concerned—those who don't know her, and those who don't like her. Worse yet, there is no place to hide on the playground.

Mary gives it one more try, "Do I have to? All the kids are so immature. I would rather spend my time with you in here."

The teacher's frustration with Mary's continuous requests is obvious: "Mary, I've told you how the others resent it when you try to stay with me every day. And when you say, 'Ms. James says . . .' to them all the time, they feel put down too. Yes, some of them may be immature, but it does no good for you to throw it in their faces and then run to me."

Mary reluctantly goes outside. She looks for the most secluded place possible, crouches into a corner, and buries her head in a book. She hopes no one will see her or, if someone does see her, Mary hopes that someone will at least stay away. Just stay out of their way until the end of the day she tells herself.

Today Mary sees a new girl who is a year younger standing by herself. Mary senses the girl is looking for her own corner to crawl into for escape. Maybe it is worth a try. Mary cautiously goes over to the new girl. "My name is Mary. Who are you?"

"Sue," the new girl says. "I really don't know anybody here."

"People are hard to get to know here and some are mean. I usually try to stay inside or read by myself when I have to go out," replies Mary.

Sue and Mary recognize similarities in their situations and begin relaxing and enjoying themselves. That ends when Sally and her friends come over. First they start talking to Sue about Mary as though Mary weren't there. Then they turn to Mary and tell her to leave. "You'll just wreck the new kid and make her a blob like you. Get out of here!"

Mary turns to go and mumbles under her breath, "You should know about ruining people, bitch."

Sally jerks her head around, "Hey, lard-ass, what did you say?"

Mary tries to keep walking, but the other girls stand in her way. "Nothing."

"She called you a bitch," says Vera, one of the older girls. "Take a lesson new kid. Some sickos like her don't deserve being here with us, but they stay anyhow. We need to teach them lessons sometimes."

Vera pulls out some matches and lights one. She holds it for an instant in front of Mary's face and then flips it at her chest.

Mary tries not to let it bother her but she is scared to death. Eventually she starts swinging at the matches as they come at her from different directions. The girls surrounding Mary keep taunting her until she finally is crying. Then they push her to send her running away.

Sue is stunned and thinks, "I'm afraid I'll be next. I knew it. I've got to make them like me right now!" She tries to get the shock off her face and works at laughing just like the other girls. She finally joins in the conversation with something she thinks they will like, "She really does run like a lard-ass, doesn't she?"

The group gets quiet as Sally says, "Just watch what you say and who you hang with. We're not always that nice to assholes."

Devon

Devon is only a freshman, but people have known for years that he would be a basketball star. Coaches, teachers, community leaders, and his mother have made every effort to assure him the best possible chance to succeed and get out of the neighborhood. Not many get out anymore.

Drugs, shootings, unemployment, gangs, and poverty are things people live with here. They don't encourage hope for a better life outside. Most will remain in the hood. Some, particularly young males, will leave for prison. Others will escape at a young age by violent death. People want to protect Devon so he can succeed and provide hope for others.

People get some relief from their difficult lives by watching Devon on the court. His motions are graceful, clean, and they inspire joy. This is the way things are supposed to be. Hope comes to those who watch.

Gangs and drug dealers are not as enamored with Devon. Sure they come to watch, but he is not one of them off the court. They aren't able to control him yet, but they wait for the time when he will be vulnerable in order to make him one of them. Then their power will be increased by having him do their bidding.

Shooter gets Devon alone and offers a "hit" outside of school. As usual, Devon turns down the drugs with a laugh and, "Man, you know they'd have my ass and my career would be ruined."

"No one needs to know man. Everyone does it. Man, you are such a kiss-ass," replies Shooter.

Devon has been trained to back away from confrontations like this, so he does. He turns away and moves toward another group standing closer to the school. He knows he is most vulnerable when he is alone and better off when more people are around.

"You know, boy, there's gonna come a time when Mr. Big Shot be more like everyone else. I'll be there to see it." Shooter's resentment and threats are made clear again as they always are.

People are not around that evening after practice when Devon has to walk home. The coach had a meeting and couldn't take Devon home this time. No one else was going his way and there is no way Devon was going to tell others he was scared and needed someone. Stars don't do that.

Shooter's gang see Devon alone that night after practice and recognize their opportunity. They catch up and circle around him; a couple with knives in their hands. "Hey, look who's walkin' the streets without all his big shot friends. It's the star. Maybe you are looking for a little high with us? What about it star?"

Devon is scared and alone. He feels trapped and freezes, not knowing what to do as they move closer.

Shooter sees Devon frozen and scared and knows he is in control. He pulls out a needle. "I think this means the star finally wants a hit. Right big shot?"

Devon knows this is real trouble and finally reacts physically. He slaps at Shooter and kicks out at anyone in front only to feel a stabbing pain from the back and then a blow to the head that knocks him out.

Shooter and the gang don't see many options now. Devon is bleeding and they will be a major target if he tells. Giving him a big shot does it. There will be no one to tell now.

THE VICTIM

Violence like that in Devon's case gets our attention. It screams at us in the headlines so it cannot be ignored—"Star Athlete Dies." Death is big news; however, the fact is that most violence related to children is not given much recognition at all by adults (Morgan & Zedner, 1993). A murder like Devon's did not start with teenagers using knives, guns, and drugs. That was the final outcome, but practice began long before.

Practice started with what adults might view as just kids stuff. Some taunting and ridiculing lead to a little pushing and maybe to a couple of fights. The rougher the place, the rougher the behaviors that seem normal and that often are ignored by adults. Not attacking these behaviors early can allow more escalation as the kids gather their friends to get revenge. Words and fists can give way to knives and guns as each side tries to get the upper hand. Now the headlines tell us Devon is dead and we wonder why it didn't get stopped earlier.

The disastrous impact of bullying in Devon's case is obvious, but what about Tom's and Mary's situations? They seem so much less severe. How much physical pain does Tom endure from Juan's punch or Mary from the matches she is ducking? What about the emotional pain they suffer from fear and humiliation? How will it change their lives?

Victimization research confirms for us what we already know from personal experiences. The objective gravity of a crime against someone is no clear guide to the impact on that person. This is particularly true in the case of children who have much less life experience on which to evaluate their personal traumas (Morgan & Zedner, 1993). We really know little about criminals and their behaviors and even less about victims; however, there is enough information out there to be pretty sure that the effects of crime are more severe than we have tended to believe (Greenbaum, 1989).

Students report that up to 81% of males and 72% of females had been bullied during their school careers. These were not even reports taken from the worst neighborhoods like Devon's. The three out of four students who reported having been bullied were actually from relatively rural environments that most people would consider safe. In fact, the numbers do not even reflect abuse at home. The numbers only refer to bullying experienced when coming to, leaving, or while in school (Hoover, Oliver, & Hazler, 1992).

Being a victim is clearly a problem of large but unspecific proportions for young people today. Although victims come in all shapes and sizes, we do find patterns of characteristics and behaviors that can help to recognize when a person is more likely to be a victim. Understanding these patterns of character- istics can be a starting place for helping prevent victimization or providing sup- port for those who are victimized.

POWER AND CONTROL

The U.S. Army has a wonderful saying that makes a magnificent sales pitch: "Be all that you can be . . . in the Army." Why would anyone in their right mind not want to join the Army or any other organization that would assure that you could "Be all that you can be"? The saying seems to offer the power to achieve a successful and fulfilling life where you are in control of your des- tiny. Who could ask for anything more?

All people want to see themselves as powerful and in control of their own life. They search within themselves and their environment for the most likely means available to gain this power and control. Consider the little boy enjoying potty training immensely. He is recognizing for the first time methods for phys- ically gaining power and control over adults. He clearly can make them react in different ways depending on what he does. A 13-year-old girl discovers for the first time how moving certain ways or giving a certain look can control the behaviors of certain boys in ways she has never experienced.

Recognizing personal sources of power and control provide many of the developmental highlights in a person's life. Unfortunately, not everyone contin- ues to develop increasingly mature methods of gaining power and control. Many times the old and immature methods of gaining power that worked at seven years old are still the ones young people keep trying to use when they are 15.

People who regularly find themselves to be victims are cheated out of much of the enjoyment and self-respect that goes along with finding healthy means of gaining and using power and control in relationships. They often see themselves as being controlled by outside forces (i.e., external locus of control) more than themselves (Seligman & Peterson, 1986). They come to believe that it is un- alterable weaknesses, the strengths of others, or "just the way life is" that deter- mines how they get along. Taking control in their lives does not seem to be an option. Instead they see power in the hands of others. It is a discouraging and frustrating way to look at life.

The most common reaction to situations where victims feel this way is to become passive or passive-aggressive. People like Tom may give up, for the most part, on the idea of trying to direct events in the way they would like. They just accept what comes and remove themselves from the situation as soon as possible (passive). Others more like Mary will quietly take what comes now while instigating more devious ways to gain a form of indirect control over her tormentors later (passive-aggressive). Mary will continue to seek ways to put down her tormentors and make them look bad. People do not give up on gaining power and control. They readjust the means used to gain whatever types and amounts of control appear to be available to them. The control they acquire might not be much or very healthy, but it seems to be better than nothing.

Once people are recognized by others as victims, they often are given labels—whimp, sissy, freak, asshole, and many more derogatory ones. These labels are not meant to be descriptive as much as they serve to further reduce the victim's power to control the situation (Goffman, 1968). The labels are tormentors' shorthand reminders of the person's weakness and lack of power. They cut off any real consideration of the strengths and good points of the individual, emphasizing their vulnerability.

Devon was victimized by what most people would consider a highly sought after label—"Star." For some, this suggested he had more control of his life than he really did. It would be nearly impossible to continue living up to this label. Then there were those like Shooter who saw the star label as a personal put-down. Shooter would do anything to show that Devon did not have as much control in his life as the star label suggested that he did. Bringing Devon down to Shooter's level would show who had the control.

Society uses labels to help shorten discussions and to use information known about one person to gain a better understanding of another; however, these same useful labels often become rigidly accepted and this rigidity inevitably leads to negative consequences. The problems come from the fact that labels emphasize only limited aspects of the person. The result is that an isolated part of a person (e.g., size, color, intelligence, sex, etc.) becomes identified as the whole person which, of course, is never the case. The "Star" is expected always to be a star and not the person who also can be weak and make mistakes. The "girl" is not accepted as a person or a woman but instead only as the connotations that her label is given. Everyone is more than the label given, but the more the label is used, the less visibility the rest of the person gets.

Depression is a common reaction by victims because they can perceive no way to gain more control of their life. They see no way to fix it and little opportunity for escape (Besag, 1989). The victims of bullies are stigmatized by labels that emphasize their powerlessness in much the same manner that the sexual abuse victim is seen as inadequate (Himelein, Vogel, & Wachowiak, 1994) even though our society says such labeling is wrong.

The physical mannerisms associated with depression can be recognized in most victims. Tom's and Mary's slowness of gait, head down, slumped shoulders posture, having little to say, and tearing reactions are not likely to be natural personal characteristics. They are signs of the depression that comes along with recognition that they were not in control. Even Devon's gregarious nature and physical stature changed when he felt he had lost control. Each of the victims felt inadequate to control their lives when they were being victimized and their felt inadequacies became apparent in their physical reactions.

Tom is a common example of many people who take the depression associated with lack of interpersonal power and control and kick themselves for being inadequate. Even this form of self-blame provides the victim with a measure of control that feels better than none at all. This is a common reaction for victims of many types of misfortune that is referred to as posttraumatic response (Floyd, 1987). There are times when hitting back at anyone or anything feels better than doing nothing at all. On his way home, Tom can blame his tormentors but he cannot make them stop or make them hurt. By also blaming himself for being inadequate, he finds a way to at least punish someone directly. Self-punishment at least provides a ready target that is not likely to fight back. The result can vary widely from the most common, simply bad-mouthing of oneself, to physical self-mutilation or potentially even to suicide.

Devon used the commonly accepted model of sports and his star status to demonstrate his power. It was all he knew that seemed to work. Mary takes passive-aggressive actions against people, which generally serves to make things worse but at least gives her some sense of power. Tom takes few actions to take control but spends lots of time thinking about everything from dirty tricks to murder. Thoughts of anger, revenge, and obsessive or rigid actions are all common for victims of bullies (Floyd, 1987). These people are hurt and perceive no normally acceptable ways to regain control of their lives. The self-destructive behaviors that accompany the fears of children (Robinson et al., 1992) may be the only means they see to show themselves and the world how they really can be in charge.

SUCCESS IDENTITY

Being labeled as victims who cannot control what happens to them often translates into feelings of personal inadequacy and failure. These feelings of failure and inadequacy occur in many different human situations. Prisoners in World War II German concentration camps frequently saw themselves as inadequate because they could not control their environment (Frankl, 1984) even though the forces against them were obviously overwhelming. Tom and Mary generally feel a similar sense of failure and inadequacy even though the danger in their environments does not objectively compare with the realities of concentration camp life and death. Most of Devon's experiences in sports and school were confirming and success-laden, but his feelings about his experiences with gangs was a different story. In these situations, he saw himself as inadequate and eventually found himself in a life-ending event where he could see only his inability to deal with his tormentors.

Victims are labeled by themselves or others because they have not successfully handled a situation, and the more often the label is highlighted, the greater are the problems that result. Their failures are likely to have a negative impact on self-esteem regardless of the degree to which they actually could have taken control of the situation. It has been shown, for example, that the more negatively experienced events a young person has, the greater will be that person's stress level and the lower their self-esteem (Youngs, Rathge, Mullis, & Mullis, 1992) Tom and Mary could be expected to have lower self-esteem than Devon just because they were picked on more often, by more peers, and in more situations. Their lack of success in life was thrown in their faces more often than it was to Devon, which makes the comments more difficult to ignore or argue against.

Victims of bullies often are found to have less confidence in their ability to handle situations than others and also to have lower self-esteem. Being bullied continues to lower self-esteem even further (Smith, 1991). Victims of bullies have tried to work things out, but have found mostly failure. It seems only human that they do not want to tell other peers or adults of their failures and further highlight their failures for everyone to see (Besag, 1989); however, by keeping their failures hidden from others, they limit the possibilities for having others contradict the view of themselves as inadequate or for getting help to improve the situation. The most common pattern is to hide one's failures, not get help to find better ways of coping, and have the continuing inability to cope; this provides proof that they are truly inadequate. The productive objective is to break that pattern wherever and whenever possible.

Bullies search for victims that have the greatest vulnerability to their own methods of bullying. Confident and determined youth are less likely to be continuing targets of bullies, although they may experience occasional or situational bullying. They are also likely to experience fewer personal problems from those times when they are bullied (Besag, 1989). Victims like Mary label themselves as victims and communicate that vulnerability to others, thereby making it more likely that they will be continuing targets. Mary's vulnerability is apparent to the bully and, as with most victims of crime (Morgan & Zedner, 1993), the greater the victim's vulnerability, the greater is the potential impact of victimization. Because Mary has become more vulnerable to attack than other students, she is identified more easily as a target and likely will have greater repercussions from those attacks.

Devon provides an example of someone who has a success identity with minimal vulnerability in most situations. Consequently, he receives few attacks from bullies most of the time; however, when his vulnerability was greater, as it was on his last evening in the street, the likelihood of his becoming a serious target also increased. He knew he was vulnerable and, unlike most of his life, had no success identity in that particular situation to call upon for ideas and strength. He was at the mercy of the bullies because he did not have his normal success identity or viable ways to gain it back.

LEARNED BEHAVIORS

The first time Devon was offered drugs by an older student he simply said, "I don't want to do that and my mom would kill me."

It was a straightforward answer, but it got only raucous laughter and unending "momma's boy" comments from Shooter and his gang. Simple honesty was only greeted by humiliation. No one is happy about being humiliated, so Devon searched for another answer next time. "Hey, I'd like to, but I can't do it. The Man will take away my future."

The new answer did not get Shooter and his boys completely off Devon's back, but it got a less negative reaction than his original answer. He found that certain answers and ways of answering got him less humiliation than others. Smiling was good if Shooter wasn't mad. Looking down was good particularly when Shooter was mad. The best words seemed to be the ones that blamed someone else that Shooter also disliked. The best answers in Devon's mind were the ones that got less reaction. They were fake answers, but this was not as important to Devon as the fact that he could reduce the degree of embarrassment. He was learning rather unnatural avoidance behaviors that got him out of situations more easily than his previous experiences, but they also left him feeling dishonest and inadequate. He would put up with the trade-off to get through the bad times even though he hated it and himself for doing it.

Devon is similar to most people in that they learn to react to situations based on how previous experiences turned out. Good experiences with positive reinforcements encourage a person to repeat the positive experiences. Devon handled his violent neighborhood, in part, by continuing to play better basketball and doing what his coach and mom told him. He got positive reactions from the crowds, his parents, most adults, and most students, so he kept on doing what earned him rewards. Those positive rewards for doing what he did naturally were not available in his reactions with the bullies. What he learned was not how to get rewarded for his true self but how to avoid punishment by acting differently from what he actually believed was right.

Devon's reactions to Shooter were no longer the strong, true reactions of the self-confident athlete but were the weak, deceitful reactions of victims. These were rare situational reactions for him, but they were common ones for Tom and Mary who made their weak, avoiding reactions a part of most of their reactions with people. This "learned helplessness" as a way of existing is a common response for victims that they develop over time rather than inherit genetically (Seligman & Peterson, 1986).

VERBAL AND RELATIONSHIP SKILLS

One common denominator for people in any victimization situation is that they run out of words or other ways to relate when they are being victimized. The relationship skills they use in other situations are not effective during these crisis times. Devon had better relationship skills than Tom or Mary in general, but none of them had the necessary skills to deal with those times when their bullies gained control of the situation.

Tom and Mary probably were bullied more often than Devon in part because they had less adequate verbal and relationship skills. Their more passive behaviors that are not responsive to what is going on around them are likely to lead to peer rejection (Lochman, 1985). This more classic victim model is an individual who has difficulty relating to peers in general and not just bullies. They tend to have poor communication skills and ineffective social skills (Besag, 1989). These weaknesses are probably a good part of the reason why frequently victims are generally less popular than others (Smith, 1991). The lack of these skills reduces the likelihood that others will want to be involved with the victim.

Victims generally come to choose some form of isolation as a means of dealing with problem situations. This isolation is one of the signals that demonstrates their potential insecurity to others who might look to bully them (Greenbaum, 1989). The combination of poor relationship skills and isolating oneself as a defense from being abused is harmful to a person's development and can continue to have impact in later life. One study demonstrated how a group of men who had unusual degrees of inhibition with women as adults were also outcasts who had poor peer relationships and often were bullied as children (Gilmartin, 1987). This confirms what most of us already know—that the habits formed in youth are likely to follow us through to adulthood where the impact can be even greater.

Another type of victimization situation that has some comparability to victims of bullies is sexual abuse. We find that sexually abused children are more likely to become sexually abused adults probably due in part to impaired social skills and feelings of isolation (Himelein et al., 1994). The trauma attached to being victimized brings on much retardation of social skills and feelings of isolation; however, it also is likely that some of these victims had fewer social skills and were more isolated than most people even before their first victimization. A nongregarious nature, little interest in others, shyness, and obsessive behaviors all are associated with victims of bullies (Besag, 1989). These characteristic behaviors often can be seen to worsen after victimization, but there is a good possibility that many were present before the individuals were actively bullied.

Some victims are referred to as *provocative* in that they not only have weak relationship skills but also the relationship techniques that they do use tend to aggravate the situation further. Provocative victims tend to be more active, stronger, and more easily provoked than other victims (Smith, 1991). Gil was a boy who could not sit still in school and was less likely to be in his seat than almost anywhere else. He was always physically butting into peer groups regardless of the group's interest in him. When they would make it clear that he was not appreciated, Gil's social insensitivity gave no recognition to the desires of the group. He would create a commotion and become the center of attention but probably not leave until the group itself either pushed him out or broke up just to get away from him. Like many provocative victims, Gil would aggravate the situation further by going to the teacher or playground monitor to complain that he was being picked on by the group while completely ignoring his part in the situation. Provocative victims such as Gil are picked on not only because they may be easy targets but also because their inappropriate interpersonal or social skills create resentment and frustration in others.

A look at young children can help one understand how persistent victims, like bullies, tend not to be effective group members or leaders because of their poor skills in negotiating and dealing with conflicts. Very young children with these weaknesses do not attract other students to them. Even the superagreeable playmates who will do anything others want do not attract other students (Trawick-Smith, 1988). These super-agreeable children tend to be manipulated and later discarded when more attractive students are available.

Jill is one of these individuals who consistently acts to please others by saying whatever she thinks they want to hear. When there are no other sources of support around for Jill's peers, she is tolerated; however, when other peers arrive, Jill becomes expendable and her aggravating habits begin receiving attention. Jill can go quickly from a marginally accepted group member to a potential victim without changing her behaviors at all. She is an example of how super-agreeable people also are likely to become victims even though they may get somewhat better treatment than those who only isolate themselves from others (Trawick-Smith, 1988).

PHYSICAL CHARACTERISTICS

No specific physical characteristics are always present in victims of bullies. Victims come in all shapes, sizes, and degrees of intelligence. *Anyone is vulnerable under the right circumstances;* however, some characteristics appear to be present more often than others.

The study of victims and bullies can apply to any age group, but it tends to focus on youth because occurrences are more frequent there. General victimization studies point out that the age group of 12 to 24 is both the most victimized group and also the group most likely to commit crimes (Fattah, 1989). Whether it is hurtful teasing, sexual abuse, robbery, or murder, young people appear to have more to worry about regarding their personal safety than do older adults who live in similar environments.

General crime statistics also show that, beyond age, other groups who suffer the most from victimization are also the most violent groups. Males at all ages, for example, are the victims of crime more often than females with the exception of sexual abuse crimes. Males also tend to perform more acts of violence than females so that male-on-male violence is the most common interaction (Fattah, 1989). These general crime characteristics appear to be consistent with research on bullies and victims in schools where more males are identified as being bullies and also victims of bullies (Hoover et al., 1992). No one is immune, but the more aggressive and violent the surrounding population is, the greater is the likelihood that a person will become a victim.

Tom and Mary have never been as good as others at physical activities. They are much more the norm for victims than is Devon who was an excellent athlete. Studies have found that as many as 75% of boys who were regular victims of bullies had coordination problems, usually of a mild nature (Olweus, 1978). Victims of bullies also have a tendency to be younger, smaller, and weaker with lower energy levels and lower pain tolerances than other students (Besag, 1989). Tom and Mary fit a number of these categories, which probably increases the likelihood that they would become victims of bullies.

Young people report that the most common reasons they felt they were bullied often included similar physical characteristics. Physical weakness was the highest rated for males and the clothes I wore was another of the five highest reasons. Facial appearance and overweight were among the most common for females (Hoover et al., 1992). What you look like and your physical abilities are clearly characteristics that have an effect on whether a person is likely to be a victim of bullies. These features are not likely to cause the bullying but they do offer the ability for people to place labels on individuals that will mark them as potential victims.

Young people like Tom and Mary are neither disabled nor so extremely different that people will have sympathy for them. They are just different enough to be recognized, and people likely will have the expectation that they can change those different aspects if they would only try. Tom, for example, no longer even tries to get into physical playground games. He learned some time ago that he was mortified when he made more errors in a game than other players. The teasing he got served to multiply the pain and frustration. Later, children began to tease him even before he made mistakes on the field, and the teasing continued after the game was over. His solution was to avoid being anywhere near the games. He did not like it but found that he could reduce the amount of harassment he got for his clumsiness.

Tom sometimes would find himself wishing he were Ed who had cerebral palsy and spent the day in a wheel chair. The idea sounded crazy even to Tom himself, so he never told anyone. What Tom recognized was that Ed got sympathy, understanding, and attention for his physical disability whereas Tom only got harassment for his lack of coordination or pain. At times he would find himself daydreaming about how to create a bad accident for himself (i.e., that would not hurt too much) so that others might give him positive attention for this severe physical deficiency rather than ridicule for his minor ones.

Tom's example seems rather consistent for victims of bullies. Their physical differences generally are not great enough to warrant obvious sympathy, yet they are enough to be noticed and have a social impact. Others may look at Tom as though he actually could change these not so different characteristics if he only tried harder. The result of this thinking is that others can blame a portion of the weaknesses on Tom himself because, as they see it, he does not work hard enough to change them. Blaming Tom then allows the bullies to say that their picking on him is "Tom's fault" and "for his own good" when the reality is these thoughts just may be excuses for their bullying behaviors.

None of these findings provide the full answer as to why someone becomes or remains a victim, but each victim does demonstrate some form of vulnerability. *It is probably not the "physical difference" itself that causes a person to be bullied but instead the vulnerability that the difference suggests.*

Consider the example of Dan and Gil who both get glasses for the first time. Dan is proud of them, talks to others about them, points them out, and has a self-confident way of joking about them. He may be teased a little, but it is not likely to turn into extensive bullying. Gil, on the other hand, hates his glasses and thinks they make him look like a jerk. He does all he can to avoid having people see him wearing them, walks away when people begin to talk about them, and hangs his head at the first sign of possible teasing about them. Gil is much more likely to become a victim because of the much greater vulnerability he demonstrates than does Dan.

SCHOOL AND ACADEMICS

All three of our victims have had *positive attitudes towards schoolwork, which is a common general characteristic of victims of bullies* (Besag, 1989). On the other hand, victims also generally fear school and the problems that await them there (Stephens, Greenbaum, & Garrison, 1988). Tom provides the most obvious example of this seeming contradiction. He always encourages his mother to collect his schoolwork so that he can do it at home to keep up with his progress; however, he wants to do that work at home where he feels more safe and secure.

It is difficult for victims to maintain concentration on work at school when they must be continually on guard to fend off potential attacks. Research has shown a clear connection between fear of assault and the desire to avoid going to school (National Institute of Education, 1978). Whether it is physical or psychological maltreatment, we know that these fears reduce self-esteem and produce underachievement in school.

Tom worries about being attacked and these worries also lead to additional thinking time focused on his anger and fantasizing about how to get revenge. These are common characteristics of how victims spend their thinking time in school (Floyd, 1987). Victim thinking patterns are far from the normal and certainly take time away from productive schoolwork. The emotional strength of these thoughts are troubling in themselves and make the situation even more difficult to handle for children. Learning suffers because victims' reactions are not conducive to concentrating, problem-solving, and doing creative education-focused thinking in the school environment.

Victims' grades suffer because of the overwhelming attention they give to their pain and the relationship problems at school. They can suffer further because good grades sometimes can add to the problem. Getting good grades encourages positive feedback from the adults in a student's life but not necessarily from his or her peers. Students have reported that they believe one of the most consistent reasons for why they were bullied was for having good grades (Hoover et al., 1992). It is probably not the grades themselves that cause the bullying; more likely it is when bullies feel put down because of the credit victims get for their grades.

Devon was successful in many ways, one of which was getting reasonably good grades. This was not a problem for most of the students, but it did have an aggravating effect on his tormentors who felt like it was an insult to them. Poor grades and statements of not caring about schoolwork had become almost a mark of honor for them. They also could use the grade issue as an argument for how Devon was not really one of the regular guys. *Any change in school status is likely to increase stress and the vulnerability of students* (Besag, 1989). Going from a self-contained elementary school classroom to a decentralized middle school or from junior high to the even less controlled high school, for example, requires major changes in student patterns of thinking and behaving. Students are unclear as to what is right to do and how to do it. Tension and anxiety make them ready targets for others who might seek to demonstrate their dominance. Added to this problem situation is the fact that 11- to 18-year-olds are at times in their lives where physical, social, academic, psychological, family, and career changes are normally greatest. Everyone will be tense and some will hope to gain control of their environment by demonstrating their power over others. The more difficult these times are, the more likely bullying and victimization are to occur in some form.

MATURATION

One reason adults worry about their lives is because of all the things changing around them (e.g., technology, the environment, transportation, economics, etc.), but children have much more personal changes influencing them. Their bodies and minds are changing many times more rapidly than adults' and they have little life experience to rely on in deciding how to deal with these new aspects of themselves. Extreme and rapid changes place tremendous demands on the young person to make sense out of their world rapidly with relatively little information to go on. The result is that the maturation process, even though it provides new skills and abilities, also causes confusion and doubt about oneself. This is a situation ripe for creating prospective victims of bullies.

Research tells us that the most common worst times children have with feeling victimized by their peers begins around the time of puberty (Hazler et al., 1991). The enormous physical, personal, and social changes going on at that time are surely a part of the reason for this increase. People of all ages going through change try to define the changes, understand them, label them, and control them. When you have little control over the changes, labels become important ways of gaining a form of control by identifying and isolating the changes until they are better understood. These labels often identify characteristics of victims which then serve to isolate not just the characteristic but also the victim.

Peer groups provide useful means of support for members, but they also serve to isolate those that are not identified as members. The major changes in characteristics that occur during maturation often are used as the means for inclusion or exclusion by peer groups. Mary often is called "lard-ass" by the girls who choose to exclude her from their group. Her size is not so unusual except that it can be identified as different from the group of girls who want her excluded. They then can use this physical difference as a way of labeling her as unacceptable even though it has little or nothing to do with why they want to isolate her.

A key factor in the maturation of young people is that people develop at different times and at different rates and people emphasize differences. Mary began her physical-sexual development earlier than most of the other girls, which leaves her even more open to being victimized. Celia, on the other hand, fits in very well right now as one of the girls whose body has not yet begun rounding out; however, she will develop these characteristics later than most and that will put her in a more likely victim situation when her peers begin to see her as different rather than like the rest of them. These two cases help demonstrate that it is not just *who* is more likely to be a victim, but also *when* and *under what circumstances* that likelihood will increase.

Growth spurts, sexual development, changes in interests, mood swings, intellectual skills development, and physical coordination are just a few of the major maturation change categories that increase insecurity in youth. Young people are highly vulnerable in these situations and do not have an adult's strength or skills to fend off the social and internal pressures created. They resort to using whatever opportunities and tactics they see available to them regardless of whether they prove to be the best or the worst actions to take.

The changes caused by maturation tend to even themselves out over time. For example, the vulnerable sixth grade boy who is shorter than others because he is maturing late becomes the norm when he hits his growth spurt later. This helps him eventually but does not eliminate the difficulties he has to overcome when he is different.

Maturing into a different person does not always solve the problems of young victims. Many people suffer as adults from the abuse they took as youth. One particularly telling example is that of a study of adult men who where extremely inhibited and avoided contact with women. These men consistently recalled much victimization by bullies in childhood and adolescence (Gilmartin, 1987). Their experiences as children appeared to have extreme, long-term negative consequences.

The previous example is extreme because most bullying is only temporary and such victims go on to lead relatively normal lives. The term normal life, however, does not mean there are no long-term effects. Most adults can think back to particularly difficult times during their development when who they were and what value they had was called into question. They know that these experiences have an effect on their lives because they find themselves making decisions, not based on who they are as adults but on the hesitancies they had about themselves during a difficult time in their maturation.

FAMILY

Families of victims and bullies probably have more in common than they have differences. An overriding factor in the families of consistent bullies as well as those of victims is the fact that the families had a variety of problems

(Stephenson & Smith, 1989). Inconsistent discipline in the home was a common problem that was often a part of difficulties in child-parent relationships. The families also suffered from financial worries, social concerns, and marital difficulties. *Abuse in the home by parents or siblings is another common factor that increases the likelihood that a student will be either a bully or victim at school.* It seems clear that the more problems and inconsistencies exist in the family, the greater the probability is that the children will fall into the victim or bully category. These can be seen, in part, as reactions to the difficulties they find at home as well as those they find outside of the home.

One area where victim families do tend to differ from others is an over-involvement in the affairs and welfare of the family members. *Families of victims tend to put significantly more energy into protection and guidance of the child than they place on encouraging independence of thought and actions* (Oliver, Oaks, & Hoover, 1995). Both children and parents need to recognize the limits of parental or family power to protect individuals from acts of abuse (Morgan & Zedner, 1993). A situation involving Tom and his mother provides an example of overly protective and unrealistic ways of dealing with his problems. Tom frequently does not want to go to school as is very often the case with victims. Each time he complains in this way, his mother reacts in a soothing manner and takes over responsibility for dealing with the problems. She takes him to the doctor, cares for him, makes him his favorite foods, collects his homework from school, and then helps him do it. She takes care of his problems but does not similarly encourage him to face his problems independently. There will be great family discussion of his difficulties and the family will make most of the key decisions for him. When it is discovered that Tom is being bullied, there will be virtually no discussion of what Tom might do. Instead, the discussion will focus on what mom and dad need to do at school and with Juan's parents to fix the situation.

Tom has become overly dependent on his family to make him feel better and solve problems. He seeks to spend his time with his parents and family more for the security of it than the enjoyment they share. He gets so much closeness and caring at home from his mother that he does not feel pressured to work at getting closer to his peers. Tom will have to acquire more independence in this area in order to start his own independent family in later life. The less practice his family gives him in this task while he is young, the harder it will be for him to learn successfully as he gets older.

Families need to be supportive of one another, but they also must encourage sufficient independence so that individuals will be able to function on their own when not with the family. Tom has learned to use his family as the way out of dealing with his problems at school. The strength of relationships and concern in his family could be much more valuable to him if it could be used to encourage more personal responsibility and independence of action on his part.

SOCIETY

The lawyer for one of the gang members involved in Devon's death put it this way, "Devon died of knife wounds and an overdose of drugs while arguing with his peers." There is not enough emotion and revulsion in this statement to satisfy Devon's family, friends, or anyone who knew the boy or the situation. The lawyer's statement is an attempt to eliminate the concept of victim from the situation, but society is not likely to buy it. Societies need to designate victims in order to clarify and reaffirm values and set limits on behaviors.

The prosecutor put it another way, "This young boy who was admired by young people and adults alike, who gave to the community, and who was a model for all of us to live by, was murdered by a band of thugs for no reason other than that he was *good.*" This lawyer wants Devon clearly and unquestionably to be seen as the undeserving victim where the bad guys are identified just as clearly. She wants everyone to know that the victim, his family, and particularly the values for which they stand deserve everyone's support.

Societies need individuals and groups that are identified clearly as the wronged party (Miers, 1990). Recognizing these people as victims allows us to make strong statements about what we believe, what we stand for, and what is acceptable behavior. Without such identified people, our beliefs and values have little practical application. Plantation owners did not want the African slave to be identified as a person for fear that they then would be recognized as the victim of the system that used them. Civil rights was only an issue for Blacks after it finally was recognized by the majority that Blacks were, in fact, people and therefore deserving of the same treatment as Whites. *Giving recognition to victimization in school serves much the same purpose of humanizing the people who are being wronged and forcing others to take a more solid stand on their beliefs.*

The labeling of someone as a victim has both positive and negative implications. The positive influence is the increased visibility given to the wrongs being done. Everyone who is forced to recognize the victim as both a person and a victim then must make personal choices regarding the values involved and how those values will be acted upon. Where do people stand on abuse? What are the words people would use to describe it? How fair is it? What actions should be taken? These are just a few of the questions that awareness of the problem creates. Without a personalized awareness, people can go along ignoring those being hurt and the values that are not being supported.

A negative of labeling is that labels can serve to keep someone in their societal place. Labeled victims can ask for support and sometimes retribution; however, victims also are looked upon as weaker or less adequate than they might be. For example, ***students often rate bullies as having higher social status than victims*** (Oliver, Hoover, & Hazler, 1994). People may sympathize with the victims, but they also see them as being less socially acceptable.

The United States is a country that values independence and making it on your own. People will stand up for victims, seek retribution for victims, and express sympathy for victims; but they do not see the individual as truly valued until they have shed their victim role. The school victim is treated in much the same way. When others are made sufficiently aware of the victim's plight, they will seek ways to support them. The negative baggage attached to that support is the impression that the victim is not the quality person they should be until they can effectively shed the label, victim.

Figure 3.1 lists characteristics of victims, issues relative to each characteristic, and resources where for information on each characteristic can be found.

Characteristic	Issues	Cites
Power and control	External locus of control	(Seligman & Peterson, 1986)
	Passive	
	Passive-aggressive	(Olweus, 1978)
	Given labels to reduce power	(Goffman, 1968)
	Depressive traits	(Besag, 1989)
	Anger, revenge, obsessive, rigid	(Floyd, 1987)
	Self-blame, self-punishment	(Floyd, 1987)
	Self-destruction	(Robinson et al., 1992)
Success identity	Low self-esteem	(Smith, 1991)
	Hide failures	(Youngs et al., 1992)
		(Besag, 1989)
	Vulnerability	(Morgan & Zedner, 1993)
Learned behaviors	Learned helplessness	(Seligman & Peterson, 1986)
Verbal and relationship skills	Poor communication skills	(Besag, 1989)
	Ineffective social skills	(Besag, 1989)
	Isolation	(Greenbaum, 1989)
	Uninterested in others, shyness, nongregarious, obsessive	(Besag, 1989)
	Provocative victims tend to be more active, stronger, and more easily provoked	(Smith, 1991)
	Provocative victims—create resentment and frustration	(Olweus, 1978)
		(Sharpe & Smith, 1994)
	Less popular than others	(Smith, 1991)
Physical characteristics	Ages 12 to 24	(Fattah, 1989)
	Males	(Fattah, 1989)
	Coordination difficulties	(Olweus, 1978)
	Younger, smaller, weaker, low energy, low pain tolerance	(Besag, 1989)
	Male—physical weakness	
	Female—facial appearance, different clothes	(Hoover et al., 1992)
School and academics	Positive attitude toward schoolwork	(Besag, 1989)
	Fear of school	(Stephens et al., 1988)
	Focused on anger and fantasizing	(Floyd, 1987)
	High grades as a labelling factor	(Hoover et al., 1992)
	Change in school status increases vulnerability	(Besag, 1989)
Maturation	Worst time—puberty	(Hazler et al., 1991)
Family	Variety of problems in family	(Stephenson & Smith, 1989)
	Inconsistent discipline	
	Financial worries, social concerns	
	Marital difficulties	
	Abuse in home	
	Overinvolvement of family members	(Oliver, Oaks, & Hoover, 1994)
	Overly dependent on parents	(Oliver, Oaks, & Hoover, 1994)

Figure 3.1. Characteristics of victims.

SECTION II
PROMOTING ISSUES
IN COMMON:
A MODEL FOR THERAPY

Promoting Issues in Common (PIC) is a model for therapy with bullies and victims in conflict. It was developed over years of practice in schools, agencies, and private practice with youth and adults having difficulties in relationships. One part of those relationship problems almost always concerned the distribution and use of power and control between participants as well as the unique practical problems that needed to be overcome. No therapy situation demonstrates these issues more than working with bullies and victims in conflict.

Much of the research and theory previously cited focused attention on the nature and dimensions of bullying. Some suggestions for general prevention methods were provided, but little was offered on techniques or models for providing therapy to bullies and victims. These early contributions, however, did begin establishing a base of common principles upon which an overall therapeutic model might be developed. The PIC method demonstrates the evolution of those principles when combined with current theory, research, and therapists' experiences.

The structure of the following three chapters rests on several concepts for its foundation. Chapter 4 emphasizes the critical factor that, before therapy can begin, participants must be involved in a situation that is perceived as more safe than is their bully/victim conflict environment. The heightened tension, anger, and frustration involved in the middle of conflicts between bullies and victims is such that the only reasonable choice is to lower it to more workable levels. The additional factor involved is that serious situations consistently include some form of punishment for bullies and sometimes victims also. The emphasis on gaining control and moderating tension levels creates an atmosphere where more objective decisions can be made and the healing process can begin. Only after emotions have calmed and standard disciplinary procedures have been followed does the therapist have a legitimate chance to begin a positive working relationship with each of the individuals involved.

The second stage of the PIC model described in Chapter 5 emphasizes evaluation of all concerned parties as to their individual needs and abilities and also those needs common to their relationship. Well meaning people often will continue to keep those in conflict apart from each other after their initial separation. Others will immediately pressure participants to shake hands and make up. Neither of these is likely to be both practical and valuable in the long run. Individuals will need both help on their own problems in individual counseling and assistance with the problem relationship, which can be handled most effectively in a joint intervention. A period of time designated to assess these individual and joint needs as well as the abilities available to work on them is essential in order to set a productive stage for future development.

Lowering tensions and assessing needs and abilities allow the active intervention stage to begin with the greatest chance of success. In Chapter 6 are the intervention steps designed to help participants eventually deal directly with their relationship problems in a joint format. It outlines the process, techniques, and criteria to be used for deciding when, how, and in what ways it is appropriate to move different individuals through the process.

It must be stressed that this model is one for assisting people with problem relationships to deal directly with those relationships. Students, parents, and, at times, professionals will question whether the time, energy, and frustration that go into improving such problem relationships are really worth it. Sometimes it is not worth it, and making such a decision is part of the evaluation process as is the question of how much progress should be sought realistically.

The greatest value of this method is far greater than simply improving one youthful relationship. The larger potential benefit surfaces when individuals can take a problem relationship and learn to improve it together. This joint problem solving of relationship problems increases individuals' skills, knowledge, and confidence in their ability to overcome future relationship problems. Bullies and victims see few positive ways of interacting with each other. Working together to develop new interaction methods that produce greater benefits over longer periods of time will expand all participants' potential for developing the many future relationships with which they will be faced.

Chapter 4

PROMOTING ISSUES IN COMMON: STEPS TOWARD GAINING CONTROL

Ahmad

Ahmad's mother fought back conflicting emotions as she and her son left the hospital. He had been there for two days recovering from the fierce beating he took from a local gang. She was relieved to know he will recover but saddened by his suffering. She was furious that this could happen to her quiet boy and even angrier that there seemed to be no reason for it. The only thing she could get from police and the school was that it was apparently a ritual beating where new gang members earned their way in by demonstrating their viciousness on a random victim.

This is not the first time Ahmad has been a victim of bullying. Throughout his 11 years in the local school system there were many occasions when he had money, jackets, jewelry, and other things taken from him by bigger boys or gangs. He had been hit from time to time and verbally abused by many of the same youth. Over time, Ahmad had learned how to stay out of the way for the most part and avoid such confrontations. He kept to safe places where other students and responsible adults were. When there was a problem that he could not handle in these ways, the intervention of school authorities was sought either by Ahmad or his mother. It was not the school life that anyone would choose for oneself or one's children, but at least it had been manageable until this latest disaster.

Now the fear of school and people in it was not as manageable as it had been. Even though some of those who had beaten him were being punished, he did not feel safer. In fact, he worried even more that the punishments given out would only make his tormentors and their friends more likely to get back at him and maybe even worse this time. Ahmad could not stand the idea of facing school, the friends of those involved, or even other students who would be looking at him as some kind of leper. He wanted out and he wanted revenge. He did not know how to get revenge, so he at least wanted no more part of school.

Ahmad's mother sympathized with him, but she knew that leaving school now would only make things worse. There would be no chance to get the education needed to get away from their neighborhood and the fear-filled life known by its residents. She knew the next few days and weeks would be critical for Ahmad and his future.

Yolanda

Yolanda's fourth-grade year was nothing special until she and others realized what things were happening to her. What made it worse was that they only seemed to be happening to Yolanda and not her friends. The standard child's straight up and down figure was now giving way to obvious curves on Yolanda. Here hips were noticeably wider and breasts were now a fact rather than an idea of something in the future. Her favorite clothes didn't fit and every morning she had to decide whether to dress in a way to show her new self or to hide it.

Hiding became impossible after the day she got up from her seat in class only to discover that there was blood on the seat and her clothes. She was horrified and more embarrassed than she had ever been. Something had to be done to cover her fear and embarrassment. Avoiding it was now impossible, so she tried striking out at people verbally. It was all she could think of to do that would demonstrate some strength, allow her to show some pride in her differences, and put some people down thus preventing her from having to answer difficult questions about what the changes in her meant.

Much giggling and many childish jokes occurred about Yolanda behind her back. She was different, and everyone could see she was uncomfortable with it. No one wanted to be browbeaten by her, and she was so unapproachable about what was happening that even the potentially supportive students just stayed out of her way. They had no idea what to do so they too chose to avoid dealing with the anxieties directly.

Yolanda's best friends also were confused. At first they wanted to help, but Yolanda couldn't accept it. She stayed away, so they talked about her by themselves. They could see that she had become physically more mature and this emphasized their anxieties about being less mature. They stayed together even more than usual for support as Yolanda became more aggressive about showing and stating her maturity. Yolanda became more stubborn, and her friends fought back every chance they got.

Now Yolanda was teased constantly for being different. Usually the teasing was not to her face. She would find notes in her desk and in her books. She was described as ugly and accused of having sex with older boys. The harder she fought back with her own name calling and accusations, the more teasing she got. Things were only getting worse in what started out as a school year just like all the others.

Allen

Allen was never the student his teachers would have liked. He had trouble sitting still in the early grades, could not seem to concentrate on work, and wasn't very good at the little work he did. His interactions with teachers always seemed to be about what he was doing wrong. Over the years Allen recognized what a relief it was to get away from the classroom and out on the streets.

Now in eighth grade, Allen already was looking forward to the day he could get out of school for good. He didn't fit in with the teachers or the students. The only place he felt appreciated was when he was with his small gang of friends, many who were older and no longer in school. He felt strong, able, and accepted with his gang, which was so much better than the feelings of inadequacy and unacceptability he felt around school and with the kids there.

It was a struggle every day to show those "damn whimpy" kids at school that they were weaklings in comparison to him. Allen could feel them looking down their noses at him when his back was turned, but he made them pay even if he didn't catch them putting him down. He did what he wanted when the teachers were not looking. He would get in line where he wanted, "borrow" their money when he liked, dunk a kid's head in the toilet, show his knife for emphasis, threaten as needed, and bloody a nose once in a while just as a reminder of what he could do to them. He didn't make real friends but he could at least get them to do what he wanted. Showing his power over others made the school day passable even when it got him in constant trouble.

PROMOTING ISSUES IN COMMON (PIC)

Bullies and victims are people in troubled relationships. The troubles usually involve difficulties in the distribution of power and control that affect the ways people see themselves in these relationships. *When either the bully or the victim acquires new information or skills that will help them revise the distribution of power and control, the relationship shifts.* Changes based on this scenario likely will emphasize the individual needs of the bully and the victim, independent of the other's needs. Attempts to gain advantage from newly found individual power in the relationship often will create battles to see whose changes can overpower the other's.

Yolanda entered puberty in an awkward way as the first and only one from her group to be going through it. She took what was a basically healthy approach to life by making changes in her thinking and behaviors to try to match the situation. Her problem was that she decided upon and implemented these changes independent of the ideas and needs of those around her. She sought only to meet the need of escaping her own embarrassment and fear by isolating herself and striking out. She gained the reprieve from discussing her fears, which she wanted, but at the cost of many friendships and the support they could have brought.

What could Yolanda and her friends have done differently and how can they be helped? The Promoting Issues in Common (PIC) method of counseling bullies and victims attempts to give direct attention to the needs of everyone involved in troubled relationships. The goal is to produce more healthy relationships based on shared needs for support and understanding between those involved.

There is nothing from research to suggest that the children around Yolanda had any desire to be mean and cruel as a group. Yolanda did what she felt she needed to do to protect herself, and those around her did the same. They just picked inappropriate tactics. The PIC method presumes that if Yolanda and her friends could be helped to understand more clearly the needs of the other (i.e., empathy) and be given opportunities to explore those needs both on their own and together, they would realize common fears and anxieties. When we see ourselves as more similar to other persons, we begin to understand and to have stronger feelings for their situations. As our perceived commonalty grows, we become more likely to recognize effective ways of supporting that person and try harder to be supportive because we can identify better with them.

Developing greater empathy for another is not an unheard of idea for professionals or for the general public. It is why family or team members are more likely to support each other in the most difficult of times. It is how the mother recognizes and supports the good part of her son who is convicted of murder. She knows he did wrong but will support him because she has a deep understanding of what is also good about him and what history, beliefs, and feelings he shares with her. They are connected by understanding of commonalties in much the same way that opposing football players who have been screaming obscenities and lashing out at each other during a hard fought game can wind up embracing after the game is over. They both feel that, to do their best, they need to play a dangerous sport in unconventional ways even though this produces great risk to their bodies and relationships. Recognizing the common risks each takes based on their common commitment to the challenge provides the basis for a comradery that can replace the animosity so obvious during battle.

PIC is only fully appropriate as a method when a better relationship actually is desired. Yolanda clearly would benefit from redeveloping positive relationships with her friends and other students making the PIC method clearly a method of choice. Ahmad, on the other hand, is a more questionable candidate for implementation of all aspects of the PIC method. He was a random victim with little previous or continuing relationships with his tormentors. Many parts of the PIC method will be appropriate, but there are real questions about how much of a relationship with the individuals in the gang that beat him is necessary or desirable. Some however, will use the situation to avoid associating with Ahmad or to tease, threaten, or even isolate him on a regular basis. Ahmad cannot continually escape all these relationships and their repercussions. These relationships provide viable opportunities to utilize all three aspects of the PIC model.

What must be kept in mind is that the PIC method of counseling is a therapeutic method that operates at its best when it is part of an overall system of dealing with these problems. PIC is not a method of discipline; however, the more appropriate and coordinated the discipline plan already in effect, the more effective will be the PIC method of counseling. A fair, well understood, and effectively implemented discipline plan increases the likelihood that counseling will be most effective for the most people. Neither PIC nor discipline methods will replace the other. They need to work efficiently together so that enforcement of rules can be taken care of in coordination with healing the psychological, interpersonal, and social damage done by those who wittingly or unwittingly break key social responsibility rules.

The PIC method seeks to increase awareness of bully-victim problems and also to bring about a better understanding of all those touched by the problems.

It does this on a rather small scale with the individuals and groups most directly involved in specific problems. An awareness building and maintenance program also must be in place to spread the concept and the positive behaviors that come from it. *Everyone benefits when people seek to understand, work with, and care for others.* These are difficult but critical tasks that require effort from everyone to have the most beneficial effects for all concerned.

The following material will explain steps in the PIC method for counseling bullies and victims. Examples will be provided to demonstrate the decisions that need to be made regarding the use of these steps as well as how to implement them. The model flows from seeing the bully first, then the victim individually, and then to potential meetings between them to the degree that progress towards working on common concerns is made. It is not a model that perfectly fits every case but is a flexible model that is most effective when the specific circumstances and personalities involved are taken into account during implementation. Suggestions will be made throughout the discussion to identify potentially differing circumstances and how the specifics of the model need to be adjusted.

STEPS TOWARD GAINING CONTROL

Counseling cannot take place until a basic level of control is in place. Only then can both reason and emotions be used together in the therapy process. For example, counseling cannot occur while students are physically fighting. Likewise, no successful counseling can occur when one person is actively bullying another. *The first steps in an overall model are therefore those steps needed to gain control of the situation in an ordered and reasoned way.* The active conflict must be halted if a working counseling relationship is to be established with those involved.

The establishment of and follow-through on functional rules and regulations are the cornerstone of this stage. These rules and regulations must be enforced by human beings, so the ways people act while enforcing them is also critical. *What is communicated while enforcing rules is often as important, or more so, than the actual enforcement of the rules.* The ideas, feelings, and beliefs communicated while enforcing rules are "human lessons" while the rules and regulations only provide the structure for the lesson. The following steps are designed to provide a combination of a fair-minded enforcement structure carried out by caring, objective, and reasonable people who are not directly a part of the conflict. The greater the success of these steps, the better the atmosphere will be for productive therapy and learning for everyone concerned.

Step 1: Assist anyone who is in danger of serious harm.

The first role of anyone attempting to assist in a situation is to assess the degree of physical or psychological harm being experienced and then to take actions appropriate to the level of danger. Ahmad was beaten seriously, to the extent that it was life-threatening. Anyone who saw that situation should have done whatever possible to stop the situation immediately. This may have included extreme steps such as calling the police or yelling and screaming to draw the attention of others to the situation. It might even have included physically defending Ahmad if one had the physical ability to do so productively. Anyone's first responsibility would have been to find some way to help protect Ahmad from serious harm.

In a previous example, Tom was picked on regularly in school; this suggests a different danger level necessitating a different reaction. A teacher or fellow student seeing Tom picked on at school or on the bus should recognize that this situation, although a serious problem, would not constitute immediate serious danger to anyone. The most serious problem here would be more long-range while the immediate situation deserves attention that is less drastic than Ahmad's example. Such an evaluation should lead someone to a recognition that physical force likely would not be necessary and that a verbal intervention probably should be attempted first. A low-level, casual physical intervention like moving closer to the youth in conflict often can be enough to distract them from the conflict.

The most important thing to remember at this stage is that one must judge the level and immediacy of serious danger in a situation. The closer the situation is to life-threatening potential, the stronger are the reactions that likely would be appropriate. Consider some examples of the extremes. A police officer is probably right to use his weapon when someone is shooting from a rooftop at people in a crowded street; however, that same officer should not be using his weapon to stop a person who stole a candy bar and is now running from the store. Likewise, one who observes bullying should not attempt to physically push, grab, or hit a bully who is verbally harassing someone where escalation to a more serious level is not likely. On the other hand, an observer who sees someone being physically beaten may find it necessary to take whatever physical steps are necessary to stop the beating.

More extreme levels of potentially immediate psychological trauma also may require stronger interventions. A middle school teacher was standing outside her room when she saw Yolanda talking to a nonassertive fifth-grader, Alice. The teacher had seen Yolanda bullying others and had recognized how

Alice was a likely target, but she could hear or see little now that would indicate that this was bullying. Her first reaction was to watch casually for the time being and, if nothing changed, not get involved. She then saw Alice begin looking at the floor and trying to move away while Yolanda stopped her from escaping and was getting louder. The major imbalance of power in this interaction where one person wanted out badly was obvious.

Recognizing the change in the balance of power, the teacher began moving closer to the girls in hopes that Yolanda would see her approaching and stop. It did not work. Yolanda was too involved and ignored the teacher's approach. She continued to become more abusive, bringing Alice to the verge of tears. Seeing that things were going downhill, the teacher intervened directly by telling Yolanda to stop. When Yolanda ignored the teacher's directions, there was little left to do but to step between the girls physically and move Yolanda back to stop the interaction. The teacher told Alice to go get cleaned up and go back to class and stayed with Yolanda until she calmed down.

The teacher in this example tried her best to stop a confrontation using the least aggressive means that would work. It is an excellent model for anyone. She knew that the less aggressive the methods she used in a successful intervention, the less negative repercussions there would be for everyone involved. It would be much easier to help the problem relationship later if the confrontation was kept at the lowest tension possible level now. Her eventual decision to step physically between the girls and grab Yolanda became the only recourse to protect Alice from an increasing level of psychological and possibly physical harm. Such a physical intervention would not have been appropriate had lesser measures proven successful and had one individual not been clearly hurt.

Step 2: Convey realistic concern without undue anxiety.

A major assumption in PIC is that, whenever possible, attempts will be made to follow-up the gaining of control with productive counseling and learning. Meeting this assumption demands that a realistic picture of the situation be recognized and also that anxiety be kept at moderate levels. The problem should not be sugarcoated or blown out of proportion. The situation needs to be viewed by all as one that can lead to more serious problems if not dealt with honestly and directly now.

People have competing natural inclinations to reduce tension as much as possible for comfort and to increase concern as much as possible to assure attention to the situation. It is a major challenge to find that realistic level of concern that helps meet some portion of both comfort and attention needs.

Intervention at this stage requires individuals to

(a) see the situation and its possible consequences objectively,

(b) recognize the participants' levels of concern,

(c) recognize the needs of the participants, and

(d) de-escalate or escalate perceptions of the situation as necessary to achieve appropriate concern without excessive anxiety.

Accurately observing the situation requires objectivity and an understanding of the people and problems involved. Seeing one person yelling at another may be just a momentary flare-up or a culturally accepted form of interaction. A similar interaction also could be one in a series of bullying acts, a prelude to more serious acts by the bully, or the final straw that pushes a victim to respond with inappropriate violence. The observer needs to understand the circumstances and culture of the people involved in order to make accurate and unbiased decisions about what actions to take.

The school principal, Mr. Denson, saw a younger boy, Seth, accidentally brush up against Allen in the hall. He could see Allen ready to take this as a challenge that it was not meant to be. As Allen began to move towards Seth, Mr. Denson decided that it would be good to move immediately before actions and emotions escalated. He quickly walked next to Allen and said, "Hi. How you doing?"

Allen didn't answer, but he was distracted from getting to Seth. The tension was lowered by Mr. Denson's action and Allen's need to think of a reply to Mr. Denson. As they walked together down the hall, Mr. Denson could see that Allen still had his eye on Seth and recognized the situation was not over. Now that he had a little more control of how things were going, the principal decided to escalate the importance of the situation with Allen just a little: "I saw Seth accidentally bump you. It made you mad, huh?"

"Damn right." Allen said.

"Looked like an accident to me." Mr. Denson said. "I don't even think he knew it happened. This is not one to get yourself in trouble over Allen. There are more important things you've got to get done in life. Don't let this little thing get in the way."

Mr. Denson was not just talking to Allen about *how to do the right thing*. He also was raising the importance of what Allen would do next in terms that Allen could understand from his point of view. Allen did not want to be in trouble with the principal at this time or in this way and Mr. Denson knew it. The principal used his understanding of the situation, Seth, and Allen first to de-escalate and then to escalate the significance of the situation in order to keep a realistic focus on what happened and the potential personal consequences of the next set of actions.

Step 3: Delay making final judgments.

One teacher sees Yolanda threatening a smaller girl while another teacher sees Allen grabbing a boy by the shirt in a threatening way. In each case, a professional will recognize that both Yolanda or Allen's behavior is unacceptable and a move to stop them is the first step. But one needs to be careful in the move to control the *situation* that snap judgments are not made on *individuals* before the whole situation is understood. One of the worst mistakes at this point is to begin judging immediately who was right, who was wrong, and what their motivations were. We have seen only a part of the situation and have little or no knowledge about preceding circumstances or what drives the participants. This is the time to reduce tension and not to make judgmental decisions.

How can deciding on immediate judgments about people cause problems? Yolanda threatening a smaller girl is wrong, but we do not know whether there was other fault or conditions that might help better understand the interaction. One teacher may know how the other girls are picking on Yolanda and the struggles she is having with her development. Another teacher without this knowledge sees Yolanda as someone who is basically mean and cruel. These two professionals are likely to take very different sets of actions if either makes immediate decisions regarding right, wrong, and the comments and punishments that follow those judgments. It is much better to delay actions based on judgments of individuals to another time when more information can be sought, considered, and used in an organized and objective manner.

Allen is very different from Yolanda in that he has never really been a successful part of the school system or school peer groups. It would be easy to tag his behavior as "that damn Allen again," assume he is at fault, and immediately implement negative consequences for him based on his record of continuing problem behavior. This is a common reaction in schools, families, and other societal groups: "Once there is a history of problem behavior, you assume the worst and act on that assumption." Unfortunately, these reactions to assumptions simply confirm again and again to Allen that, "He is not liked, not trusted, and not treated with the objectivity and consideration that others get." He has done wrong but, unlike others who have done wrong, he is judged based on the past rather than on a fair and thorough look at the present.

Withholding judgments, even on people with a problem history like Allen, demonstrates that all people will be treated in a similarly fair and concerned manner. Delaying judgment encourages trust on everyone's part that the system will deal with all the present information rather than only past history. It conveys the belief that people and situations can change in positive or negative directions. No one is relegated to being the person they have always been in such a system, and this provides greater encouragement to change.

Allen will probably be found to be at fault later in the process, most likely because he probably was at fault. By delaying judgment on him, however, we demonstrate our belief in his ability to change and encourage him to take an active role in a system that has never worked for him in the past. We keep offering opportunities to change without giving up the responsibility for the system to make the eventual necessary judgments about right and wrong behaviors.

Step 4: Attempt to develop positive working relationships with everyone.

The delay in making personal or official judgments about participants while diffusing the problematic situation allows us better opportunities to develop positive working relationships with everyone involved. Additional first steps are ones demonstrating that we care about those involved, want to hear all sides, will listen closely, and will work as hard as possible to give fair and equal treatment to all concerned. At this stage, we are not trying to take the roles of best buddies, counselor, or parent. Instead, the attempt is to do whatever possible to demonstrate that we are willing and able to listen and work fairly with everyone and that more will be done *when things calm down.*

What does it take to convince someone that positive working relationships are possible? First of all, we need to recognize that it may not be possible to convince everyone that a working relationship can happen. We do not have control over what the other person chooses to do, but we can do everything possible from our side to show the positive possibilities. Taking the first three previous steps is the starting place for gaining people's confidence: protecting all those who might get hurt, conveying realistic concern and anxiety, and delaying judgments. ***Showing genuine confidence in the system to deal with these problems, using good listening skills with everyone, and assuring each person that help will be provided are the additional things that should promote the best chances for developing continuing positive working relationships.***

This is not the problem-solving stage. The system is set up to deal with long-range solutions when emotions have been calmed and that time is not now, not during or immediately following the conflict. The current task is to convince all participants that there is a working system and that the system is ready, willing, and able to help each person when the emergency is over. Explaining honestly, briefly, and specifically that each person will have a chance to tell his or her story and to gain assistance in making things right in the very near future is the task. The system is actually set up to do this and people need to understand the system well enough to make it work for them. This will allow a genuine presentation with assurances that such help will follow.

> "Allen! Stop it! No Seth, I don't want to hear your side either right now. I know you guys don't agree about what is going on here. There will be a time and a place to give your side. This is not the time or place. We'll talk about it at the end of class. Right now I just want everyone to calm down and go about your business for the time being. If you can't calm down right here, then I'll get you to a place where you can get yourself together. We'll get back to this at the end of class. I'll have the principal there too."

Using good listening skills at this stage does not mean long discussions about all the details. Good listening now focuses on hearing from each participant, a recognition of a problem without trying to define all the dimensions of the problem immediately. One also needs to listen for a recognition that there is a process that will take place to follow-up on ways to solve the problem. Seeking to gain control of the situation at this point requires confidence that three critical questions can be answered by all parties:

(a) Do the students recognize why the situation is deemed a problem by some, if not all participants?
(b) Do they know why those seeking to gain control of the situation are doing what they are?
(c) Do they understand what will happen next and why?

The teacher who has broken up the disturbance says, "Do you two understand why I see this as a problem?" "Allen?" (Shakes his head yes, but with a disgusted look.) "Seth?" (Looks down at the floor and shakes his head.)

The teacher needs a more specific assurance of where the two students thoughts are. "Let me try again. Allen, you were grabbing Seth by the shirt and yelling at him. That is not acceptable. Seth, this type of thing has happened before and you need to be a part of us getting it straightened out. I don't know all of what happened to bring this about, but I know it is not okay to let it continue. Do you understand?" (Both boys shake their heads yes.)

"I'll ask Mr. Thompson [the counselor] to see each of you individually because I know he has helped others with these situations in the past."

"Allen, tell me what I've said will be happening."

Allen replies with a still angry look on his face, "We'll talk with you and the principal after class. Then Mr. Thompson will probably see us, but it's not gonna do any good."

Assured that Allen and Seth know the process, the teacher gives one brief but hopeful view of its value, "Doing things this way has helped other people with these kinds of problems and it can help you too. I hope you'll give it a chance."

The teacher also involves Seth by asking, "Seth, why are we doing this with both of you?"

His head down, Seth says, "Well, I didn't do anything, but you say I need to do stuff anyway."

Frustrated but controlled and persistent, the teacher continues: "I don't know whether you have done anything or not. The point is . . . this is a problem for Allen and a problem for you and I want you both to help find ways to stop it from happening again. Do you understand?"

Allen and Seth both reluctantly say, "yes."

No problem was cured but the stage was set for getting the problem out in the open with the right people at the right time. That is the primary purpose of the gaining control stage. The teacher, provided a confident, brief, and knowledgeable picture of what would happen and why. He let both boys know why now was not the time to fully hear everyone out or to decide who was at fault. He asked both Allen and Seth to try to state some portion of the basic process in order to get a degree of assurance that they understood enough to move the process along. They each got some parts right and some wrong, but this allowed the teacher to confirm what was accurate, correct what was not, and repeat what was missed.

Allen and Seth are too upset at this point to be expected to have complete understanding and commitment to the process. This situation is normal when emotions are high; however, we generally can get participants to attend to the major details and reasoning of the process even if they do not want to agree with it. Keep in mind that the major desired outcome is to set a stage for a better working relationship and this does not require that all of the details of that relationship be immediately in place.

Step 5: Designate authorities who will carry out all official actions as quickly as possible.

Any group of people (e.g., communities, schools, classrooms, counseling groups, families, etc.) can spend most of their time determining how to deal with each problematic situation that arises or they can design rules, roles, and procedures that apply to many problems. Effective rules, procedures, and designated roles needed to carry out decisions form a plan that can move people more quickly to the productive work of improving things for the future. Laws, regulations, elected and appointed officials are the ways we make groups operate more efficiently and thus allow us to work on new things rather than re-deciding how to do things that had been decided before. Chapter 7 discusses the basic ways to develop such a plan.

Gaining control of a problematic situation requires that people have confidence that each person will be treated as he or she would be treated. People can move more quickly to working on personal and relationship issues when rules, responses, and roles are clear and followed efficiently. Allen and Seth would have argued all day about what should be done if the teacher had allowed it. The official actions identified by the system are designed to reduce the time spent on this type of argument and move people to more productive work.

The teacher knew the process, explained it, and moved immediately to see that it was carried out as prescribed. These actions had productive effects on gaining control and moving the situation in positive directions.

(a) Time was not wasted in arguing over procedures that were already in place.
(b) Questions about what actions officials should take were eliminated because roles were understood and implemented.
(c) Questions of which student did what, why, how, and what needs to be done to improve the situation were put off until a time and place where more objectivity and less emotion could be arranged.
(d) Confidence that the system would be carried out efficiently and equally for everyone was conveyed through the teacher's words and, more important, the teacher's actions.

(e) Delaying the decisions to notify the principal and counselor about both boys would only have led to speculation among Seth, Allen, and their classmates as to who would get what and when?

The system demonstrated it was moving quickly to do what it always does in a consistent and honest manner. The teacher's actions also confirmed that the system can be expected to do the same next time. The result is that confidence in the system has been increased both in terms of what it is doing now and what it will do in the future.

The teacher not only knew the system and followed through with it but also recognized the need to stay within his designated role. He saw the interaction and intervened in predesigned appropriate ways. Then he briefly explained what would happen including his role, the role of the principal, and that of the counselor.

It can be tempting for a genuinely concerned professional to try also to make administrative decisions or to be the witness, judge, and counselor all in one. Trying to assume more than one of these roles is, at least, counterproductive and has the potential to be very harmful. Teacher, administrator, and counselor positions have evolved precisely because they work best when they are kept as separate as possible. The administrator gets to be the heavy by handing down major punishments so the teacher and counselor can have less conflictive relationships. The counselor does not have to make decisions about grades, placement, and so forth that the teacher does. This allows even more opportunity to focus on personal issues without punishment or academic evaluations being a part of the therapeutic relationship.

Participants involved in any hostile situation are anxious, nervous, angry, scared, frustrated, and their adrenaline is flowing at a rate so high that all their reactions will be extreme. Gaining control of the situation requires lowering the levels of each of these to a point where realistic understanding and reasoning can occur. The time when counseling and healing truly can begin is when control of a situation has been achieved and calm restored. Reasoning and emotions then can take their rightful place in the counseling and learning processes.

Chapter **5**

EVALUATING THE PEOPLE AND PROBLEMS

Ahmad

Ahmad has recuperated from the physical aspects of the beating he took. The two boys who beat him had been in much trouble in school previously, and this event was the last straw. They were expelled from school for the remainder of the year. It is not likely they will return. Each of them had previous charges against them in juvenile court and they will face those charges in the next two months.

The psychological trauma suffered by Ahmad from this and previous events have not healed as well as his physical problems. He wants his mother either to get him out of school so he can find a job or at least "home school" him until he graduates. Almost any choice seems better to him than facing those who have bullied him at school.

Yolanda

Yolanda had plenty of reasons for why she was in trouble again. She told the counselor, "That damn Alice just doesn't get it. She ought to know by now that her and her friends better quit talking behind my back or I'll take care of them. How come no one cares what they do?"

Yolanda had already been to the principal and this time there would be a meeting with the principal and her mother as soon as it could be arranged. Now she has to see the counselor. "Why do we need to go through all this anyway? Why not just do whatever you are going to do and get it over with? No one cares about my side anyhow."

Allen

Allen liked the idea that Seth was more worried by the talk with the principal and the teacher after class than he was. These discipline talks were common for Allen and he resented Seth for being one of those whom no one ever blamed for anything.

OVERVIEW OF THE EVALUATION STAGE

A more serious approach to therapy for bullies and victims can begin once order has been restored, emotions moderated, and formal steps followed. It is not expected that everyone, or perhaps even anyone, will want to be involved in therapy. All participants most likely would like the whole situation just to go away immediately. It is tempting for professionals to give in to this desire to avoid working on the problem. Difficult problems with unwilling participants are emotionally draining and frustrating; however, an organized approach to evaluating the scope of the problems involved can provide ordered therapeutic direction and increase the likelihood of success in overcoming those problems.

The process of evaluating bully/victim problems and their relationships begins with interviewing each participant individually. The purpose is to get to know as much as possible about each individual including the areas in which they individually or collectively need information, support, or skill building. Determining their willingness and ability to work on the problems at hand and the relationships involved are also critical.

Identification of common concerns among participants and setting a stage for joint counseling are the major goals of this stage. Persistent bullying of one student or group by another is a way that people use relationships to meet their individual needs. A clear choice is made to use relationships for personal fulfillment even though the way they do it may be highly inappropriate. The PIC method uses this desire to get needs met through relationships to develop more appropriate means to reach the desired positive ends.

Exactly how this model might work in specific relationships depends on the dynamics of the individuals and the situation involved. A thorough understanding of the people and circumstances is critical in determining the extent that direct interactions between bullies and victims can be used, how and when they can be used, and under what circumstances the interactions will be most effective. The importance of these determinations makes this evaluation stage a critical one that must not be bypassed.

Another key reminder is that all problems of individuals cannot be dealt with through joint counseling between those involved in the conflict. Where students have unique problems or are unwilling or unable to work together, there is little likelihood that participants will be counseled together eventually. The evaluation process is designed to identify the factors that preclude or delay the use of joint counseling of bullies and victims as well as those factors that indicate the appropriateness of joint sessions with bullies and victims.

The evaluation steps that follow serve to lower the pressure on each student, give attention to personal needs, seek true understanding of the situation from all points of view, and test how well each student can begin understanding the other person's view of life and their relationship. The overall goal of this stage is to accomplish this evaluation in a way that also will set a cooperative tone for future sessions both alone with the counselor and potentially together with those on the other side of the conflict.

Step 1: See the probable bully first.

The ideal first step in counseling a bully and a victim is to see the bully first. There are probably many circumstances outside the therapist's control that preclude doing this, but, to the extent it can be obtained, it offers a much more preferable first step in the process. Seeing the bully first helps the counselor in building a relationship and also adds protection for the victim.

Ahmad's mother took him to school to see the counselor. He did not want to go. All he could think about was that time in seventh grade when a student everyone called Tiger took a couple of dollars from him before math class. Ahmad was upset, the teacher recognized it and appropriately let the school counselor know how upset Ahmad appeared. Midway through the class Ahmad was called to the office where he met with the counselor. The discussion was about how he was doing in school and problems he was having, but it did not deal with being forced to give his money to Tiger. It felt good that someone cared about him. Having someone to talk with where there would not be any repercussions was a nice feeling and Ahmad left with a more positive view of the future than when he came. It wouldn't remain that way.

Shortly after Ahmad came back to class, Tiger was called to the office and Ahmad immediately knew this was going to be a problem. Everyone saw the deadly look Tiger gave to Ahmad. A short time later Tiger returned looking just as angry. He and the counselor had talked of his bullying others and, even though no mention was made of specific students, Tiger was sure where the blame for this session fell: that wuss Ahmad had squealed about the lunch money. Other students in the class watched the interaction out of the corners of their eyes. They did not want to get in the middle of what surely was going to be an explosion between Ahmad and Tiger. Ahmad was going to be made to pay for whatever happened, and no one wanted to be another target for Tiger's anger. They did whatever possible just to stay out of the way.

Professionals handled the current situation much better than the one with Tiger. Ahmad would find he was much less likely to be perceived as "getting someone in trouble" in the current situation because he was being seen last and privately. This time the bullies who beat him up already had been seen by administrators, the police, and therapists, and that was unlike the seventh-grade episode with Tiger.

Ahmad got to see the counselor privately this time rather than both he and Tiger being called out of a class where everyone would guess at what was happening. The added social pressure of having everyone see the problem building in class put Ahmad in an even more embarrassing situation. The same pressure pushed Tiger into a place where he became even more committed to getting revenge and demonstrating his power for everyone to see. The current situation relieved Ahmad from worry that what he said in private to the counselor could be interpreted as getting the others in trouble as it had been with Tiger.

What Ahmad did not know is that two other boys who had bullied him from time to time also had been counseled regarding their bullying of Ahmad. The counselor realized that, if the two bullies were seen first, they would be less likely to blame Ahmad and therefore less defensive and more open to a positive counseling relationship. This also would set a productive stage for the counselor to discuss with Ahmad the possibility of improving his relationships with these boys instead of continually seeking ways to escape relationships like these.

Step 2: Identify concerns regarding the problem.

It is very important to build a level of trust at this stage. Both bullies and victims know there is a problem even though they may not want to admit it.

Much of their tentativeness and anxiety will be caused by the fact that they do not know how the adults in their lives will react to their thoughts and behaviors. They are just as unclear about how much control they really can exert over the process. Will adults take it into their own hands? Will they ignore it? Will they tell me what to do? Will they really want my opinion on what to do, or will they just want me to say what they think should be done? Will they let me do what I think is best or force me to act their way? These concerns about the problem and how others will take those concerns create an initial lowering of trust in the counseling relationship. Those doubts will be confirmed to the extent the counselor conveys the idea that they will not be truthful about what this counseling is really about and what will be happening in the future to the bully.

Counselors help confirm their honesty by not beating around the bush about why a student has been asked to come for counseling. This is also the time to briefly lay out the general but important information the counselor actually has about this particular bullying situation. Being up front about these things early in the first counseling session relieves students from wondering why they are there, what is known, and what information they will need to provide.

Allen's counselor, Mr. Jones, provided a good example of the problems caused by not identifying concerns early in counseling. Mr. Jones spent a long time in rather casual conversation with Allen. He then asked how things were going, to which Allen replied, "Fine."

Mr. Jones came back with, "Are there any things I can help you with?"

"No," replied Allen.

Trying to find grounds on which to begin a significant discussion, Mr. Jones said, "Surely there must be some ways we can help you make the best of your time in school?"

Allen stuck to his story, recognizing that there was another agenda behind Mr. Jones's seemingly innocent comments. "There's nothing you can do for me. Everything is okay. Can I go now?"

After several more unsuccessful attempts to engage Allen, Mr. Jones finally said, "What are we going to do about your problems with Seth?"

Allen figured all along this was why he was sent to the counselor. "So that's what you really want me here for. I'm not doing anything. Seth is not my problem."

Mr. Jones lost valuable time, and his honesty now will be questioned because he did not get to the point for the session earlier. Everyone knew what had been going on and here was a counselor trying to pretend that it was not the main issue. Allen recognized that Mr. Jones was avoiding the real reason for which he was here. The smirk on Allen's face was just to let Mr. Jones know that he was fooling no one. Allen saw that the general discussion and the expressed concern for how he was doing was just a trick to get him talking about the situation with Seth. Allen didn't trust most adults in school even before this session. Now he had another example of how adults couldn't be trusted, which he could use to show why he too need not be truthful. It now would be even harder for other adults to develop a trusting relationship with Allen in the future.

Mr. Jones's motives were good. He just wanted to give Allen every chance to initiate the direction of counseling. This is generally an excellent tactic but not when the situation is very specific and the therapist has a definitive agenda. Asking a young person to come to therapy to explore key issues obligates the therapist to confront those issues in an efficient manner.

Ms. Kline provides a more effective direct approach to a similar situation with Yolanda. After a brief discussion about how Yolanda was getting along, Ms. Kline stated, "Yolanda, I have heard that you have been having trouble getting along with several girls, putting them down, and most recently pushing Alice in the hall. I've asked you to come here because these problems seem to be hurting your grades, getting you and others in trouble, making school less enjoyable for everyone, and increasing the possibility that somebody will be hurt badly. I'd like to see what we can do about these things. I hope you are willing to work with me."

Ms. Kline quickly made it clear that Yolanda was here for a specific reason. Yolanda might not like that reason, but at least she knows Ms. Kline is being straight with her. Little blame was placed while still stating the basics of the problems and Yolanda's role as Ms. Kline knew it. Finally, she sought Yolanda's support in working on the relationship problem rather than Yolanda's problem. The result is a strong statement that establishes an honest relationship, provides the basics of what the problem appears to be, and places as little blame as possible without eliminating knowledge of the apparent roles.

Yolanda understood but still had an expected defensive reaction: "How do you know what's going on? So what else do you think happened? Do you know why? Did Alice squeal? What makes you think this is my fault?"

"No. I haven't talked with Alice. I hear things from a variety of students and faculty who all are concerned about helping people. I don't really know much more, and that's part of why I would like you to help me understand and work on these problems."

Ms. Kline has given her most relevant information to Yolanda without getting into a discussion of all possible details. Had she actually gone on to tell everything she knew, Ms. Kline would have focused the session on herself, her knowledge, and how accurate it was. Giving all her known and perceived details would have been a bad mistake because it would have taken attention away from Yolanda and her perceptions of what occurred and why.

Those who are not professional therapists might wonder why a therapist would not want to prove to Yolanda how she was at fault and that she must change. It is the job for the more judicial aspects of the intervention program to judge and prove the judgment quickly and efficiently. It is the job of the counselor to develop a relationship where seeking deeper understanding of the people involved can lead to healthy change regardless of the judicial punishments that may need to be taken as a result of problem behaviors. Ms. Kline was right to focus on building an honest working relationship with Yolanda under the conditions of a direct and caring approach to the issues.

Mr. Jones was more direct and more effective when he saw Seth, having learned from his frustrating experience with Allen. "Seth, I know there have been problems between you and Allen that are causing trouble for both of you. We need to do something about this for everyone's sake: Your sake, Allen's, and the rest of the class who also are worried about what is going on. This is affecting lots of people. So what's the story?"

Seth was uncomfortable with this discussion, but he understood that the problem could not be avoided. Mr. Jones was pretty clear about that. "Well, you know . . . I didn't do anything. Allen just has this thing about me . . . and, well, he's an ass! I hope you're not going to say anything to him about me saying this stuff. Are you?"

"No," Mr. Jones calmly assured Seth. "I won't be saying anything you don't want me to say. As a matter of fact, I've already talked with Allen and let him know that I hadn't even talked with you yet, but I am working with Allen too. I'd like to see if we somehow can solve whatever the problems between the two of you are. I've seen things get a lot better between people like you and Allen when I can help get people really working on it."

Mr. Jones's directness with Seth set a sound stage for working directly on the problem in an honest way. Dealing with interpersonal problems is not a pleasant situation and seldom pleasant in the beginning. The relief, confidence, and strength that can come with successful therapy are not immediate gifts but are achieved in the end from work. Seth recognized that Mr. Jones's honesty and directness were going to push them into difficult issues quickly. There would be little room for spending time thinking about how to avoid the issues because Mr. Jones obviously would not allow much of it. They had set a sound stage for efficient use of therapy time.

Step 3: Gain the individual's understanding of the situation.

Mr. Jones has made it clear to Seth that to begin work on these issues Seth's side of the story is needed. "So what's the story?" Much more information about Seth and his relationships will be needed beyond a simple "who did what." Because this is likely to be the easiest place to begin, however, it makes sense to start here.

The counselor probably has knowledge of some things that occurred and other people's opinions as to what or who caused the problem. These are all going to be limited views and, to differing degrees, biased accounts. Counselors must be careful not to continuously seek the most unbiased accounts of the situation in order to get at the truth. Judges need the truth and only the truth. Therapists, particularly at this stage, most need the highly biased and probably very different accounts of the people involved.

The school principal or perhaps even a judge needs unbiased accounts much more than the therapist does. These people are responsible for making objective judicial decisions and seeing that those decisions are carried out whether people like them or not. Therapists will not be making these judicial decisions nor are they responsible for their implementation. Decisions and the likelihood of them being carried out through therapy come not from the directive power of the counselor but from the amount of agreement and commitment given to decisions by the participants. Lasting agreement and commitment can be achieved only when participants fully recognize first their view of the problem and second how their biased views compare with others' views. The counselor must follow this necessary order and focus initial attention on gaining a full understanding of how the individuals involved view the situation.

Gaining understanding of the situation from the participant's view is traditionally known as seeking empathy for the individual. Empathy is an attempt to identify with another person's situation and feelings. The current step emphasizes the first aspect of empathy, which is an understanding of the content or happenings of the situation. The next step (Step 4) emphasizes the person's feelings related to the problematic events. Some students or counselors might choose to begin with feelings either because of the type of person involved or because of a high level of emotion that is overriding more cognitive functioning. This is a very reasonable alternative when the specific situation demands it; however, beginning with content generally will be easier because what happened is usually easier to explore and less emotionally charged than beginning with participants' feelings.

The content of a situation makes a good starting place for evaluation because it allows for the development of scenarios that can be matched with the observations of others. These scenarios involve who, what, where, when, and how things occurred. They can be checked with the student for logical progression of events as well as for match with the observations of others.

Many problems between people will move much closer to settlement as participants simply come to greater agreement on the evolution of problematic events. For example, if Seth and Allen can come to agree only on the specific time that the problem started, then they will have found agreement on common events. On the other hand, the two protagonists might perceive that things actually started at very different times with one believing that the start was with the current event and another believing that problems started long ago. The result here would be that Seth might be seeing the main issue as what happened in the hall while Allen could be focusing on a perceived slight that occurred minutes, hours, or even days before. By obtaining a clear picture of the evolution of the situation from differing points of view, the counselor is better able to recognize those places that will need more attention in therapy.

Seth is explaining his view of the situation to Mr. Jones. "It all started when Allen came up to me in the hall and just punched me for no reason. Then he started yelling at me."

"So this seemed to come out of nowhere. First there was nothing wrong with you and Allen and then all of a sudden he is on you in the hallway. Is that it?" Mr. Jones reflected the content of Seth's statements directly but he also recognized that things would not be this simple. He expressed this confusion, not by stating it, but by the look on his face and the texture of his voice. He was letting Seth know that, although he believes what Seth is saying, it certainly sounded like a peculiar scenario.

"Well, yeah," Seth said. He paused and then continued, "Well, we had other problems before and we never really get along, but that don't have nothin' to do with this time."

Mr. Jones recognizes that Seth would like to limit the issues to this one event but that Seth also knows this is not the case. Expressing his understanding of all the content Seth has offered thus far, Mr. Jones promotes further exploration of the events. "So there have been other problems, but you don't think they're connected to this one. Maybe we should think about some of those other problems. A lot of times there can be similarities that might tell us something important even when they are not directly connected. Maybe we should talk about some of those other problems that happened recently or maybe even other problems something like this one with other kids."

The counselor must not appear to conduct an interrogation of the student at this time. It is easy to get into a mode where the therapist asks question after question about details, gives little feedback on the student's answers, and directly challenges many statements based on what the therapist knows or has heard. Challenging statements and beliefs is important, but it is of much less importance at this stage. Gaining understanding of the student's point of view is more important here than reaching agreement on which point of view is correct. Rather than pose a long list of challenging questions, the counselor should encourage the student to talk, reflect the content of student comments, and help the student to recognize where there is confusion in the story. This pattern should help gain the clearest view of the situation while continually strengthening the alliance between counselor and student.

Another key point to keep in mind at this early time in therapy is to keep the emphasis on the student's view of the situation and not on what other people believe. Mr. Jones is using numerous appropriate counseling skills to help Seth explore the situation. At the same time, he is using reflection to show understanding while increasing Seth's trust and confidence that the therapy and the counselor are truly working towards his best interests. Should the counselor immediately begin stating things such as, "Well, that's not how the teacher saw it," and "Allen has a different story," Seth likely would see the emphasis of the therapy shifting from focusing on him to others. This would make him more likely to believe people were not actually trusting him or concerned about his needs. Such a pattern produces lowered involvement and less commitment to the process, which makes for unproductive counseling. It is more appropriate to keep comparisons to other people's views and direct questions to a minimum at this point in therapy.

It is to be expected that bullies and victims will see the events surrounding the problem in very different ways. The successful counselor will have a clear perception of both the similarities in views and specific differences. Similarities in bully and victim views will act as the glue that puts the individuals together on common ground. Specific differences will identify those places that have the greatest relationship to the problem and therefore deserve significant attention. These similarities and differences in the way events are viewed also will give the counselor critical clues as to where and when emotional responses will be strongest and mildest. Those emotions and feelings are the emphasis in the next step of the evaluation process.

Step 4: Explore the feelings of the individual being seen.

A thorough knowledge of problematic events and the way in which they occurred is seldom enough information to make for effective PIC counseling of bullies and victims. Nathan Farris in DeKalb, Missouri was a mild mannered youngster who surprised everyone when he brought a gun to school to kill those who had been teasing him but not physically abusing him. Adults and youth alike were shocked when these things happen and shocked again as they came to realize how wrong their views were that this boy was "only the target of a little teasing." It was the type and strength of the emotions experienced that drove these disastrous actions and not the objective outsider's view of the situation.

Bullying and victimization do not take place because some people are bad and some are good. Were this the case, our society would be set up to get rid of the bad people and keep the good ones. Instead, it is organized on the basis that everyone has the ability and responsibility to take actions that can be either good or bad. Judges, courts, and legal systems focus on the actions of people to encourage good actions or more likely punish bad ones. Therapists, on the other hand, must spend their time focusing on the underlying reasons for why these behaviors occurred. The underlying reasons found are generally tied closely to emotional or thinking issues rather than just the facts of the case. *The role of the counselor in the PIC method is to get beyond the objective facts to the feelings, thoughts, and emotions that are behind the behaviors of each individual involved.*

Mr. Jones had discussed with Allen the events of the situation in which he appeared to have been bullying Seth. Allen's picture of the events was that Seth had conveyed numerous slights to him before this current set of events and that this last brush was on purpose and the final straw. Mr. Jones's next step was to explore some of Allen's emotions surrounding his picture of the events. He made a statement, which was really more like a suggestion, that Allen continue to talk further about his feelings. "It sound like these slights and other things that Seth does really get to you."

Allen was still wary of exposing his real self. "No. They don't bother me. He's just a jerk."

Using a mild form of confrontation based on a conflict in Allen's own statements, Mr. Jones says, "I'm a little confused. You told me it was what Seth does that caused the problem, yet nothing he does bothers you? How do these go together?"

Allen tries to have it both ways: "Well, I mean I can handle it, and he is no big deal. But yeah, he makes me mad and I need to put him in his place."

"What is this mad feeling like?" asks Mr. Jones to help them both get a better picture of the emotions involved.

Allen unconsciously tries to hide as much information as he can, but Mr. Jones's tactics get him closer and closer to his real feelings. "Hey, I'm in control, man. I do what I want. . . . The little jerk needs to learn a lesson once in a while, and I got to show him."

Mr. Jones stays with his first idea but catches on to the new one Allen presented. "Well, I didn't get the mad part, but it sure is important for you to feel in control isn't it."

Allen confirms Mr. Jones's accurate reflection of his feelings. "Damn right it is. Letting people know you are in control is what it is all about."

Mr. Jones finds out a great deal more about Allen's feelings as the session progresses. The key general recognition is that Allen is very much afraid of losing control of the people and events around him. He begins to put this together with other information about how Allen believes he has little ability to control people's ideas, that he is a poor student, or that he has almost no control over the chaos at his home. He seeks a form of control by dismissing academics and home as unimportant to him and also by showing other students like Seth that he can make them do as he likes at any time he wants. When the control Allen seeks is in question, Allen's anxiety and insecurity rises and he looks for some way, any way, to assert his control over something or someone.

Mr. Jones's discussions with Seth provided a very different picture. He was a boy very much ready to say he was not only afraid of Allen but also that he felt no support from others and was on his own in this situation. He did not believe that adults or other kids wanted any part of the problem, even though they hinted that they wanted to help. The feelings Seth experiences—of being alone, isolated, and helpless to do anything that would not wind up causing him even more hurt—are common ones for most victims.

Mr. Jones's experiences at school did not support the idea that Seth should feel this way. He knew how much teachers wanted to take the right actions; other kids had come to say something needs to be done; and he had been in touch with the principal several times. He also knew enough about this type of problem, however, to recognize that Seth's fears were real for him and common for victims. This understanding allowed him both to recognize the legitimacy of Seth's feelings and at the same time to understand that they were not directly connected only to the specific bullying events being discussed.

These examples demonstrate how evaluating the emotions of those involved in bully-victim problems often provides a very different picture of the individuals involved than would a thorough knowledge of the events alone. There is more going on inside Allen than the fact that he did wrong and has done wrong regularly before. The emotional parts of Seth also tell us that we must work with more than the objective fact that people really are there to help him. Allen and Seth both have seen the same events, but they have interpreted them and emotionally reacted to them in very different ways. The result is that the actual physical events and the emotionally viewed events are so different that understanding one alone will not be sufficient for effective therapy to take place.

Exploration of the feelings of involved individuals provides even more than the necessary understanding described. It also offers direction for further exploration of both emotions and content. The frustration over lack of control that Allen feels at home is the same frustration he feels at the very different school situation. Recognizing that home and school are very different situations where Allen has similar reactions to Seth's should direct the therapist to explore home, school, and the common emotions together, if not immediately, then at some future time. Any time common emotions can be identified in uncommon places, there is fertile ground for gaining understanding of both sets of events and their impact on the individuals involved.

Step 5: Explore potential feelings and situations as seen from the other participant's point of view.

A key transition point arises when the therapist attempts to help the student explore the other individual's point of view. Steps 5 and 6 focus on this transition from self-exploration to developing empathy for others. Up until this point, the student was only asked, "How do you see things?" This position is highly supportive of the student who is given recognition for knowing his situation better than anyone. The student's importance and personal power are emphasized, which creates an excellent environment for relationship building between counselor and client. Students who are bullies or victims, however, have problems not in isolation but in relationships with others. They also need to recognize information about how others perceive the situation and integrate that information into their interactions. This change from seeking self-insight to gaining insight into the lives of others can be a difficult one.

Very often the transition from looking at oneself to understanding the world as seen and felt by others occurs after the break between sessions. A counseling session where the client has shown great progress in struggling to understand himself or herself deserves to have that progress emphasized by not changing to another topic and by allowing the feelings of success to go with the client after the session. This is particularly true of younger clients who have a shorter attention span and more difficulty generalizing. They need more reward and processing time to observe, think about, talk about, and take some action to verify individual gains. *The task of considering the other person's feelings and situation often had better come early in a counseling session* rather than near the end or directly after some other major gain.

Sometimes bullies or victims move quickly to an interest in understanding the other person's point of view. This is particularly true when there has been a previous positive relationship between bully and victim or when the bullying was recognized and handled before a long-time pattern has emerged. These cases can be moved along more quickly but not in a way that would reduce the importance of evaluating one's own view and feelings first. Some students will desire to shift the emphasis off themselves in any way possible. Counselors must be wary about those who want mostly to talk about others rather than about themselves. This may well be more a defense mechanism than humanitarian action.

This transition stage can be the point at which the counselor decides that further steps designed to bring bully and victim together to form a better relationship may be inadvisable. Whether to bring them together, how quickly, or the decision to not bring them together at all are decisions that depend a great deal on how willing and able the individuals are to consider the other person's point of view.

The PIC method is not designed to bring bully and victim together for a major confrontation. Instead, PIC would bring them together when the counselor is confident that they have enough interest in, concern for, and recognition of the other person's world to meet the challenges of these meetings. This more positive evaluation suggests a situation where the probability for relationship building is maximized and the potential for argument based solely on self-interest is minimized.

Mr. Jones nears the end of his first session with Allen. He feels his relationship with Allen has progressed even if it didn't get off to a great start. One hopeful sign is that Allen has begun to express more things about himself and in more productive ways than his usual defiant "I don't care about anything" communications with adults. This beginning was not all that Mr. Jones would have liked, but he does see enough positives and progress to be encouraged about the future.

Mr. Jones summarizes what they have talked about, provides encouragement, and suggests that he would like to see Allen again tomorrow. He ends the session by saying, "Meeting again tomorrow should be good. A lot of times people will think of some other important things about themselves or the situation when they have a little more time to think. Also, I'd like us to talk a little about what might be going on in the minds of some of the others involved, particularly Seth. I'm understanding where you are better, but I'm less clear on Seth. The better we understand both you and Seth, the better will be our chances to make things work out in positive ways for both of you."

Allen is not enthusiastic but he agrees. "I don't know what I can say about Seth. You have to ask him."

Mr. Jones is simply trying to set Allen's thinking in motion and not to convince him of anything right now. "Don't worry about it. I will talk to Seth but sometimes people, like you, see some things or can figure out things that the person themselves cannot see. We'll talk more tomorrow about the situation and see where it leads. Then we'll make some decisions on what would be the best things for you and me to do."

The purpose of Mr. Jones's closing was to give basic encouragement for work done and to plant a seed for the kinds of directions they could take. Before tomorrow's meeting with Allen he will have met with Seth and gone through much the same process. He then will have a better picture of the two boys' personal perspectives and their individual needs. Also, the two boys will have had time to think about the fact that today's session was not too bad and that, according to Mr. Jones, tomorrow's holds some promise for each of them getting more control of eventual outcomes.

The next day, Mr. Jones reviews with Allen what they discussed the previous day and asks Allen what other things he might have thought about that could be important. Following some discussion on these issues, Mr. Jones leads Allen into a discussion about how Seth might feel and why he acts the way he does.

Allen's initial reaction is pretty typical: "I don't know what he thinks. I'm nothing like him."

Mr. Jones emphasizes a broader approach to reduce the pressure but also to get some ideas on the table. "Right, but you've been around him and others a lot. What are some of the ways anybody might feel in this situation? How would you feel?"

This transition to talking about the life and feelings of others often raises a good deal of anxiety. The therapist will need to be patient and creative in finding ways to encourage this exploration without telling the student that "you should recognize this." Brainstorming in which the counselor can play a role, extremes are legitimized, and evaluation is minimized is one effective technique at this point. Mr. Jones used another common technique of asking Allen to imagine what his feelings, thoughts, and reactions might be if he were in Seth's situation. These both give direction and support for coming up with ideas without emphasizing judgments on the correctness of the ideas.

Later in the session, Allen responds to Mr. Jones's request to summarize what he thinks are key things about Seth's feelings. "Well, he is scared of what I'll do. He's embarrassed about me bossing him around. He probably wants to get me back, but he knows he can't do it by himself, so he is probably thinking of how he can get me in trouble or something like that."

"Good thinking. I imagine that is pretty accurate," replies Mr. Jones. "What other things we talked about do you think he might be feeling? What kind of life do you imagine he has at home or at school?"

"Probably he is pretty lonely too because no one goes around him much. Partly that's because he is a nerd, but other kids are afraid of me getting on them too, so they stay away. I don't know about his home, but I bet his mom is always taking care of him. I'm sure he's a momma's boy."

The examples above show some of the progress that can be made in this step. Switching to an exploration of the other person's feelings and perceptions is seldom an easy step for the therapist but is one that must be taken if participants are to develop a better relationship that includes more than anger and frustration hidden through avoidance of each other. Once they begin to think about the other person as one who has a life and feelings that they can understand, that person becomes more of a human who deserves concern and becomes less of an object without human qualities. Step 6 attempts to take these perceptions of other person's human qualities as well as the client's self-perceptions and compare them to see what issues in common are present.

Step 6: Explore bully and victim issues in common.

The final step in assessing the potential for bullies and victims is for them to be seen in therapy together. By so doing, the identification of common issues or concerns that the individuals might have in common can occur. The PIC method emphasizes gaining an understanding of issues in common to bullies and victims in order to increase understanding and the potential for improving relationships. It presumes that every reasonable attempt should be made to improve relationships between bullies and victims because success will translate into self-confidence in one's ability to deal with other relationship conflicts.

A simplistic analogy that emphasizes the reasoning for this step can be seen in marriage counseling. Everyone knows that in marriage counseling the participants are the couple. No professional or layperson would think of having a partner from one troubled couple meet with a partner from another troubled couple. The relationship problem is between partners, and it is those partners who must identify their common problems and common advantages for being together. Only then can they improve their relationship. Similarly, bullies and victims in conflict have relationship problems with each other and true solutions can be fully recognized only through their joint understandings.

The need to identify common problems and advantages of their relationship holds true for bullies and their victims if it is decided that improving their relationship is possible and desirable. The policies of our society often promote the idea that people who have a conflict should disassociate themselves from each other in order to avoid future conflicts. Criminals are sent away to jail. Abusers are forced to stay away from those they have abused. Students with immediate discipline problems are told to leave the room while those with extensive problems are told to leave school. Parents, too, commonly use the idea that, if you are having a problem with someone, then stay away from that person. Each of these examples serves a valuable societal short-term purpose of removing the potential for conflict and allowing healing time. That procedure,

however, is less valuable when used over the long-term because those in conflict never have the chance to improve relationships or even their inappropriate
self-perceptions about those relationships.

Some important negative results of not resolving conflicts can be continuing denial of reality, inappropriate self-concept, a continuing cold war of
sorts, waiting for the opportunity to get revenge, and a continuing fear that the
conflict will return. Perhaps the most damaging result can be a continuing
reminder that one was unable to resolve the conflict. The more individuals or
groups have hidden from or given up on conflicts, the more likely they are to
be fearful of the future and to avoid those challenging situations where conflicts could arise. On the other hand, people and organizations who find ways
to resolve conflicts, gain reality-based confidence in their abilities each time
they succeed. Confidence gained from successfully overcoming conflicts increases the likelihood that people will seek new challenges and have less fear
of changes that are normally associated with conflicts. People have a greater
chance for success when they have a belief, supported by their own experiences, that they are able to overcome most, if not all, potential conflicts with
others.

Seth has feelings of powerlessness related to Allen, whereas Allen sees few
traditional ways in which he can impact how he is treated at school or at home.
Until now, both boys have given into these feelings of powerlessness by avoiding them and striking out in other ways. Seth could continue to take the advise
of some who suggest his whole strategy should be to "stay out of Allen's way
and forget about it." Allen, too, could continue acting on the assumption that
making some people do what you want allows you to ignore those people and
things you cannot control. Neither one can really ignore those situations where
they feel like failures however. The starting place for overcoming the powerlessness is where they begin to realize that their troubles are not so unique and
may even be shared by those very people with whom they are having conflicts.

The counselor working in a bully-victim situation might use a variety of
methods to begin an exploration into finding common issues depending on how
things have progressed to this point. What all these ways have in common is an
emphasis on relating the previously identified self-perceptions to perceptions of
the other person's feelings and life situation. New information may be identified at this step, but the starting place will be the combination of previously
recognized information.

Mr. Jones is in his second session with Allen and tentatively seeks issues
that Allen has in common with Seth that could provide a solid starting place for

their relationship. "You know, Allen, you said you think Seth is probably lonely and doesn't have many friends. I guess he has some, but not a lot. You also talked before about you being bothered some times because you thought kids made fun of you behind your back and that's why you need to teach them lessons. This problem with other kids seems to be one that both you and Seth have in different ways."

"I don't have no problem with friends anymore." Allen knows this is not true, but he cannot admit it right now because it would feel too much like a loss of face. "I've learned to take care of it. Seth is the one with a problem."

Mr. Jones understands that Allen's denial cannot be confronted too strongly right now, so he ignores it in order to allow more profitable work to continue. Instead of directly confronting or dropping the issue, he continues the conversation with the belief that Allen may be able to be more honest later. His tactic is to use Allen's ideas to increase understanding of his commonalties with Seth. "You may be right, Allen. How was it different for you before? How was your life different? How did you feel different? Maybe what it was like for you before has something in common with what it is like for Seth now."

This was an issue that seems fairly common: Allen sees Seth as lonely and he at least admits that in the past there also was some loneliness for him. Recognition of these commonalties increases the chances that Allen might find positive ways of identifying with Seth, and in this particular example, perhaps might consider how to help Seth.

Useful commonalties can be based on similar situations and events such as the example given; however, others that can prove useful may take place in similar situations (e.g., family, school, friends, etc.) but with greatly differing events. For example, Allen mostly is ignored at home whereas Seth's mother is forever doing things for him that he would rather she not do. The boys' future relationship could be built, in part, on the realization that they both perceive problems dealing with their parents even though those problems are opposite in nature. In this case, they have the potential to see a common problematic situation (i.e., dealing with their mothers) where discussing their differences could help each person get new ideas about ways to deal with their own situation. The common situation can serve to provide a bond that can be used for understanding and growth.

The examples show how therapists can combine information already identified to suggest new directions and ways for identifying commonalties. The more successful Allen and Seth are at recognizing their similarities, the greater the likelihood will be that they will accept common issues to discuss together. Bringing bullies and victims together can succeed only if common ground is recognized. *When common issues cannot be recognized or accepted by participants, it is probably best to continue individual therapy only.* The effective therapist assures participants' recognition of that common ground before they are brought together. Only then can the therapist be confident in a productive outlook for future joint sessions.

Chapter 6

DIRECT INTERVENTIONS

Ahmad

Ahmad has seen his counselor twice, developed a positive relationship, and explored some of his pain and fear surrounding the beating. He also has talked a little about others who have bullied him, but Ahmad cannot talk much with the counselor about other students before he becomes very emotional and shuts down. He feels good about the therapy relationship, but continues to experience major anxiety attacks including cold sweats, panic, generalized fears, and hyperventilation. These attacks also have come at school and home without any particular initiating factors.

Yolanda

Yolanda has developed confidence in her counselor, but it took some time to get over the incorrect idea that Alice "told on her." She has confided in Ms. Kline about a few of the problems facing her and how she feels treated badly by other students. They also tentatively have given recognition to the hurt Alice probably feels by being embarrassed by Yolanda and how Yolanda has some of those same feelings from her interactions with other girls.

Allen

Allen has used bullying others to get his way for some time. His methods have been reinforced by his parents and others who either have ignored these actions or punished him but not given recognition when he would make positive changes. There was no support that Allen could see for interacting in any way other than as a bully. The punishments he received felt as if another person had the "power," which he too could acquire when he had the chance to be the bully. It appeared to him that the real task of getting along with people was simply to gain enough power to make people do what he wanted them to do.

Therapy for Allen was more difficult than for most. He had many long-standing defenses and beliefs that had been reinforced over time; however, Mr. Jones recognized, from both verbal and nonverbal reactions, that Allen was thinking about more issues than he could admit to at any given time. What used to be strong denials and blaming of others for every problem, in just two sessions, had become tentative denials and some consideration of the idea that he might have played some small role in his own difficulties. Mr. Jones was encouraged by this progress, but they were nowhere as far along in the process as he would have liked.

OVERVIEW OF THE DIRECT INTERVENTION STAGE

Directed attempts at interventions in the bully-victim relationship should begin only after control of the situation has been established and the problematic situation has been evaluated with all significant people involved. PIC interventions begun prior to the establishment of control and a thorough evaluation are simply hit or miss shots in the dark. Interventions tried before these steps are taken have the possibility of working, but they also could fail miserably and produce an even worse situation.

Individuals are more likely to be harmed than they are helped by trying to go too far, too quickly, and the same holds true for their confidence in the therapy process. When people are not helped by therapy, even when no clear harm is done, their confidence in the process and their ability to deal productively with issues within the system is damaged. Gaining control and evaluating everyone's views of the problems in a professional manner is essential before moving on to decisions as to what intervention directions would be best.

A variety of therapy theories and specific techniques can be used in the direct intervention stage. Specific interventions that apply directly to bully-victim situations are provided in Chapter 9, Therapy Actions. It is the process of providing direct interventions more than specific therapeutic tactics that is emphasized by the PIC method. A series of counselor decisions regarding what direction to take in therapy, who to involve, and how individuals should be involved are the key factors discussed in this chapter.

Decisions on direct interventions in the PIC method begin with a determination of how much each individual involved is in need of personal, social, or psychological therapy. No attempt should be made to move onto work with pairs or groups of clients until the therapist is confident that individuals are independently prepared to do so. It may be appropriate to see some individuals on an individual basis only. Others may need to be seen alone for a period of time to gain strength and knowledge necessary to deal with paired or group work. Individuals often can move quickly to deal with each other under the therapist's supervision. This is most often the case when the problem can be caught early enough or when people have confidence in the PIC method through past experience. The best direction to go and the timing involved are dependent on the individuals, their specific situation, and the availability of professional therapy.

Once a decision has been made to have individuals in conflict come together, a need remains for individual work prior to joint meetings. Individuals need to have their personal concerns clearly identified. They need to see clearly how this next step will help them. They also need to recognize issues they have in common with the other individual or group so that these can form the basis of a working (i.e., not necessarily friendly) relationship. Finally, they need to be prepared for their work with others so that the specific process is understood. Insuring these accomplishments prior to any joint meetings will create a productive atmosphere focused on specific directions for work and a realistic view of potential positive outcomes for everyone involved.

The goals and the process of how joint therapy will progress should be emphasized immediately as participants are first brought together. Establishing a working relationship between all parties is the primary therapy goal of each joint meeting. It is from this base that issues can be explored, plans beneficial to everyone can be developed, and specific actions can be decided upon for implementation. Plans and actions need to be reviewed, modified, and expanded as necessary in follow-up therapy sessions so that a process and method of improvement is learned rather than an expectation that relationships are "fixed" by one change at one point in time.

The PIC direct intervention method emphasizes an ongoing model for improvement that decreasingly relies on the therapist for relationship development. Clients are directed towards reliance on themselves as individuals and as pairs or groups to continue improving their relationships. This emphasis then must require a formal termination of therapy where it is made clear: (a) the progress that has occurred; (b) the improved skills that have brought about the progress; (c) the work done on their own to improve things; (d) their individual and paired plans for the future; (e) the actions and skills they will use to work on further progress; (f) feelings of anxiety, loss, sadness, excitement, and relief are not unusual to have about a final meeting; and (g) specific people who are available to help them when they are having difficulties.

Step 1: Decide on individual therapy needs.

Reactions to the psychological trauma associated with victims of bullying comes in forms similar to other victimization cases. Victimized young people and adults often suffer from generalized and situational anxieties, fear, isolation, and lowered self-esteem. The severity of the trauma reactions is generally associated with the extent and duration of the abuse suffered as well as the coping capacity of the victim. The greater the extent of an individual's trauma and resulting problems, the more therapy will need to address his or her individual needs rather than the joint relationship factors of the abused and the abuser. People need basic levels of strength, confidence, and control to work on relationship problems, and individual therapy generally is needed to assure the establishment of these basic intrapersonal levels.

Of the victims in our three examples, Ahmad has had the most severe reactions to being bullied. A major factor in his reaction is the severity and continuing nature of his victimization. He was beaten badly enough to need hospitalization and has been a victim over the years of several other bullies. A therapist should see clearly that Ahmad would have continuing fears of future victimizations based on past experiences. Moreover, the situation is worsening since the latest beating progressed to a more severe nature than anything in the past. Simple reassurances that these things will not likely happen again will not be of much comfort to Ahmad.

The counselor recognizes that Ahmad feels totally unable to change his victimization status. It has become a way of life that Ahmad sadly accepts for himself. Inadequacy and failure in relationships are how he sees his life unfolding and the best alternative in his view appears to be avoidance of these difficult situations. All he requests from authorities and others is to be left in isolation where he at least feels in control, if not happy, about his life. Being home-schooled and avoiding as much contact as possible with others does not sound like a fun life for Ahmad, but it has a sense of security that, right now, he wants more than anything.

Ahmad provides a clear case of someone who needs more than cursory individual therapy before dealing directly with those who are a part of the problematic relationships in his life. Attempting to put him together with his tormentors quickly would arouse so much fear and feelings of inadequacy in Ahmad that little productive work is likely to emerge and substantial harm might result. His current therapy needs would benefit more from individual therapy where anxieties and situations could be controlled. Smaller steps designed to build his confidence and thus allow him to look at himself, others, and the future in more positive and productive ways are essential. The goals are to help him become more self-confident and more realistic about himself and the future. The more Ahmad's intrapersonal characteristics strengthen, the greater is the potential for a joint meeting to deal with those he finds threatening. The time for such a meeting is not right now, but it could well be in the future.

Professionals need to be aware that there may be people other than victims and their tormentors in need of individual therapy. Many people in Ahmad's peer group, for example, either saw his beating or have heard of it. They know of how he has been treated and may be identifying with him. It is wise for professionals to keep a watchful eye out for individuals whose behaviors change at such times. Bystanders are often overlooked because they are not seen as being directly involved. The fact is that bystanders also can suffer the problems of victims, because it is the fear of future victimization that causes greater psychological problems than the actual victimization event.

Yolanda certainly can benefit from individual therapy, but probably not to the extent necessary for Ahmad. Bullying has not been an ongoing pattern in her life and her problematic relationships with her peers are relatively recent. She has gotten along well at school in the past, has a positive home environment, and desires more interaction with peers rather than less. Furthermore, the physical changes that have caused her such embarrassment are developmental in nature and, although they make her look different now, will become more the norm as her peers mature. There is a strong base for eventual joint meetings with the other girls, which should move things along much faster than Ahmad's situation would allow.

Individual work with Yolanda could be relatively brief. First, her relationships are suffering primarily because of the discomfort of a developmental situation that will be experienced by all her peers. Also, she has the personal strength and motivation to work directly with her victims on improving their relationships. Barring unforeseen problems arising, individual therapy might quickly become less productive than joint therapy. Promoting peer relationships in cooperative ways as quickly as possible would appear to be the most efficient form of therapy for Yolanda.

Allen is the client most hostile to therapy of the three examples. An accurate evaluation of how much individual therapy is appropriate for Allen depends, in part, upon the quality of the relationship he forms with his counselor. A high quality therapy relationship may encourage him to explore areas and issues of himself and his life that he has kept suppressed. The impact of his disengaged home environment and his reactions to it would be obviously productive areas for individual or family therapy if an adequate therapeutic relationship can be established.

It is possible that Allen and Mr. Jones may not be able to form a sufficient therapeutic relationship at the present time to indicate the jump to joint sessions. Allen's situation is long-standing and difficult enough that his defenses may not allow such exploration now. The best Mr. Jones may be able to do in individual therapy is to demonstrate listening, trust, caring, and a willingness to continue when Allen is ready to work on his personal and interpersonal issues.

Ahmad, Yolanda, and Allen provide three very different situations that call for different approaches to individual therapy. All three could benefit, but to greatly differing degrees. Whether individual therapy is accomplished, and for what length of time, will be dependent on the need level, willingness of the client and the client's parents, the abilities of the therapist, and the availability of therapy time. Each of these factors plays an important role in the potential productivity of individual therapy for such individuals.

An important procedure is to give first attention to the need for individual therapy in bully-victim situations. Such therapy may last a few minutes, a few sessions, or long-term. Situational circumstances and individual needs will decide whether individual therapy is stopped when joint therapy occurs, continues after joint therapy, or if it is to be the only form of therapy deemed appropriate. Whatever the case, counselors must realize that the pain, anxiety, and fears experienced by individuals may require individual attention regardless of the need for joint work on relationships.

Step 2: Have individual discussions of common concerns.

This step should be a smooth transition from the last stage of the evaluation. The last step in the evaluation stage was an initial exploration of how well the victim could recognize problems in common with the bully and visa versa. The potential for improving any relationship increases dramatically when individuals begin to identify more accurately aspects of their own life, ideas, or feelings in others. Identification of commonalties with others is a basis for the expectation that joint therapy indeed can provide mutually valuable benefits. In Step 2 are efforts to solidify identified commonalties, find potential new ones, and explore how working on them jointly could help both individuals.

The goal of this stage is to lay the groundwork in preparation for individuals to meet jointly. Enough significant commonalties must be identified and their implications for improved relationships understood to convince the counselor that a joint meeting will be a positive experience. Those expectations include jointly recognized meaningful substance, a picture of how things will go, and generally expected positive outcomes. All possible commonalties between individuals do not have to be identified prior to a joint meeting; however, enough commonalties are needed to assure that something positive can evolve from the meeting. Observable progress is more important in early meetings than trying to arrange a meeting with the unrealistic hope of solving the problem once and for all.

Step 2 can be as brief as a few minutes or last up to several sessions. The difficulties in helping students see issues, complexities of the situation, the length of time problems have been in place, and previous relationships between individuals are a few of the factors that will determine how long preparation may take. Yolanda and Alice provide an example of a situation where this stage might move very quickly. They have had a positive relationship in the past, many common peers, are in different stages of the same puberty problems, and both feel pressure to be liked by others. Easily identifiable common ground that is not burdened by a long-standing history of problems either as individuals or in their relationship make the potential for preparing them to work together soon a strong possibility.

Allen and Seth provide different types of problems that could delay their ability to work together. Allen has had problems for a long time and his defenses are strong. He probably will be hesitant to admit to commonalties or to consider positive options for improving his relationship with Seth. Experience tells him that meeting with people about his bullying behaviors bring him punishment and criticism, not better relationships. His defenses are built around shutting ideas and people out of his life when they do not reinforce his bullying behaviors. Through this thought process, he manages to feel as if he has kept some form of control of his relationships.

Seth also may be hesitant about getting involved. He has little confidence in his ability to solve relationship problems on his own, in part, because his mother always has intervened to fix things for him. Experience has taught Seth that the model for handling this type of situation would be for his mother to meet with people and to deal with the difficult issues rather than himself. He will need much reassurance from the counselor about the value of the process and his ability to be strong and effective in a joint meeting.

Seth's mother is just one example of the many factors from the individual's environment that have the potential to influence this process. Allen's family too will probably play an important role, though a very different one. They probably will not even be informed of the situation by Allen, because he has no real belief that involvement is something that they would want. The different family styles serve mostly to complicate the situation. One family provides a model where parents take primary control of the situation whereas the other is quite the opposite, in that little to no need for involvement by parents is recognized. The counselor will probably find that Allen and Seth's family experiences provide them with widely varied pictures of how to settle problems. These pictures may need to be modified somewhat before they can work together effectively.

Another possibility is that Allen and/or Seth's parents might decide to become actively involved. Parental involvement should not be allowed to take the therapy direction away from Allen and Seth working out their own problems; however, it does have positive potential for working on the issues on two separate fronts. The counselor might be able to help the parents of each boy identify areas of common concern they have about their boys. Once these are identified and the structure for a positive joint working relationship established, it would be very appropriate to bring the parents together. The potential positive effects on young people can be great any time a more productive learning and working relationship can be established between their parents. The PIC method can provide the process model for helping their parents be productive in the situation in addition to serving as a therapy model for their children.

Meeting jointly to discuss the common concerns of bullies and victims naturally produces anxiety because of past experiences. Preparation is required to provide these individuals with the knowledge, skills, strength, and motivation needed to deal effectively with meetings and to lower anxiety. Therapy goals for individuals prior to having them meet together should confirm for therapist and student that they are ready to take this next step, that they know what to do, and that they expect things to go well. Step 2 should end when the following are in place:

(a) common issues have been identified by each individual,
(b) the PIC process is understood,
(c) the potential value of a joint meeting is recognized,

(d) the potential outcomes of a joint meeting are identified,

(e) the specific process of how a joint meeting will go is clearly understood (outlined in Step 3 to follow), and

(f) agreement is reached on the willingness and ability to take the next tentative step of meeting jointly.

Step 3: Meet jointly.

No matter how much one individual is at fault and another is not, a bully-victim problem remains an interpersonal relationship problem rather than an intrapersonal one. Two or more people are affected by the problem and the more they are commonly involved in the solution, the greater will be the benefits for each. In some cases, people, groups, or nations in conflict are better served by forcing avoidance of all contact with each other, at least in the short term; however, this choice of forced avoidance is never as potentially productive as when it is possible for the parties to work out things together. Joint meetings between bullies and victims are to be encouraged, when the time is right, whenever possible so that individuals can see relationship building as more valuable than relationship avoidance. Productive joint meetings may not always be possible, but they are the aspect of the model that can provide the most benefits to the greatest number of people.

The critical purpose of joint meetings, and particularly the initial meeting, is to make progress in identification of commonalties and to gain confidence in the joint meeting format. Only limited productive steps need to be achieved at this first meeting although it is quite possible that more substantial progress might occur. Even limited progress along with successful implementation of the meeting can provide the critically needed confidence in the process and in everyone's ability to make it work. It is most important to have individuals come away with a recognition that this will work rather than to be disappointed with not achieving major changes.

Joint meetings are presented as problem-solving sessions with a common structure. Individuals then can have realistic expectations of the meetings and see that those expectations are met. The consistent phases of these sessions are as follows:

(a) The counselor briefly reviews the problem, goals, and progress that has been made, and restates the purpose and structure of the meeting.

(b) The counselor seeks input from everyone to find common recognition and potential differences regarding how things have progressed.

(c) The bully first is asked to express in sincere and positive terms an understanding of the victim's situation. The victim then is asked to express personal thoughts and feelings about the bully's interpretation. If the responses are positive, a good start is underway.

(d) The first situation is now repeated with a change of roles. The victim is asked to express in sincere and positive terms an understanding of the bully's situation and the bully is asked to react. Positive reactions to common understandings are very hopeful signs for continuation and progress.

(e) The counselor gives recognition to the differences, reinforces specifics of the progress made, states clearly the positive actions taken by all concerned, and requests suggestions for what they can do next to improve the situation.

(f) Potential goals and next steps are discussed and agreement sought on which one(s) are achievable and agreeable to the bully and victim. How, where, and when such actions will be carried out and evaluated for effectiveness are agreed upon.

(g) The counselor emphasizes the need to continue previously successful actions, clarifies the specific new actions that the students will take, reviews the benefits of the actions for everyone, and restates the agreed upon next meeting time, place, and focus of the next meeting.

(h) Finally, people make mistakes and someone may not do all they have agreed to do. Forgiveness and tolerance for mistakes as well as how to get back on a positive track must be emphasized rather than penalties and sanctions.

This problem-solving structure is designed to give maximum attention to making progress towards common benefits and to minimize blaming and rehashing of past actions. The pattern is not a natural one, because the lack of agreed-upon cooperative behaviors is a hallmark of bully and victim relationships. This structure gives bullies and victims a new way to work with each other. It increases the attention given to the benefits of taking positive cooperative actions while also reducing tension and emotions to levels that do not interfere with making sound relationship decisions.

Step 4: Identify common goals.

Every joint meeting from first to last needs to focus on the common goals held by bullies and victims. These common goals serve as the picture of what they are seeking together and why it is necessary to continue. They provide the reasons for doing the work needed to develop necessary new behaviors. Without common goals to work toward, there is little reason to carry out common actions. Goals need to be clarified early in the process, reviewed regularly, and modified when necessary. Goals must be identified early in the process because they provide direction for the relationship and the basis for evaluating progress.

Agreeing on realistic common goals requires understanding of one's own goals and understanding of the other individual. This is one of the reasons why all parties were first asked to try and understand the other person's view as well as their own prior to the first joint meeting. Steps b, c, and d in all joint meetings (Step 3) reemphasize this by asking individuals to demonstrate understanding of the other person and accepting feedback on how accurately they do understand. Promoting individual and later joint exploration of each other's feelings in these ways increases understanding of each other, how the relationship has developed problems, what would be a more effective model for a relationship, and how well they are moving towards that more effective model.

The model that develops should not be interpreted as being idealistic or as having unrealistic goals. Joint exploration to increase understanding of each other also helps to maintain a realistic picture of what is possible versus what might be ideal in the way of goals. Allen and Seth, for example, likely would find through joint exploration that they do have some common goals, but many other factors probably mitigate against "good friends" as a realistic goal. They do not hang around in the same groups, live in the same neighborhoods, or feel the same about what they want out of school—just to name a few of their differences. Recognizing these differences through joint exploration should relieve them of the pressure to seek a good-friends relationship and allow them to set as a goal a relationship that is at least not harmful and possibly helpful to both of them.

A hopeful model for Seth and Allen with low level but reasonable goals might include (a) encouraging separation during high stress times, (b) emphasizing recognition and avoidance of actions and situations that are particular problems to one or the other, and (c) identifying situations and topics where positive interactions have the most potential for being valued by both boys. Such broad goals are a viable starting place for any individuals or groups in conflict because these goals provide directions leading out of difficult situations and toward more mutually beneficial outcomes.

The situation for Yolanda and Alice suggests that they would move further towards a truly positive relationship in a shorter period of time than Allen and Seth. The goals for Yolanda and Alice should reflect these differences with an emphasis on higher levels of friendship expectations and less emphasis on avoidance of problems. Their goals might be to (a) identify places where they could do things together based on mutual interests and past positive experiences, (b) find time to talk of their common fears and frustrations, (c) recognize those times when fears and frustrations are becoming a problem, and (d) agree on productive ways of dealing with those difficult times.

Adults know that the worst of relationships can turn into close friendships or even marriages, although this is not normally the case. In the case of bullies and victims, it is appropriate to have an ultimate goal for them to become friends, but such extreme goals are seldom helpful in the process of rebuilding a hurtful relationship. The distance between the bad current relationship and a best-friends relationship is too far to provide realistic day-to-day hope. Moderated goals ranging from (a) a low of enemies who avoid each other, (b) to a middle ground of non-enemies who interact effectively as necessary, or (c) to a high ground of people who are helpful to each other, are likely to be much more productive. These may not be as spectacular as going from enemies to best friends, but they do offer more realistic hope of actually achieving a better relationship.

Extreme goals can be recognized as important without accepting them as the primary measures of success. Yolanda and Alice had discussed their understandings of the situation, the problems, and each other's point of view in a joint meeting. Things went well as the girls communicated very effectively and recognized their commonalties. Yolanda made it clear that she felt so good she wanted to make Alice her best friend: "Really, we are like sisters because we have so much in common that we just forgot. Now that we know how we feel, we are gonna be best friends. I'm so happy!" Alice was smiling and nodding her head in agreement.

Ms. Kline was aware enough to recognize that this euphoria was related largely to enjoying the positive interpersonal reactions during therapy. It felt especially good after all the anger and tension they had been experiencing; however the girls' reactions were not accurate reflections of the realities of Yolanda's relationships in general or the relationship between her and Alice in particular.

Ms. Kline's reply was designed to recognize Yolanda's joy while modifying it into a more realistic short-term goal at the same time: "These are exciting possibilities for both of you, aren't they? It's good to see so many nice things in your future. Now we need to make sure that you don't get caught in some of the same traps that got you into these problems before. They are easy traps to fall back into, even for those who have been best friends for a long time. What are some smaller goals we can work towards that are better than the enemies you've been, but a little smaller and easier to accomplish than 'best friends for life?' What are some of the ways you can picture getting along better even in the next few days?"

The counselor is doing her best to help the girls see that, although the ideal goal is worth keeping, more limited goals will allow them to share the feelings of success more quickly. A common analogy is that of a 250-pound woman who gets excited about diet and exercise and pictures herself at 130 pounds for the first time in years. It is a wonderful goal but not likely to sustain her efforts during the many hard months and years of forming new habits needed to lose the weight and keep it off. She can keep that extreme goal but also must set realistic short-term goals that can be achieved sooner and more easily. Achieving these short-term goals will provide the continuing encouragement of success that the long-term, 120-pound weight loss will not. Yolanda and Alice will be better served by focusing on goals such as encouraging each other, seeking better understanding of each other, and finding ways of supporting each other.

Step 5: Agree upon actions, time frames, and conditions.

Goals provide the pictures people need to envision better ways of living for themselves. A set of actions, time frames, and appropriate conditions are needed to make these goals obtainable. Yolanda and Alice will not make any progress towards becoming friends unless they take the necessary actions at the appropriate times and places. The counselor's job is to help the girls identify what they will do, when they will do it, and under what circumstances it will be done.

An early joint meeting ended with Yolanda and Alice both happily accepting a goal of supporting each other. A week later, at the next joint meeting, Ms. Kline recognized that the girls had lost the closeness they had shown at the close of the previous meeting. It didn't surprise Ms. Kline that things had not gone exactly the way the girls had hoped. In an attempt to be supportive, Yolanda overreacted to another friend's comment about Alice by tracking down the girl after school, hitting and kicking her, and threatening her with worse. The next day all of Alice's friends were angry at both her and Yolanda. Alice felt the need to take sides and so joined her friends against Yolanda. What Yolanda had done to be supportive had backfired. Ms. Kline realized that they needed more exploration of how to accomplish their goals in more organized and mutually agreeable ways. These needs would provide productive directions for this next joint session.

Yolanda's physical threatening of Alice's friend was not seen as the supportive act that Yolanda had thought. The girls and the counselor realized that they needed clarity on what actions were accepted as supportive by both girls. They realized that physical support was not acceptable to Alice unless she was in immediate physical danger. She also wanted Yolanda to ask her whether she needs support before deciding to do something extreme. Yolanda wanted Alice to invite her to go with her friends sometimes instead of always excluding Yolanda. Agreeing on more limited actions in specific situations was not as exciting as planning to be best friends, but they are the starting points that will lead to becoming real friends instead of enemies. Best friends may need to wait until more progress has been made.

Seth and Allen were working towards the limited goal of not getting in trouble. They recognized that their conflicts usually started in certain situations, one of them during and immediately after math class where they sat next to each other and got on each other's nerves. They agreed to try to find mutually acceptable actions to meet this limited goal in this particular problematic situation as a first-step effort. The teacher would not agree to move either boy so they agreed not to talk to each other or those around them during class. They also agreed that Allen would leave the room quickly because his seat was closest to the door, and Seth would wait until Allen was out the door before he left. Leaving in this manner would assure that one would not get in the other's way, which they knew was sometimes a problem. The counselor emphasized that these were not long-term solutions, but that they did assure both boys that neither would say or do the obvious things that caused conflict during this particular problematic situation. They agreed to try this for one week and then discuss how it went.

Making progress in a designated time frame is more important than trying to solve a major problem in one giant step. Mr. Jones knew that keeping the boys out of trouble in agreed-upon ways would lower tension levels, give them a small sample of success at working together on a common goal, and create a better atmosphere for further progress. He knew that the rigid actions agreed upon would not be very acceptable to anyone over a long period of time but would be useful in the short run. He emphasized one week, even though the boys were originally talking forever. He knew it could not be the long-term solution the boys wanted. One week would allow them to work on the actions, see how they progress, and develop further ideas on what to do next. The actions can be kept easily as is or changed from meeting to meeting. Thus, it is not necessary to set a long time frame for actions with such limited value.

Another goal Allen and Seth agreed upon was not to show disrespect for each other. One of the agreed-upon actions is that neither boy would call the other negative names either to his face or behind his back. This action called for a different time frame and conditions than the previous one emphasizing avoidance in the classroom. It was agreed that this should never happen and that it would be in place forever. It was also recognized that someone would probably slip, in which case an apology would be offered in a way and a place that would not embarrass the other person.

Avoiding calling each other negative names was an action easily agreed upon as long-range and one that could be done anywhere and anytime. There was no need for the boys to set a more limited time frame or only certain situations where they would carry out their actions. These specific actions fit Allen and Seth only. It is possible that, in a different situation, a goal with similar ideals would need more limitations based on the circumstances and the relationship. The most important factor is that Mr. Jones recognized the actions, time frame, and specific circumstances that best fit these boys and helped them to set up a situation that best matched those circumstances.

Step 6: Evaluate and redesign goals and actions regularly.

People in relationships, people in therapy, and people who are growing have one major thing in common: change. There is every reason to expect that young people who are growing physically, socially, and emotionally; involved in therapy; and trying to improve relationships will experience extensive change on a frequent basis. The result of change is that decisions and actions taken at one point in time will very likely not fit the same people as change takes place. Regular evaluation of goals and actions is necessary to know where, when, and how changes need to be made. Therapy in bully and victim relationships requires evaluation and a redesigning of plans through regular joint meetings to maintain plans that continue to reflect the current status of the individuals involved.

Therapists and supporters must understand that acceptance of some short-term actions is often necessary in order to reach long-term outcomes. Situational circumstances usually dictate the use of smaller steps are necessary in the beginning of the healing process to pave the way for more large scale changes.

Ahmad does not want to come back to school and experiences serious emotional and physical problems when the subject is even mentioned. It is probably a good choice to let him stay at home for a time considering the severity of his reaction and the current nature of his peer relationships. We know this is not the effective long-range decision anyone would like, but, at the moment, the security it provides may well be necessary for lowering anxiety to a level where greater changes can be considered. Therapy should help him gain better control of these reactions and develop skills for building better relationships. At one point, it may be acceptable for Ahmad to think he will not go back to school, but it also will be necessary to reevaluate that decision regularly and change it as circumstances warrant.

Joint meetings of bullies and victims should never end after one positive session, no matter how good the results. Relationships in transition need to be watched for the impact of changes. *This developmental model requires that therapists make time for observing variations in thinking and behaving and for helping those involved recognize and adjust as needed.* As logical as this might sound, it is never accepted that easily by those involved. People tend to be euphoric over positive changes and resigned to negative changes. Both reactions can promote unproductive stagnation in relationships if they are not modified to more realistic positions.

The development of families provides an appropriate analogy to view this need for continuous revisions based on change taking place. Families that exist effectively over the years come to learn that neither the euphoria of the wedding day nor the deep depression of the death of a loved one can be allowed to last if productive family life is to continue. Attempting to maintain extreme emotions when the situation no longer calls for them is unhealthy to individuals and to the family as a whole. Long lasting, effective families find ways to reevaluate their goals and actions and to make changes that facilitate progress. On the other hand, families that become harmful do not recognize that change is needed or are not willing to make the adaptations necessary for positive continuation. One family grows and another withers because of the way they come to deal with change.

The structure of joint meetings need not change greatly, but the areas emphasized will fluctuate. Starting each session with a review of the situation and gaining understanding of each other can be shortened in later meetings compared to early ones. This content still needs to be included, however, because their presence is a reminder that monitoring for understanding rather than assuming understanding of oneself and others is critical to maintenance and growth of relationships. There will be many times when this portion seems unnecessary and the motivation will be to bypass it but, just when it no longer seems necessary, something will occur that demands another formal look at each other and how those understandings have changed.

Changes in perception of individuals identified through the exploration stages provide a foundation for evaluation and planning. The situation and behaviors now can be judged to be "the way we want it to be," or "not the way we want it to be." This exploration is also the way to identify what needs to be different and the ways of getting there. The goals and next substeps stages of the session often become a larger portion of follow-up joint sessions as people search for the next productive steps. Participants compare how actions turned out to what they actually desired. Adjustments then can be made in goals and future actions based on their joint conclusions.

After several meetings, sessions tend to spend most of the time increasingly on making these adjustments to goals and actions. Participants begin to recognize the pattern of the sessions and often begin thinking individually and sometimes talking together about what changes need to be made even prior to sessions. This is a healthy part of the process that encourages a transition from only working on relationship issues during therapy to doing these things outside of therapy. The counselor emphasizes the occurrence and value of this transition as a way of empowering the individuals and reducing their dependence on therapy to promote further growth.

All therapy sessions should end with some recognition of progress, what is to happen next, and an understanding that forgiveness and tolerance of mistakes continues to be needed. Every relationship has ups and downs. The people who are not overly surprised by these fluctuations and recognize the value of attending to them will be better able to weather the difficult times and enjoy the good ones. Bullies and victims have had significant problems in their relationships and need to be continually aware that either the old problems or new ones are likely to arise again. Successes achieved in dealing with their problems should serve as reminders that they can overcome other problems if they are willing to use the skills and processes they have learned to work at them in an organized way.

Step 7: Successfully terminate joint meetings.

The PIC method emphasizes a model for improvement that increasingly relies on clients to take control of their relationships as their understanding, skills, and the tension level improves. Clients are directed towards reliance on themselves as individuals and as pairs or groups to continue monitoring and adjusting their behaviors. They are attempting to at least maintain nonabusive relationships and to improve on them as much as circumstances and motivation allow. This increasingly independence-focused direction must lead eventually to ending dependence on the therapy relationship as the primary means for promoting additional gains. The counselor needs to assure that termination takes place in an organized way that recognizes the value of gains made, reinforces skills learned, confirms the ability to self-control, and establishes sources for additional assistance if they become necessary.

Yolanda and Alice have had four joint meetings with Ms. Kline. Their relationship has become stable in that they know they are not best friends yet they do spend considerable friendly time together. They have learned how to be supportive of each other without antagonizing their other friends. One important dimension of their growth is that they find a little time to talk alone at least once a week on Friday afternoons over the phone. These discussions may be about many things, but they always check how they are getting along first. Relationships with girls, boys, and their looks form the bulk of the remainder of their conversations as is normal for most females their age.

Termination is a process and not an event. It begins well before the last meeting and provides follow-up opportunities. Ms. Kline recognizes that the girls are doing many of the monitoring, reevaluating, and revising of their relationship independent of her just as she has encouraged them to do. The girls do not want to end their sessions with Ms. Kline, but they no longer need it as much as others do. It is time to draw these joint meetings with the counselor to a close, and Ms. Kline has been quietly preparing them for it during past sessions. She has been shortening the length of previous meetings and increasingly focusing only on gaining updates, emphasizing the benefits of their progress, and reinforcing the good work they are doing outside the sessions. The girls see termination as the last joint meeting, but Ms. Kline knows that it has been going on for some time. Preparation began by clarifying the reasons for these sessions at the first meeting and progressed to the point where the last meeting was little more than another logical step toward independence.

The last two joint meetings signify the timing of the termination process, but specific events and content make up the work within these steps. Setting the stage for the final meeting is a key outcome of the next-to-last meeting. The rationale for termination, preparation tasks to be done between sessions, and a preview of the last session should always be a part of the next to last session. These normally will take a very short period of time but they are necessary to reduce the anxiety associated with ending a therapy relationship.

Yolanda expresses her concern about Ms. Kline's statement that they need to consider ending joint sessions: "We've been doing really well. I like these sessions. If we stop, things could go wrong again and besides, there are other things we could talk about here."

The anxiety is a natural part of the termination process. Ms. Kline tries to convey that to the girls: "Yes, you have done very well and you keep doing better all the time. I've been pleased to see how well you get along and deal with both the good things and the problems. But you are doing that almost all on your own now. Most of what we talk about are things you have already worked out together before you got here. That is just the way it is supposed to be and you need to be proud of that. I'll always be here when you need me again. All you have to do is ask, but right now other people need me more."

Ms. Kline deals with the girls' questions and emphasizes her confidence in them. Then she goes on to set the stage for the final joint meeting for the three of them: "Next week we will meet one more time and do some reviewing of how far you have come and how you got there. Before then, think about what you have learned and how it will help you in the future. Look at yourselves and the other people in your lives this week to see how things have changed and what you think could still get better. We'll talk a little about how it feels to stop these meeting too. I'm pleased about how far you have come, and I'm excited to see where you are headed."

The final joint meeting is not too different in structure from others if the groundwork has been laid well in the previous meeting. One difference is that, although the subjects stay much the same, there is an emphasis on review of long-range development rather than just those occurrences since the last session. Clients will be led to recognize the full extent of their development rather than focusing on the small changes that took place from session to session. This big picture of progress should look even more significant and encouraging to everyone. The topics that should be discussed formally in the final meeting are as follows:

(a) the progress that has occurred;
(b) the improved skills that have brought about the progress;
(c) the work they have done on their own to improve things;
(d) their individual and joint plans for future growth;
(e) the actions and skills they will use to work on further progress;
(f) feelings of anxiety, loss, sadness, excitement, relief, and others that are not unusual to have about a final meeting; and
(g) that specific people are available to help them when they are having difficulties.

These topics and format of the final meeting are designed to review, encourage, and solidify progress, and to provide confidence that additional help is available if it becomes necessary. Some time in the last session needs to be given to the feelings of separation associated with this termination. The end of any relationship is an emotional experience and a therapeutic relationship is no different. A regularly scheduled support system is ending, and there is every reason to believe people will be uncomfortable about it. Emotions can be positive or negative, strong or mild, and no two people can be expected to have the same set of feelings. What can be expected is that everyone will have some form of reaction and that those reactions should be recognized as acceptable.

Yolanda's tears and her words convey to Alice and Ms. Kline that these joint meetings have been one of her favorite parts of the week, which she will miss a lot. Ms. Kline shows understanding but does not try to eliminate the sad feelings. She goes on to explain that many good things have happened around these meetings and that feeling sad about ending is normal. Recognizing that Alice does not feel as strongly as Yolanda, Ms. Kline also says, "People react in all different ways to relationships starting and to relationships ending. You can never tell exactly how you will feel, but it is important to understand that different reactions are just an individual's way, and they need not to be the same for us to get along."

Termination is designed to cut the strings between counselor and clients so that independence is strengthened; however, independence does not mean that people can no longer ask for help. The last step in the termination process is to assure those involved that sources of help continue to be readily available when needed. The counselor is an obvious source of help, but teachers, parents, peers, and others also can be of assistance. The effective therapist spends time helping clients recognize these sources in their own lives and establish the general criteria to use to decide when and how to use specific sources.

SECTION III
DIRECT ACTIONS FOR
INDIVIDUALS AND GROUPS

Therapists, teachers, parents, and other concerned adults need to translate the information and general model presented in the first two sections into the specific practical actions that best match their individual roles. Section III contains examples to assist in that translation from ideas to application. Those concepts and suggestions offered do not stand in isolation as helpful measures. Their value is apparent only when implemented within an organized effort. Using any one action by itself with no support from other coordinated actions could prove harmful in dealing with the problem instead of being helpful. Problems are not simple and neither are solutions. Taking coordinated actions is essential in order to be confident the results will be those desired.

Actions presented in Section III range from general to specific groups and actions. These actions are specific and they are likely to be useful in some form for most situations and for implementation by many professionals; however, there is no reason to believe that every action will work for each school, community, or student in the same way, at the same time, or when implemented by different individuals. Judgments of when, where, and how to use them should be based on a thorough knowledge of the general problem, the PIC model, and the specific situation and human resources available to you.

Actions are presented in the context of the specific groups that would employ them most commonly. The many groups that should be involved in the solution include school and community, teachers, many types of professional therapists, and families as well as bullies, victims, and bystanders; however, the value of any individual action is not isolated to one specific group. It is expected that individuals from one group will find many beneficial ideas for use in their particular situation listed under a group other than their own. It is also important for each group to know what the other groups could be doing. Coordination of actions and positive consultation outcomes become increasingly common as more individuals understand how best to work with those in different roles.

Key actions that schools and communities can take to help implement their portion of the model are presented first. The actions of these groups most directly affect the first phase of the PIC model that emphasizes gaining control of the situation through creating awareness and developing cooperative relationships. Through these groups, an effective system of reducing harassment and violence must be organized. Schools and communities effectively involved in this way will be the most likely to focus on breaking the cycle of violence through preventive measures. Those schools and communities with little involvement most commonly give either no attention to the problem or focus only on remediation for those most affected by the worst forms of violence.

Teachers spend the most time with students and, therefore, have the greatest opportunity to impact on the greatest numbers. The development of a healthy, organized, learning environment within individual classrooms is a key role for teachers. Rules, relationships, methods of work and play, manners, and moral behaviors are some of the issues that are dealt with either formally or informally within every classroom environment. The actions provided for teachers emphasize their critical leadership role; however, teachers must recognize that they cannot be all things to all students. Counselors, psychologists, social workers, principals, and others are hired precisely because of the widely varied roles, responsibilities, and specialized training required. Teachers need to focus their energies in the roles and places where they can do the greatest good for the most students and the actions provided emphasize this focus.

Counselors, psychologists, and social workers are the professionals most responsible for overseeing the psychological and social needs of students. Their time is set aside for seeing that these needs are met rather than teaching academics, discipline, record keeping, or monitoring groups. They are commonly among the first to recognize the scope of bullying and victimization problems through their role as therapists. They also are likely to be critical professionals in the organization of forces to attack the problem, train people in productive ways of helping, and of course they must provide therapy as needed. Actions described for this group emphasize their consultation, coordination, and therapeutic roles.

Parents and extended family can play an important part in reducing violence, harassment, and bullying, yet they are a minimal part of the child's life at school. The actions provided for parents and families are therefore less directed at the problem events at school and more focused on the ways that families can either reduce or add to the problem. Examining family relationships, emphasizing support mechanisms, learning new ways to interact more productively, and changing aspects of family relationships that may be adding to the problem each receive attention.

Skills and actions that help bullies, victims, and bystanders to better understand and improve their immediate situation also are likely to help them in other aspects of their lives. The general model and specific activities presented are designed to provide a means for just such situational and more broadly viewed life improvements. Specific, yet generalizable actions are provided that have been shown to have positive results with many students. It must be emphasized that these actions are not nearly as likely to be effective and may even be harmful if done outside of a coordinated and systematic approach. They are meant to be used by conscientious adults who understand the problem, the child, and the means to achieve solutions. In this context, the well-informed parent may be able to use these actions in conjunction with the work of the professionals at school. Counselors, psychologists, social workers, or teachers who have understood both the model and the individual situation should be able to encourage the appropriate actions for the right student, at the right time, and in the right situation.

Chapter 7

SCHOOL AND COMMUNITY ACTIONS

OVERVIEW

Bullying and victimization effects those involved plus everyone who sees or hears of the problems. The level of anxiety is raised for everyone because who will be the next target is always in question. Even those who do not know of the problems are affected, because those around them go about their lives in more self-protective ways. The environment is changed and neither the school nor the community is the place of safety that is expected of it.

Creating a safe climate in a community requires everyone's involvement. One angry person does not make a community angry and one caring person does not make a community caring. Many people live, work, and play in a community and the more of them who are willing to take joint action, the greater the likelihood is that the community will be the way people want it.

Schools are communities in themselves and they also are part of larger communities. No single staff member, student, or parent can change that community by working in isolation. That single individual can make a major difference; however, when actions are taken that promote the involvement of others. Increasing the number of people working towards similar goals and employing coordinated actions directly improves the possibilities that a school or a larger community will become the safe and productive environment everyone wants it to be.

Actions suggested in this chapter are designed to raise consciousness, develop behavior standards, and implement those standards in schools and communities. The greater the number and frequency of the actions used in an organized way, the greater will be the probability of creating the necessary public support for building a safer environment. Safe communities come from the active awareness and involvement of its members in the design and implementation of actions that support both individual and group needs. This is no small feat in our society where many people have many different needs. The key objective is to get as many school and community participants as possible involved in the work.

Who will lead? Someone must take a leadership role in the development of these actions. Superintendents and principals are logical leaders for schools as are elected officials for communities; however, bringing people together seldom is started or finished by the official leaders alone. Formal leaders often are moved to action by individuals and groups that demonstrate credibility, motivation, and a willingness to do the necessary work. Energetic teachers, therapists, parents, students, and business leaders consistently have proven that each can produce movement in formal systems and acquire its support. Organizing people, spreading out the work, and seeing to its implementation are the true jobs of leaders and those tasks can be done by anyone with the will and ability.

Formal school and community leaders are certainly the most logical individuals to promote the following set of actions; however, obtaining their support is more important than whether they would initiate actions on their own. Everyone should look at the following actions as ones that they can initiate on their own and with others in order to get things started while also seeking additional support through formal channels. The most effective communities are those where people recognize their potential for influence as individuals and groups and then find the ways to make that potential a reality.

ACTIONS ASSOCIATED WITH GAINING CONTROL

"I'm so upset about the way kids are acting in our school. No adults seem to care. It's like they're all just burying their heads in the sand. When I say something about it, everyone looks down at their feet and then goes on as though nothing happened. Why doesn't anyone care that these things are going on?"

The parent expressing her frustration wanted nothing more than to enlist the support of others in helping her daughter's friend overcome a problem with bullies. It is not only a parent's dilemma. Similar statements can be heard from students, teachers, counselors, psychologists, social workers, administrators, friends, and the list could go on. People in need want others to recognize and do something about it. But getting by from day to day and week to week in our hectic culture often leaves little time for the problems of others. Consequently, what should be a large scale, coordinated approach to a problem often becomes something that individuals must struggle with on their own, leaving those like the mother above feeling frustrated and ignored.

The more awareness and involvement created in the school and community, the greater will be the potential for positive actions. A first major goal for total school and community involvement in a program to reduce violence, harassment, and bullying is to create as much awareness and inclusion of as many different groups as possible. Commitment to carry out actions is created during the development of the programs that guide those actions. This involvement stage is critical to assuring long-range effects of any antiviolence programs.

Take a strong and consistent stand against the abuse of power.

Frustrated parents often get acknowledgment of frustrations but no strong commitment for school or community efforts. What would be the difference if the school and community took a public stand on people who abuse physical, social, emotional, or even economic power over others? Such stands emphasize the fact that bullying, harassment, and abuse are inappropriate for all people and not just for children.

Consider the possibilities if all school groups agreed to and published a mission statement similar to the following:

> "Our school environment will be a physically, socially, and emotionally safe environment. Every individual and group in the school will be responsible for maintaining this safe environment by continually showing understanding and respect for others. Every individual and group also will be responsible for calling attention to those instances where an individual's or a group's feelings of safety are jeopardized. Individuals and groups are expected to respond to these issues both informally in those situations where possible and by using the formal procedures of the school as they apply."

A mission statement conveys a school's or community's strength of commitment and direction in a formal way. It does not assure that action will be carried out. It does promote and encourage individuals in the development of policies to deal with human abuses that reduce the feelings of safety in a school. The exact nature of the policies that evolve will vary based on the needs and style of the people and cultures that make up that specific school, classroom, or community.

Provide regular opportunities to freely discuss all sides of issues.

A mission statement such as the one above will not make schools a safe place by itself. It is a statement of commitment that needs to be followed by actions that create better understanding of issues and people involved and move people more toward further planning and action. All this cannot be accomplished in one big meeting. People at meetings often want to hear quickly what they need to know and then move on to other things. The result for this type of problem would be that everyone might walk away from a meeting feeling good, but those most directly affected by the problem quickly find that information and agreement do not necessarily turn into quality actions. Making the transition from information and ideas to consistent actions needs time, discussion, and practice.

Regular opportunities for discussion are essential when the positive actions begin to happen. As the environment improves, people will have different reactions. Some will feel their work is done and the potential loss of their commitment is a danger. Some will feel that the improvement is not enough, whereas others will claim things have gone too far. Success also causes new people and groups to seek involvement, which can be very positive, but it also requires considerable attention to all the problems surrounding inclusion and leadership. These factors increase the importance of providing opportunities for as many people as possible to get together and discuss the best and worst aspects of the issues on a regular basis.

Encourage participation of those outside the system.

Obtaining the active involvement of those who are outside the system greatly increases support for decisions, but it is not without its headaches. People are busy, most work during the school day, and helping the school is not likely to be a top priority for their free time. There is also the problem that people often don't understand enough about how the school works and why things are done the way they are. Thus, suggestions from those outside the school may well be in conflict with the directions or abilities of the school. These are just a few of the problems in a long list.

Problems associated with involving more adults in the school are also the reasons we need to include them in school activities. Lack of involvement is one of the reasons that outsiders do not understand the school's position on many issues. Outsiders deal with rumors and one friend's opinion about school rather than a wide variety of opinions including those of the people who work and study in schools.

No one wants an unsafe environment in schools. This basic assumption should tell us that the more people of good will we can actively involve in the school's activities, the more people there will be trying to make it a safe place. Overcoming the disagreements on how to do this is a part of the process that needs to be encouraged rather than avoided. Only when you get people together can they work at gaining common understanding and overcoming their potential disagreements.

EVALUATING THE PROBLEM

"What's the big deal here? We live in a nice community and the kids are just regular kids. They get along sometimes and sometimes they don't. This is the way the world is."

This gentleman speaks for many adults who have trouble seeing why kids picking on kids sometimes is a big problem. "Isn't it something that has always been that way? I've seen it and I grew up just fine."

No matter how committed an individual or group is to solving what they feel is a significant problem, many will not be easily convinced that it impacts them. People need the extent of a problem clearly demonstrated rather than just being told to accept it as reality. We want and expect proof of issues that will make us change our ways.

National and international statistics are a fine starting place at helping people recognize the problem; however, no reason exists that these statistics will convince everyone that the problem is true in their own school or community. A local assessment needs to occur within a school or community so that the members can evaluate the immediate impact on themselves, their children, and their community.

Communicate the firsthand local concerns.

Statistics and data serve a major purpose in assessment, but they will not convince people by themselves. People need to see how real people in their environment are being hurt. A good starting place is to present general examples (i.e., if possible without names) of those who are suffering. People do not like to see others hurt, and the more personally they come in contact with the pain of others, the more likely they are to seek ways of preventing it.

This is not the time to showcase school victims and their parents where the situations would be most volatile for everyone. Instead, it is the time for less involved individuals—those who no longer have such a problem, but have had one in the past, or those people who see the problem through their interactions with those directly involved. These could be students, parents, teachers, therapists, or others who would have knowledge and exposure to the problem, but who would not be seen as the individuals with the problem.

The reasons for not immediately involving bullies, victims, or their parents is that this could convey the idea that the problem is isolated to these people and perhaps a few others. Actions might turn quickly into focusing on a single person's problem rather than the overall issues. Being able to speak to the specific problems and needs through knowledge of examples in the school and community is a much better way to begin a true assessment of the overall problem.

Avoid placing blame.

Assessment at this stage should be about finding the extent and nature of the problem and not to designate who is at fault. People will be looking for a convenient scapegoat with the unconscious hope that, once action is taken on this individual, group, or organization, the problem will be solved and then they can go about their normal lives. Many attempts at good assessment of a problem are derailed when high emotions combined with busy lifestyles cause people to seek the scapegoat rather than truly assess the size and nature of the problem.

It is important to keep this stage as objective as possible. Whether it is a specific statement or a general guideline, the following comment gives the appropriate direction for this stage of assessment: "What we know for sure is that we need to know more about the problem in general and what it really looks like here. Everything we can find says it is likely to be a problem and that no one person or group is at fault for it."

Increase awareness of the information available.

People need to know whether problems are theirs alone or whether they are only samples of larger problems. This broader information serves two major purposes. First, the recognition that violence, harassment, bullying, and victimization are problems across the country and around the world gives emphasis to its importance. This is not just a problem for a few select people in a few unusual places. Feeling part of a larger fight is more encouraging to people than feeling they are in it alone.

Credible information about bullies, victims, violence, and harassment decreases the possibility of one person, school, or group being labeled as somehow uniquely bad. People want to believe that they are good, at least normal, and hopefully better than normal. We shy away from issues that suggest we could be labeled as abnormal. Understanding that our problems are not so unique is a standard way of helping people admit to their needs in preparation for work on them. It increases the possibilities for solving the problem both because it is admitted and also because now it can be seen as something that can be overcome.

Much of the information about bullies, victims, and the problems surrounding them provided in the first section of this book should fill this need. The information is presented in an academically defensible manner so that those who would present the ideas can clearly demonstrate the quality of the information. The examples provided should help make what could be dry data more personally relevant and understandable to most people. The two aspects of defensibility and personal relevancy should be incorporated in any presentation of information designed to inform in both a general and personal manner.

Raise awareness of the problem through assessment.

Bullying and harassing behaviors frequently go unrecognized. Even when the behaviors are seen, it is often difficult for adults and youth to decide on how to interpret the actions. Was it bullying? Does that person feel harassed? Did someone really get hurt or was it just play? Did it just happen this time or does it happen regularly? These are difficult questions even when we do recognize the potential problem. There will be much confusion and differences of opinion on how great a problem these issues really are for a school or community.

A local survey is an excellent tool to begin clarifying the extent and nature of the problem while also raising awareness and encouraging discussions. Students are the most obvious individuals to survey, but it is also valuable to include education and mental health professionals, parents, and other community members. The idea is to get as many perspectives as possible on the extent and nature of the problem in the local environment.

A Bullying Survey is included in Figure 7.1 that can be used either as the actual survey or as the starting place for developing an instrument that more specifically meets your local needs. A good starter survey has several critical ingredients:

(a) *Keep it short and more people will answer it.* This is designed to get some basic ideas of the overall picture in your location. It is not designed to get every detail that might be interesting.

(b) *Provide a specific definition of the problem.* You want to have people answering questions from the same frame of reference.

(c) *Collect minimal information about those completing the survey.* Getting general information about the school or community as a whole is the issue. Don't try to identify specific individuals and groups as problem areas.

(d) *Ask how many people have been bullied or seen it, when, and how much of a problem it causes.* This is the core information needed to assess the extent of the problem and its local impact.

(e) *Ask about the ways people are bullied.* Later discussions about what bullying looks like here, how it is different from play, and how to observe it will benefit from this information.

(f) *Ask about the reasons people feel they are bullied.* Many reasons why bullying occurs will be substantiated here. People will see that solutions will not be simple and that ways of overcoming the problems must deal with people's perceptions as well as their behaviors.

(g) *Ask about peoples' actions and feelings when seeing someone bullied.* People will have many ideas on what should be done when people see bullying occur. The greater problem is that people often actually do little or nothing. These results help focus attention on identifying and practicing individual actions and emphasizing individual and group responsibilities.

(h) *Ask how well adults deal with the problems.* Results will probably show that few believe adults intervene effectively. Most adults realize this as true for others, but they will have more difficulty seeing the same deficiencies in themselves. The answers to these questions may encourage people to talk about what adults can do and ought to do and to plan for what they will do.

(i) *Leave room for comments.* Many examples will come from this and the extent of people's reactions will become more evident through their comments.

Instructions

In this survey, you will be asked questions about bullies and being bullied. By the word "bullying," we mean (a) repeated (i.e., not just once) harm to others by hurting others' feelings through words or by attacking and physically hurting others, (b) committed by one person or by a group, (c) occurring on the school grounds or on the way to or from school, and (d) deemed as an unfair act. The person doing the bullying is physically stronger or more verbally skilled than the person being bullied. Give the answer that best tells how you feel or what you know. Do *not* put your name on this survey.

1. If you are a student, circle your grade level.

   Grade: 1 2 3 4 5 6 7 8 9 10 11 12

   If you are a parent, teacher etc., write that here. _____

2. Circle which you are: male   female

3. Have you ever been bullied during your school years? Yes ____ No ____

4. During which grade or grades were you most bullied? _____

5. What problems have you seen that bullying causes yourself or others? (Circle each type of problem caused by the bullying.)

a. physical problems (hurt or made to feel sick)
b. social problems
c. emotional problems
d. academic problems (the bullying produced problems with learning in school)
e. family problems
f. others _____

6. When you or someone else is being bullied, what did the bullies do?

	Never Occurred			Always Occurred
a. ridicule or teasing	1	2	3	4
b. verbal attacks other than ridicule or teasing	1	2	3	4
c. practical jokes	1	2	3	4
d. vandalism of property	1	2	3	4
e. physical attack	1	2	3	4
f. other (please describe):	1	2	3	4

_____
_____
_____
_____
_____
_____

7. Circle the reasons listed below that you believe cause yourself or others to be bullied.

a. facial appearance or features
b. overweight
c. underweight
d. because of who your friends are
e. physical weakness
f. illness or handicapping condition
g. good grades
h. bad grades
i. where you live
j. clothes
k. race
l. ethnic group
m. speech problem
n. religion

o. a scar or mark
p. who parents are
q. who brothers or sisters are
r. family is poor
s. have a handicapped family member
t. height (too tall or too short)
u. don't "fit in"
v. have a handicap or are in special education
w. short tempered
x. cried or was emotional
y. lack social skills
z. new to the neighborhood or area

Other (please describe) _____

8. How often do other students try to stop it when a student is being bullied at school?

a. I do not know
b. Almost never
c. Sometimes
d. Almost always

9. What do you usually do when you see someone your age being bullied at school?

a. Nothing, it is none of my business.
b. Nothing, but I ought to try to help.
c. I try to help him or her in some way.

10. How many kids in your classes do you believe are being bullied? (*Circle just one answer, but count yourself if you have been bullied.*)

0   1   2   3   4   5   6 to 15   more than 15

11. Which statement below describes how you think school personnel handle bullying?

a. The school handled the problem very well.
b. The school handled the problem adequately.
c. The school handled the problem poorly.
d. The school doesn't know what is going on with kids and bullying.

12. Please write any comments on the back that would help people in our schools better understand the problem of bullying and its effects on young people.

Figure 7.1.   Bullying survey.

DIRECT INTERVENTIONS

"The system stinks! Someone needs to stop this stuff from happening!"

The problem is that a system describes a plan and an organization to make things happen or not happen. A system is not the someone of which this parent wants to take charge and make things right. The objective for school and community involvement is to develop a plan and an organization that will provide many individuals and groups with the direction and support they need to do what will be most beneficial.

Productive direct interventions for schools and communities are those that will clarify values and policies in addition to the procedures necessary to carry them out. Direct action on specific problems will be provided most often by individuals and groups of students, therapists, teachers, administrators, and parents. The actions suggested here give these people the tools and support necessary to do their work. Quality actions should require follow-through that continually pays attention to the values and goals established.

These steps lay a foundation for action that is often appropriate in situations that do not directly target bullies, victims, and others more directly involved. For example, if we want children to operate more cooperatively in a school, then we should model similar behaviors in the adult community. A fully effective program that fights abuse of power with children also must identify and fight similar abuses among adults as they operate in school administration, neighborhoods, service organizations, businesses, clubs, and political organizations.

This is the adult community's chance to demonstrate that we practice what we preach. Even young children recognize that, when adults say to do something and then consistently act in that way themselves, the message is highly believable and has great power. Likewise, they recognize that when adults say, "Do not cheat," and then go on to cheat on taxes, in sports, at the store, or in other ways, the message has little power except to make youth more suspect of adults.

Be clear and consistent in the enforcement of behavior standards.

Everyone plays by the same rules. Policies, rules, and regulations should never be designed only by certain people or for certain people. Whenever standards are enforced selectively for different groups, tension, frustration,

separatism, and disunity will increase. Whatever policies a school or community designs to fight violence, it is most important that everyone is included in
the design, and that everyone is treated the same by those who enforce the
policies.

People are angered and frustrated when they believe others are treated better than they are. No group can eliminate these feelings completely because all
of us feel wronged from time to time. The way to deal with this is twofold.
First, the policies for enforcing behavior standards must be made clear and agreed
upon by as many people as possible. When majority rules, then almost half the
people can feel as if they are not a part of the system. Majority-wins voting on
enforcement policies does not create unity and confidence. Complete agreement
would be great, but that is not always realistic. Not being satisfied with any
percentage of agreement, but always looking for ways to include more people
in the agreement, is the most productive approach in the long run.

The second aspect of creating higher levels of confidence in behavior standards is to make opportunities available for open discussion of policies and
actions. People with the heavy responsibility for enforcing behavior standards
dislike being second guessed in part because their task is difficult and, like all
human beings, they will make mistakes. When the practice of having regular
open discussions regarding policies and enforcement can be maintained, however, there will be less simmering hostility left to blow up at a later time. Dealing with people's immediate frustrations publicly, openly, and honestly creates
a situation where regular work goes into handling small problems rather than
having to deal with enormous and often uncontrollable problems at a later time.

Never overlook acts that appear abusive.

No rule seems to fit every situation perfectly because rules cannot recognize the intricacies of human feelings and behaviors. Situations will arise where
the rule, who is to enforce it, or how it should be enforced is unclear. These are
the times of difficult decision making. "Jimmy is such a good boy. He's not
like Tommy. Surely he couldn't have meant to hurt that person, could he? What
can I do? Am I supposed to do anything? Are these people my responsibility or
someone else's?"

There are no perfect answers to questions like those above, but there is one
general answer that overrides all others: *Never overlook an act in which someone is abused*. It is better in the long run to do the wrong thing and be embarrassed than it is to do nothing when an act of abuse is seen. The worst pains

people involved in abuse suffer are those that result from the isolation that follows. People get hurt a second, third, fourth, time, and so forth because no one got involved. It is better to get involved in any way that demonstrates your concern and moral values than not to get involved at all.

Provide assistance for perpetrators and bystanders as well as victims.

Our culture tends to take a legalistic approach to most problems. We decide who is right or hurt and support those people. We decide who is wrong and punish the wrongdoer. Everyone else who was not directly involved is ignored. There is a basic fairness logic to this approach, but fairness alone does not provide for a supportive and healthy environment. Programs designed to deal with violence, harassment, and bullying need to undertake strategies that recognize that everyone is helped by reducing these problems and everyone needs help in dealing with them.

Everyone knows that victims need assistance, but so do bullies, and they are not the only ones. Those who observe violence are increasingly being recognized as being affected negatively. Even those who have no exposure to violence are affected negatively because they must live with those who are touched more directly. We are all in this together. *A successful overall program provides opportunities for everyone to get help.*

Victims need support and bullies need to be punished. Bullies also need support for dealing with the problems that put them in this situation. Victims, too, can benefit from learning more about the reasons why people are bullies or victims and how to deal with those reasons more productively. Bystanders need to learn what they can do because continuing difficulties can result from their feelings of inadequacy stemming from standing by and not acting when they know something is going wrong. The more that each of these groups can feel as if they are important, supported, and in this struggle together, the greater will be the overall influence of the program.

Always seek understanding others as the first step.

Top leaders and negotiators have learned that the way to change another person is first to understand that person. The more you know about a person or a group, the greater will be your chances of having a positive influence on what they think and do. First steps in helping bring about change in another focus on observing and listening to that individual or group. This is difficult when someone has been hurt and anger pushes us to ignore the needs of those that caused the hurt and attend only to the victims. Giving into this anger-motivated approach probably will help the victim in some ways, but it generally will do little for helping change the perpetrators or those who were bystanders.

"I just cannot understand why they do those things." We all have heard this statement many times, but how often have we sought out "they" and tried to get to know them better? The more common reaction is to dismiss the people who we don't understand. Seeking understanding first is a simple model to employ when we can remove a degree of our personal emotions from the interaction for a time. We can do it with bullies and bystanders as well as victims. It can be done at board of education meetings, faculty meetings, town meetings, and day-to-day interactions with friends and family. The more often we put our emotions and opinions aside to truly hear and understand others, the more likely it is that we actually will come to understand. Then the chances for making a significant positive difference are increased.

Demonstrate assertive behaviors as opposed to antagonistic ones.

We teach assertive behaviors, but do we follow our own teachings? Teaching assertive behaviors as opposed to aggressive or antagonistic ones is an important concept to convey to the next generation. Schools and communities need to be able to demonstrate these more productive forms of action as well as espousing them.

Consider children who are taught a lesson on how to assertively make their displeasure known to another person. The lesson goes well and the children see the logic, but they will need to see it work in real life before they fully accept it. They leave the classroom to find that their teacher, Ms. Anderson, is not speaking to the teacher next door, Mr. Tucker, because he consistently lets his class out before hers. Ms. Anderson is talking to another teacher in earshot of the students newly trained in being assertive: "Tucker is a jerk. He should know better, but it's not up to me to tell him. When I get a chance I'll get him good. He'll never know what hit him."

Ms. Anderson's threats and unwillingness to approach Mr. Tucker directly completely contradict the lesson she just taught. The assertiveness lesson will be seen as only one that people talk about in class. It does not appear to be the way adults really believe one should act.

Adults should use all possible means to demonstrate how to get individual needs attended to assertively. We need to act in the ways we teach others to act. If we believe these things will help our children, then they also should help us. Demonstrating assertive behaviors, reaping their benefits, and calling attention to when, where, and how they work will do more for teaching children positive behaviors than all the lessons we can offer.

Enlist students, parents, staff, and others in cooperative activities.

It is often easier to do a job yourself than to enlist, organize, and coordinate the actions of others. This is why we often find schools and communities where a handful of dedicated people are doing most of the work that was designed for everyone. The amount of energy, time, and money these people put into making our environments better can be enormous. They are appreciated while they last, but burnout is a regular occurrence. When mental and emotional exhaustion catches up with them or when they move to a new area, their positions seldom are filled and much less gets done.

A thriving group needs to have as many quality-shared activities as possible if they are to be their most effective. People need to know the responsibilities that go along with being a community member and participate in those tasks in order to feel like an important, active part of the whole group. Few people in busy societies are looking for more things to do and most would be very happy to give up some tasks. The pressures to avoid involvement make it necessary to encourage, recreate, invite, and support people in as many ways as possible to get involved through both work and play activities. You cannot stand by and hope for it to happen.

Block parties, art shows, sporting events, academic activities, painting parties, and cookouts are just a few of the activities that promote community cohesion and involvement. They do no good, however, if they are only planned and attended by the regular group. The hard part is to continue seeking ways to involve both those who normally are involved and those who are not.

One way of involving groups not normally in attendance is to go to places the nonattendees go and do things they do instead of asking them to come to you and do your thing. Well-meaning organizers often can be heard to say, "I don't understand why they don't want to do this. It's great fun!" The most important piece of missing information in this statement is that the planner doesn't understand the other group. The answer is to go out and get to know those people on their grounds and doing their things. At the other person's home is where true understanding begins to emerge.

Try holding meetings or other activities in the local church, meeting hall, picnic area, basketball courts, or apartment complex whose members seldom get involved with traditional school or community activities. This allows people to be in a place where they feel they belong and where they are most comfortable. The local school or town hall may not be such a comfortable place at all for those who have had little positive interactions there. Having others come to your home to see, learn, and understand you and your life is enormously appreciated. Opportunities for communication increase tremendously in these situations and that communication can lead to more unity in planning and follow-through of any actions taken.

Create opportunities for different age, culture, ability, and social groups to work toward common goals.

We tend to spend our time with others who are most like ourselves. Age, sex, culture, ability, and social preferences are common ways we divide ourselves into work and social groups. These actions make us more comfortable, but they also reduce communication between groups and often promote rigid thinking on issues. Every attempt should be made to increase the number and quality of interactions between different groups so that unity of purpose and common planning and understanding is more likely.

An International Street Fair takes place at Ohio University in Athens, Ohio, every year. One objective is to celebrate the people of many different nationalities who live, go to school, and work in the area. The most traveled main street provides the setting where many will become involved by accident as well as those who come on purpose. This is a mixing of cultures who normally remain separate most of the year. For one day, everyone has the opportunity to see everyone else show their best food, clothes, music, dance, and customs. The benefits for building a stronger school and community go well beyond that one day. It is the joint planning, recruiting, dealing with problems, negotiating, putting aside prejudices, and even clean-up duty that give these separate and sometimes antagonistic groups the opportunity to understand each other better and practice actions of good will.

An international group is not needed to create the unifying benefits of the preceding example. Every school and community has groups with differing customs, foods, activities, and accomplishments. Different races, churches, occupations, recreational interests, athletic groups, and grade levels in schools all lend themselves to similar groupings. Increasing positive interactions between differing groups, where each can see and learn about the value of the other, promotes unity and reduces the fractionalism and distrust that encourages conflict.

Balance competitive activities with cooperative activities.

The more you do, the better you do it. The greater the value of what you do, the greater your rewards will be. Our country has operated quite successfully on the competition principle for centuries. It has made us productive and moved us and the world as a whole to great advances. Competition appears to be necessary for human beings, but it needs to be balanced with cooperation if joint survival is to be the end product.

One person wins a state high school golf tournament and five others are on the floor when the city basketball championship is won. Were these examples of competition or cooperation? The golfer was supported and challenged by her teammates who continually pushed her to greater accomplishments. The basketball team had 8 additional varsity players, 12 junior varsity, 15 freshman, 6 coaches, trainers, cheerleaders, and a cheering section that all played significant roles. The schools and the communities felt achievement in the supporting roles they played with these athletes. The events were clearly competitive, but the success was achieved through the cooperation of many. Certain families or communities continually produce outstanding achievers in specific areas precisely because they cooperatively work towards competitive achievement. It is not the competition alone, but competition with the cooperation of many that is most productive.

Schools and communities need to seek a balance of activities that teach both competition and winning as well as cooperation and group achievement. Habitat for Humanity provides an example of where many people with different types and levels of skills can all find a place to support the overall achievement. Everyone can enjoy the outcome and their part in it just as the cooperative community can recognize that they had their part in supporting the individual golfer who won the state championship. The specific examples of cooperative projects are no secret. Deciding to do them and take the necessary actions to make them a reality is where we often fall short.

Emphasize the need for shared leadership responsibilities.

Many leadership functions are performed in any group, and those groups with multiple people in those positions tend to be more effective. Cooperation and supportive behaviors can be encouraged better when more than one or two people are seen as taking leadership responsibilities. Taking these roles can be encouraged at school, at home, on the playground, at church, on the ball field, and anywhere that people interact.

Parents who leave no family leadership responsibilities to their children will raise no leaders and no one with any practice at being responsible in a family. Sharing chores, decisions, and play activities with children gives them a feeling of significance in the family. They know that they make a difference. The same holds true in a school or classroom where the more real leadership responsibilities that are shared, the better.

Establish coordinated prevention and intervention programs.

Any of the actions presented should have a positive effect on the problems of violence, harassment, and bullying in schools and communities. One person or one group doing one thing can make a difference. A much greater difference can be made, however, if a coordinated program of both prevention and interventions are established and carried out by a number of different people.

Metal detectors in a troubled high school will do little to curb violence if they are the only technique used. Those who would be violent will simply find other ways, means, times, and places to be violent. Programs are needed to prevent the development of violent attitudes as well as programs to stop violent attitudes from becoming actions. We need to look not only at the high school but also at the elementary school where somehow young children learned the attitudes that evolved into carrying guns at an older age.

Discipline, caring, action, discussion, understanding, rules, feelings, beliefs, and facts cover a wide range of factors that all need attention if we are to overcome violence, harassment, and bullying among young people. The task sounds overwhelming, and it is for one person to accomplish in a short time span. It is not likely we will make everything the way we would have it in a month or a year or maybe in a lifetime; however, the more comprehensive and well thought out we make our efforts, the more success we will see now and the better world our grandchildren will experience. Our impact as a coordinated, concerned, and reasonable group far outweighs what we can do as separate individuals.

Chapter 8

TEACHER ACTIONS

OVERVIEW

The classroom teacher is put on the spot more directly than anyone else when it comes to dealing with violence, harassment, and bullying in schools. Society asks teachers to be experts at an enormous variety of roles within their classrooms. At any given time, someone will be expecting them to be instructors, detectives, group leaders, enforcement officers, judges, mediators, counselors, encouragers, disciplinarians, academicians, laborers, friends, parents, nurses, writers, speakers, and the list could continue easily. Even superhuman cartoon characters would have difficulty filling this many roles. The reality is that no one can perform all these roles with equal effectiveness and that includes the world's best teachers.

Teacher burnout is common precisely because there are so many roles that need to be performed and the task for one person can be overwhelming. Teachers need a support system around them and an understanding of how that system can accomplish the most. They need to rely on those people who can take formal or informal roles in making the system work more effectively. The focus of the actions presented here is to give teachers specific functions and activities that are manageable and effective when taken as a part of a larger program. Roles and situations that are better left to others are pointed out in order to reduce the pressures on teachers to more reasonable levels.

Division of responsibilities within a larger program is easier to envision and accomplish within a school rather than within a classroom. The reason is simple: There is usually only one adult in a classroom while many adults with various official roles function in the overall school. Division of responsibility can appear impossible when one adult is alone in the classroom of 20 to 35 young people. Teachers need to recognize actions that can be taken to develop an organized and supportive classroom environment where students also know their responsibilities and feel obligated to take them in specified ways. The actions for teachers suggested here should help when alone with students and also demonstrate how they can deal with students in the context of the whole school and community.

The support teachers need in order to deal with violence, harassment, and bullying fall into three main categories:

1. an organized program in which to work,
2. a support system that is available when needed, and
3. a set of realistic boundaries on the roles and responsibilities expected of them.

Implementing some of the School and Community Actions provided in Chapter 7 should go a long way in creating the organized program and support system necessary. It is well worth a teacher's time to invest energies in these broader activities as well as the ones designed more specifically for teachers and the classroom in this chapter. Most of the School and Community Actions also can be translated into classroom actions where those in the room are considered as a community. Emphasis will be provided in this chapter on ways to help create such a supportive community within the classroom while also recognizing the classroom's part in the larger school and community.

No person in school spends more time with more students than the teacher. This full-time involvement makes teachers the most visible models for either positive or negative behaviors. Much like a family relationship, teachers will have a significant influence on how children see and relate to others, whether they want the influence or not. Effective teacher actions will be those that encourage positive behaviors, discourage negative behaviors, provide opportunity for students to practice and reflect on behaviors in school, and put teachers and other adults in the position to be positive models of similar behaviors.

GAINING CONTROL

Several girls surrounded Tia in the hall to let her know their anger in no uncertain terms, "Wait 'till we get to the shower after gym. We'll see how much your fancy clothes and sucking up to the teacher means when you don't have someone to cry to."

Physical education class is four hours away, but nothing productive is going to happen between now and then for these girls. Schoolwork will be the last thing on their minds. Other girls are doing all they can to avoid Tia and her tormentors. These bystanders are planning how to be out of the shower room when the confrontation happens. A few are excited by the confrontation and thinking of ways to be there without getting in the middle of it. Most of the bystanders feel sorry for Tia, but they don't know what to do and they sure don't want trouble themselves. Bad feelings and minimal thoughts for schoolwork are the norm.

Both students and teachers face a difficult situation. What should be done? Who is responsible? Should we avoid discussing this in class since it happened outside of class? How do you start to deal with something that no one wants to deal with in the open? What happens if we do nothing?

Gaining control of the situation requires that people know their most basic responsibilities and have access to a few basic actions. Complex ideas, intricate techniques, and devising new programs do not work at this time. To gain control, people need confidence in a few good ideas and the support of a well understood system that tells everyone how to take calming actions.

Take action when bullying occurs.

The actions of recognized potential models (e.g., teachers, parents, other adults, and strong peers) will serve as a primary learning tool for young people. Teachers, administrators, school staff, parents, and adults have more long-term credibility attributed to their actions than to their words. Allowing verbal or physical abuse to occur, because the situation is not comfortable or because one does not know how to act, is not acceptable. It is better to demonstrate distaste for the situation by doing something not totally appropriate than to do nothing. Even an incorrect action conveys that you care and will act against perceived wrongs. *Conveying the moral commitment through your actions to fight injustice is more important than making the perfect response.* The specific action taken will be different depending on the circumstances, but there are some reasonable guidelines that should help.

Approach the situation to only the degree necessary to diffuse it.

The model in Chapter 4 on gaining control of the situation provides examples of how to begin gaining control through approach techniques. Many times adults simply need to make themselves noticed by participants using minimally intrusive means. Attention from adults is not generally what a bully wants. At other times, adults may need to take much more active verbal actions, physical actions, or both using more intrusive methods. The general principle for approaching a problem situation is to use the approach that will reduce tension to an acceptable level with the least possible involvement of the intervening person. Some examples of less and more intrusive approaches are offered in Figure 8.1.

Use the formal policy for dealing with bullying.

The way to teach students the importance of fairness and values is to make and enforce policies that are logical, public, and implemented consistently and to involve students, parents, teachers, and others in the development and regular reevaluation of policies for reacting to bullying and harassment. Gaining consensus and public understanding of the policies may not be the easiest way to make rules since everyone will have differing opinions on what is best; however, consensus certainly makes carrying out policies much more effective since everyone feels they have a personal stake in developing, implementing, and changing policies.

Effective polices that are understood by all must be carried out the same way for every student. No special favors should go to the nice kid who breaks the rules over the problem student who does the same. It would be best for these policies to be school-wide, but they also can be developed for a single class or grade level.

Means were suggested in Chapter 7 for developing school and community policies for violence, harassment, and bullying. Individual teachers make a great mistake if they show disregard or disrespect for these policies. Many people reading this book probably will say, "That's a nice idea, but some of our policies are just stupid!" Yes, a lot of stupid policies and rules are out there. Expressing your opinions on these problem policies using all the logic, facts, and human support you can muster in every appropriate forum will demonstrate your commitment to change. On the other hand, complaining about them without taking actions and not enforcing them when appropriate communicates a disregard for the process and the rules that emerge from it.

Adults never should be seen as advocating change without having the drive to work actively for change within the system. Teachers, students, and parents need a system of policies and people to implement them in order to maintain a structure that promotes safety for all. They also need to be involved in creating

Minimally Intrusive Actions

These actions are designed only to get people's attention with minimal involvement of the outsider. They leave great leeway for participants to reconsider their actions and save face while stopping their problem activities.

- a cough, a laugh, a sigh, or a sneeze
- a look in the direction of the situation
- beginning an unconnected conversation with someone not involved
- ruffling of papers, tissues, books, tools, or toys
- changing position by standing, sitting, or taking a few steps, but not giving direct attention to the situation

Somewhat Intrusive Actions

People involved in a conflict may be too involved to readily recognize someone attending to their conflict. Getting the attention of participants and expecting them to cease once they know another person has become aware of their conflict is still the purpose. Actions at this stage are still designed to allow participants to break off their conflict without any follow-up by the adult.

- looking directly at the participants (showing disdain in one's look adds additional emphasis if desired)
- walking (not running) towards a situation
- short general questions to the participants such as "What's the problem?" or "Need some help?"

Clearly Intrusive Actions

Emotional involvement may be such that one or more participants will not be stopped simply by knowing another person recognizes the conflict. Loud verbal arguments, on-going problems, and physical confrontations often can fit this group. In these cases, adults need to demonstrate that they are willing to take direct intervention actions if necessary, but that they would rather not, if possible.

- moving quickly or running to the scene
- loud comments telling the participants to stop (general comments—not focused on any one participant)

- loud comments generally followed by questions about the problem situation (questions do not attempt to determine guilt or fault)
- stepping to the edge of an argument in an authoritative manner
- getting additional people involved by bringing them to the scene

Extremely Intrusive Actions

There are times when subtlety will not get the job done. At these times, only direct and strong intervention is appropriate. There are still significant variations on how extreme the intervention is and the exact level should continue to be determined as the least intrusive that will put a stop to the present threatening situation. Extreme action should be taken only under one of the two following conditions: (a) other forms of less intrusive interactions have not worked or (b) someone is clearly in immediate danger of significant physical or psychological harm.

Extreme actions raise the emotional, physical, discipline, and legal stakes for everyone so they should be used with caution. Inappropriate use can endanger conflict participants, bystanders, and also interveners more than increase safety.

Extreme actions should not be used often. The more they are used, the less effect they have each time they are tried. People become accustomed to even extreme interventions or discipline techniques. If used again and again, they lose their power.

- threatening participants with punishment if they do not stop
- bringing several adults physically and verbally to the situation
- physical interventions that, depending on the nature of the situation could range from pulling participants apart, to pushing, to holding someone down, to attempts at disarming participants
- calling disciplinary authorities such as the principal or the police

Figure 8.1. Approaching problem situations: Less intrusive to extremely intrusive actions.

and changing the system where necessary. Teachers and parents who want children to follow the rules and work within the system must model these beliefs actively and consistently both inside and outside of class.

Have everyone take a specific role that matches a personal position and ability.

Everyone must identify a personal role in the formal and informal policies that seek to reduce violence, harassment, and bullying. Administrators, counselors, teachers, and parents should be clear on their roles as model adults and authority figures. Students must be aware of the legitimate roles for themselves that emphasize their significance and importance to overall outcomes. A major drawback to such efforts comes about when people realize that someone is supposed to do something, but who the someone is or what that someone's responsibilities might be is unclear.

Individuals and groups must be aware of the formal roles, which they are expected to take, and also the informal roles, which are often more dependent on their unique strengths and weaknesses. Specific information on roles and actions are available throughout this book and are emphasized in Section III, but a review of basic roles is provided here for teachers who frequently find themselves in a position to provide such information.

Parents have more time at home with children than anyone, and the roles teachers might promote for parents should emphasize that opportunity. They also can be encouraged to make regular contact with the school through local opportunities that allow and encourage parent involvement. Finally, parents are sometimes in a good position to contact the parents of students with whom their child is having conflicts. Much progress can be made when one parent directly contacts another, not to blame or criticize, but instead to solicit discussion and explore issues. School personnel should be involved only in such communications when parental anger and frustration are such that they only will lead to blaming and criticizing each other and their children, which is not helpful for anyone.

The role of administrator is best suited for those actions that include the interpretation and enforcement of policies and, whenever possible, they should be left to the administrator to enforce. Administrators have broader involvement with policy than teachers and they are in a position to be responsive to the greatest number of groups both inside and outside the school. This puts them in the best position to make major final judgments about activities or people who have encountered conflict with school safety policies. Great power can come with this position but it also carries baggage that reduces the ability of administrators to do other things. Being seen as judge and major disciplinarian reduces the ability of administrators to be the individual to whom people will come with smaller and more personalized problems. Teachers must assume some administrative baggage within the classroom, but they should not take on these tasks any more than necessary outside the classroom.

Counselors, psychologists, and social workers are the professionals in the school whose training, experience, and time commitments put them in the best position to deal with individual and group problems. Teachers need to make sure they use this resource rather than assume the extra burden of attempting to be therapists as well as teachers.

Students can be encouraged to take a wider range of roles than simply ignoring the situation or just telling the teacher. Both of these limited views promote a feelings of helplessness and inadequacy. Instead it is strength, importance, and relevance to the outcomes that we want to encourage in students. Roles that promote appropriate student involvement include speaking up in difficult situations, supporting those who are being hurt, attempting to diffuse problem situations, and seeking an authority figure when necessary. Students who recognize that they can learn skills and then practice to better fulfill important roles will be more likely to fill those roles than those who do not know their roles or how to attain them.

Teachers may be expected to do it all, but they must avoid the temptation to try and meet this expectation. The challenges of running an academically focused classroom, implementing high quality teaching techniques, evaluating student progress, and conveying all this information to students and parents should be plenty, if not too much, for any human being. The teacher in the classroom will need to take on a variety of roles because no other adult is there, but they also must recognize and use the additional support available to them from students, parents, administrators, and mental health professionals.

Separate recognition, enforcement, and counseling roles.

Three basic roles need to be established and accounted for in any effective violence prevention program. Asking everyone to perform all the roles equally will not work. Person(s) who enforce the rules and determine the penalties (i.e., usually administrators for serious offenses and teachers for minor ones) are not likely to be effective as counselors of those involved. Those who are final arbitrators of major conflicts are unlikely to be in the best position to be given unbiased or truthful information by individuals who want things to go their way. The result is that recognition, enforcement, and counseling roles need to be separated in programs and people's minds as much as practically possible.

Everyone plays a part in recognizing violence, harassment, and bullying whenever it occurs. Every individual and group should be aware of personal behaviors and those of others that cause pain and suffering. The focus of awareness-building activities is not simply to provide information. It should demonstrate how someone can recognize problems and why everyone should be attentive to what they observe. Only when individuals are aware of a problem can they begin to consider taking action.

Enforcement of established policies should be limited to selected individuals. The criminal justice system establishes police forces and a judge and jury system to meet this need in the community. These systems actively discourage people from taking these roles who are not formally trained and not evaluated as competent to handle the high stress level. When police need help, they ask communities for the types of help they need where and when it is appropriate. They do not ask them to be civilian police officers. It is a difficult role with major fairness and danger implications, and it needs to be left to those in officially designated positions.

Enforcement roles in the school and classroom have similar although generally less severe implications than those in the criminal justice system. Effective antiviolence systems need to have processes and procedures that are carried out in the most consistent way possible by the same individuals in each case. Those people will have their credibility questioned regularly because virtually all their major decisions make someone feel misjudged and mistreated. Administrators need to be the final determiners of major judgments regarding violence, harassment, and bullying in schools because their role is always schoolwide in nature and does not include the many individual academic and personal decisions about students that are made each day by other staff.

Enforcement in the classroom falls mostly to teachers when it includes consequences limited to the classroom. For example, a boy is picking on another on a continuous basis, which clearly is not allowed based on classroom rules. It is the teacher's place to move one child away and make it clear that this was caused by a violation of room policy. If the student needed to be removed to the principal's office for a major violation, this would be a place where the teacher was taking the most severe response available and handing future decisions over to the appropriate authority. Such a major step also conveys the message that enforcement was not a typical matter but one that needed to be referred for additional judgment at a level outside the room.

Students and parents are generally not appropriate for enforcement positions within the school environment anywhere but at the lowest of levels. Even when students or parents are given the responsibility for evaluating problems in a court-like atmosphere, their decision-making powers must be limited and reviewable. Students and parents cannot be given this total power of enforcement in the school because they do not have the physical, social, and legal authority to carry it out. Parents can and should, however, be recognized as having the major enforcement role at home.

Bullies, victims, and bystanders each have relationship problems and they need therapeutic support from professionals. Professional therapists must be in a position where they will not be determining student punishments or making other public judgments on them. Teachers and administrators often have the willingness and skills, sometimes the training, and occasionally the opportunity to interact in caring and helpful ways with children or parents. Although they may be very helpful in these interaction opportunities, they should not allow themselves or others to begin seeing them as the therapist. Providing information, advice, and guidance must be kept separate from the more complex therapy role.

All professional organizations for therapists speak directly and unequivocally about the avoidance of dual relationships. The nonjudgmental and client-focused nature of the therapeutic relationship demands that all other social, friendship, discipline, and evaluation components of a relationship be set aside. There has been much written about whether, once someone has been a client, it is ever appropriate to have another type of significant relationship with that person. Although controversy over the "forever" term remains an issue, there is complete agreement that someone, most likely the client, will be harmed when a dual relationship exists while a client is receiving therapy. All ethical and legal guidelines direct professionals to allow only trained therapists who have no other formal roles with clients to do therapy with that client.

EVALUATING THE PROBLEM

A new student has made his first friend and is asking him about what the kids are like at this school, "At my old school there were a lot of kids that got picked on. If you weren't in the right group, you got pushed around all the time. The teachers didn't do anything. It was like they didn't even see it. Kids didn't try and stop it either. You just kept quiet and minded your own business. What is it like here?"

Students will attempt to size up the situation at their new school so they can fit in the best way possible; however, they may not receive much quality help because the problems of violence, harassment, and bullying usually are discussed quietly and spread through rumors. Seldom are the discussions open, honest, and based on reliable information. Everyone wants to know as much as possible about their environment so they can make the best of it. An evaluation process is necessary to reduce inadequate and inaccurate information so that everyone has consistent information and overall awareness of the problems will be increased.

Teachers should be aware that attempts at evaluating the problem in their room or school should be tied closely to raising awareness of the problems. This should not be approached as a research project where the amount, degree of significance, and strict objectivity are the primary factors. Instead, evaluation can be approached as the means by which the questions that need to be asked are brought out and the process for seeking answers is begun.

Each of the following actions is tied into the evaluation section of the model presented in Chapter 5 and also will help the classroom teacher implement the intervention concepts presented in Chapter 6. The activities are best used at stages and situations where introduction of the issues and their implications are the primary issue. Raising awareness, recognizing needs, considering problem origins, examining the scope of the problem, and giving initial consideration to what could be done are the major goals of the evaluation.

Introduce the issues with emphasis.

Demonstrate the importance of the issues by starting on a large and comprehensive scale. This process will not work by talking quietly with a few students, teachers, or parents at a time and hoping things will get better. Rumors, talk behind people's back, down-playing hurtful acts, and having in-groups and out-groups are primary symptoms of the kind of environment that promotes violence, harassment, and bullying. To reverse these trends, open communication where the importance of the topic is communicated clearly is essential. People need to know that they are in an important struggle and that they must overcome it together.

Arranging faculty meetings, school-wide or grade-level student meetings, and Parent Teacher Organization meetings for initial discussion of the problems are a good beginning. An introductory speaker, a survey, or a film could kick off the effort at getting people to recognize the problem and a role for their own involvement. Hand out any current school policies and other reading materials that will help people gain a perspective on the scope of the issues. The same procedures can be used on a smaller scale within an individual classroom.

Hold regular discussions on the subject with all students.

National and international statistics, as well as individual accounts, make it clear that violence problems are widespread. Adults are more likely to be surprised that fear and violence are common in our school than students who live there every day. The only surprise students will have about open discussions is that adults are allowing them to talk about the problem in public.

Students will doubt the commitment of adults to continue this openness. Past experiences will cause many to question whether this movement is "Just another one of those big issues that gets a lot of talk for a little while, but then things go back to the way they were." If the plan is to hold one or two meetings to solve the problems, then you might as well not begin. A halfhearted effort is not sufficient and will reinforce the idea that adults cannot be counted on to follow through with their beliefs. Only a strong start with clear commitment to continue the work in public forums will convince students that "The adults really mean it this time!"

Class and small group discussions with students and parents need to be planned and held on a regular basis. These discussions are designed to air issues and examine classroom or school progress rather than to solve or judge individual problems. When discussions are held regularly, they may be as short as 5 to 10 minutes each and still prove informative and encouraging of further actions. Having discussions on a regular basis will help keep students, parents, and faculty in touch with both old and new issues and emphasize their continuing importance.

Conduct a simple survey as a good starter.

Good content for starting discussions and developing awareness can be gathered through a survey of students' experiences. Researchers are generally happy to send a sample copy, but designing one of your own is not difficult. The survey in Chapter 7 (Figure 7.1) is a good starting place.

Ask yourself what kind of information would help start a discussion? For example, you can ask questions about whether, when, and where people have been a victim, a bully, or a bystander. Other general questions might be as follows: What form did the bullying take? What brought on the bullying? What caused the bullying to stop? What could be done about bullying by other students, parents, teachers, or school administrators?

The purpose of the survey for the teacher is to provide an impetus for discussion and secondarily to provide a basis for local information. Students will have many ideas, thoughts, and fears. They will have fewer ideas of how to begin a discussion and what is appropriate to discuss in the open. The questions on a brief survey, even before the results are established, will give direction and permission to deal with specific questions that would not normally be open topics of discussion.

Emphasize real-life experiences.

Students and adults generally know what is right and what is wrong regarding the treatment of other people. Good books and lectures serve to clarify and confirm what they have intuitively known and seen but were not able to express or implement in their day-to-day life. The best awareness building requires that students and adults examine their own experiences and those of others to understand the situation rather than only seeking information through a book or speaker. Emphasis should be placed on discussing, writing about, drawing, role-playing, and acting out actual student experiences, beliefs, feelings, thoughts, and action plans regarding these issues.

Some people like to lead into personal discussions by beginning with questions such as "How do you think people in the book we read would feel about their problem?" The use of books and outside examples is designed to reduce tension by avoiding discussion of one's own situation. Doing this is most useful when you are trying to work your way into a discussion that could be difficult to approach. What must be kept in mind, however, is that to be effective, the discussion must progress from talking about others to talking about oneself. The sooner this occurs, the better because it is the attention to the individual's real world that is most likely to move people to take significant action. The longer discussion of personalized immediate examples is delayed, the quicker interest will be lost and commitment will diminish.

Emphasize understanding of all sides.

Awareness activities must emphasize more than just concern for victims and denunciation of bullies if they are to build a solid base for change. Bullying, harassment, and violence are likely to have been a part of every person's actions or thoughts. All students must examine what factors might have in the past or in the future push them into one of these roles. Productive awareness activities focus on trying to understand how victims, bullies, and bystanders feel and why they act the way they do. Bystanders need to be included because there are always more of them who could get involved than there are victims and bullies who are involved.

This is no time to take sides and only consider the negative aspects of those we judge bad and the positive aspects of those we judge good. Awareness building requires that we do everything possible to see the commonalties between people as well as the differences. How can the same person be a bully, a victim, and even a bystander at different times? Why does someone behave in a particular way? Why do individuals who want to do the right thing wind up sometimes doing the wrong thing? General questions such as these need to be applied to bullies, victims, and bystanders alike. They are not three different animals but three ways that any human being can behave at one time or another. Once people are more aware of the common motivations for these behaviors, then they can begin to identify and implement ways to change inappropriate behavior patterns.

DIRECT INTERVENTIONS

Two girls are talking about the outcome of a fight between two other girls. Tension had been building up over time as one was always picking on the other. Finally things blew up and now there is a mystery about what is happening. "I know both of them were suspended for a while and then I think they both had to go to the psychologist. I don't think it will do any good. Nothing has changed around here. The same people do the same stuff they always did."

The girls in the example above are not clear about what is supposed to happen after an act of violence occurs and they have little hope that anything different is going to happen. They may recognize that someone intervened and they also may be aware of the problems in the school, but they do not see a role for themselves in dealing with the issues. Everyone in a united effort needs to be knowledgeable and skilled in behaviors that have a positive effect on the overall situation. These are not things that need to be learned through one-on-one therapy. They are skills based on knowledge and practice that enables people to know how to improve potentially violent situations. These things can be taught in small groups and classroom groups.

Teachers can begin by helping students develop the critical skills of understanding, cooperation, and assertiveness. Counseling interventions are left to the mental health professionals. These intervention actions are intended to influence groups of students by increasing their knowledge base and skills in areas in which they may have had little previous exposure.

Provide assertiveness training.

Bullies, victims, and bystanders have difficulties in this area. Young people tend to see things in black and white, which increases the probability of using behaviors that are either demanding, aggressive behaviors or the opposite, acquiescing and withdrawing. Most young people learn by trial and error that these extreme actions do not get the desired results. As they begin to experiment with new behaviors, they find which ones get better results than others and the ones that get the best results tend to be repeated. The trial-and-error process eventually leads towards assertiveness rather than aggression or withdrawal simply because assertive behaviors are more often than not the most effective in the long run.

A major problem for young people is that they do not have the 30 or 40 years of trial-and-error experience that adults do. Consequently, they may see that, for a relatively short time, the bullying, aggressive style of a stronger student really does allow them to get their way over a weaker one. For short periods of time, isolation and withdrawal also can work to make a situation better. Neither aggression nor withdrawal works over an extended period of time. Years later, when they have seen the results of regular aggressive or withdrawal tactics, adults often look back and say, "I wish I had done things differently." Unfortunately, it is experience that is the greatest teacher of these skills.

Teachers can help students gain experience by emphasizing on a daily basis through lesson plans, reactions to students, and modeling the methods and benefits of being assertive. Teaching the importance of and ability to assert yourself without demanding complete acquiescence to your desires is a major life lesson that also will have a direct positive effect on reducing violence and harassment in school. The earlier students learn this lesson and the skills that accompany it, the better they will get along with others both as young people and as adults.

Practice reverse role-playing.

Prevention and remediation of bullying and victimization requires the development of a better understanding of yourself and the other person. The greater the depth and ability to demonstrate that understanding (i.e., empathy), the greater are the chances of overcoming the interpersonal problems that are present. Reverse role-play is a technique designed to put people in a position where they need to identify with another individual in order to react as that person would.

People expect to be asked for the right answer or for their reactions to a situation. They are less often asked to demonstrate their reactions or feelings. We therefore grow up doing a lot of thinking and talking about information and ourselves, but with less encouragement to demonstrate our feelings, thoughts, and emotions. We get even less encouragement to consider another person's situation so closely that we can identify with and demonstrate personal feelings, thoughts, and actions. Reverse role-playing asks students to take the role of the other person, act out a situation, and then discuss how it felt to be in a position different from your normal one.

Students should be provided opportunities to role-play the thoughts, words, and feelings of bullies, victims, and bystanders. Reverse role-play helps students recognize and relate to the feelings that drive different people, how they are similar, and how they are different. Increased empathy for another person improves the chances that students will be willing and able to intervene in problematic situations. The greater the understanding of the people involved in a conflict (i.e., why they do what they do, and what might change their behaviors), the easier it is for a person to decide what interventions would be most helpful.

Encourage cooperative group work.

Give regular opportunities to work in groups where cooperation is more critical to success than are individual skills. Emphasize that success in cooperative group activities requires students to give positive attention to the needs and abilities of others in order to receive rewards themselves. These actions cannot and should not replace the individual and competitive activities that are a cornerstone to our society and our educational system. Instead, teachers need to communicate and follow through on the concept that there is a critical need for both individual and group efforts and achievements.

Cooperative education efforts have been found to promote the prosocial skills in people, which are often missing in situations where violence, harassment, and bullying are problems. People become more supportive of each other when they learn how to work cooperatively and have ample opportunities to put that learning into practice. They are learning how to recognize and use the best aspects of others to benefit the whole; however, in order to achieve these understandings and make them practical skills, there must be ample opportunities made available to practice them under supervision.

Teachers commonly encourage these activities as part of student projects while studying basic curriculum. They are also used as means to get common chores around the school done as a group rather than simply giving tasks to individuals. Other creative approaches are to use groups to identify problems in the school and community, collect information on them, develop potential solutions, and cooperatively work to see those plans through.

Whatever cooperative projects a teacher uses is less important to prosocial skill development than the emphasis given to the skills and benefits of working effectively together. Having recognition and providing respect for the qualities, dignity, and sensibilities of others go a long way in helping people work effectively together. These are both membership and leadership skills that can be demonstrated and encouraged in cooperative group projects more effectively than in individual work.

Develop a classroom action plan.

One project that demands cooperative group work is the development of a classroom action plan for dealing with violence, harassment, and bullying. A thorough introduction and follow-up discussions of the issues should lead to the question of "What should we do about this?" No teacher, parent, administrator, or student can effectively answer this question in isolation. A teacher action plan for the class will not be effective. What will be effective is an action plan that students feel is "*our*" plan.

Students need to feel a personal investment in their plan of action. The more the plan is perceived to come from them, to meet their needs, and to give them responsibilities in carrying out the plan; the more investment they will feel. This is no time for a classroom plan that worked in another class or one that is well thought out by authorities. It is critical that students be given the time and responsibility to make an action plan of their own.

The teacher should assure that awareness building and evaluation activities surrounding the problems have been extensively used before starting to develop any plan. One occurrence will be particularly recognizable as a clue to the best time to start planning approaches. The class will begin to reach agreement on the problem and issues. It is at this time that reaching consensus on some ways to act and how to treat others will become more clearly possible. These common agreements and areas of consensus will be the core of a formal class action plan that everyone can agree to support.

The teacher can be most helpful by providing time and coordinating abilities to assist students in planning. They will need to know what has been tried other places, what the school rules are, what kinds of support are available, and the boundaries of their potential actions. The teacher can help the class find these answers without answering each one for them by considering beforehand where such information can be located.

Another valuable step in developing a classroom action plan is to have everyone sign the completed plan. This is another opportunity to reinforce the importance of personal commitment to decreasing violence through a self-designed and agreed upon plan. The majority of discussions in schools and on the job are seen as only exploring ideas. Having a written plan and putting one's signature to it help clarify the difference between such discussions and making personal commitments to action.

No plan was ever perfect! The plan your classroom designs will have flaws that will cause it to work less well than you had hoped. To counter the nothing-is-ever-perfect reality, a good plan must build in provisions for regular review, evaluation, and revision. This does not need to be anything extensive at all. Planned follow-up discussions on a regular basis to determine how well the plan is working and what might need to be changed is the major requirement.

Read about and discuss historical figures as examples.

History books and current news publications have many examples of adults and countries who have acted as bullies toward others. Each case includes victims and bystanders with many similarities to young people on the playground. For example, the actions of Adolph Hitler and Germany in World War II provide classic examples of bullying tactics and the use of violence to get one's way. People (i.e., Jews, gays, and non-whites) and countries (i.e., Poland, France) were clearly victims of this bullying. History also has taught us that other countries (i.e., England, Russia, and the U.S.) remained too long as bystanders. Vice President Hubert H. Humphrey stated this clearly in a 1965 speech: "Today we know that World War II began not in 1939 or 1941 but in the 1920s and 1930s when those who should have known better persuaded themselves that they were not their brother's keeper." Highlighting examples from the regular curriculum and emphasizing the connections between historical concepts and current student actions will increase learning.

Discussing historical or even fictional examples of bullying, harassment, and violence also can help in lowering anxiety over the discussion of these issues. It is particularly threatening for young people to admit directly to having those personal situations, feelings, and behaviors that they see as negative. The worse the behaviors seem to the individual, the greater will be the anxiety related to talking about them. Discussing historical or fictional figures with similar characteristics allows people to ease their way into considering personally difficult areas. It is easier to begin talking about the problems of a person who is not really here than it is to start by admitting that the problems are your own. Once a person has a better understanding of the problems and how people will react to them, they then will be more likely to deal with their own related issues.

The study of historical bullies and people of violence clearly will demonstrate that they always fail in the end. Although it may be months, years, or even decades, these tactics have been proven to be ineffective over time. The reason bullies became historically important figures is that they did get people to follow them for some period of time; however, bullying tactics lose their effectiveness eventually and the bully winds up forfeiting most or all of that gained, and usually is punished severely as well. Other individuals, groups, and countries eventually get together, and through cooperative efforts, defeat the bully. This is a process backed up by traditional values that is demonstrated in myths and history as well as being taught in school.

THERAPEUTIC ACTIONS

OVERVIEW

The PIC model for therapy with bullies and victims as presented in Chapters 4, 5, and 6 provides a detailed description with examples of how the process is to work. This Chapter 9 is designed to highlight actions for the attention of mental health professionals within that overall process.

Mental health professionals need to be either the driving force or at least key participants in programs to reduce violence, harassment, and bullying. Their training, close contact with schools and communities, and ability to speak to the mental and emotional needs of youth, put them in a major position to play a variety of roles from consultant, to coordinator, instructor, and certainly professional therapist. Previous chapters provide information on the problem, prevention systems, intervention techniques, and educational concepts that should have value to mental health professionals. This chapter focuses on specific therapeutic actions related to the therapist role that may not be identified as clearly elsewhere.

The ideas presented here will attempt to avoid the extensive training and information that professionals traditionally receive. The therapeutic ideas presented are offered on the basis that those who would practice them already have a sound theoretical therapeutic base, a solid understanding of human development, assessment skills, a clear recognition of professional ethical behaviors, and substantial supervised experience. That solid background is needed to see the practical and additive nature of the actions presented. Without such a background, the information may prove useful but is unlikely to produce consistent positive results for young people or adults.

Teachers, administrators, parents, and others who might have many informally developed helping skills must recognize that these concepts may have applications to their work, but they are not designed for them. Consistency of success in assisting others with personal, social, and emotional problems is a critical difference between a helpful person and the professional therapist who knows how to produce positive results on a regular basis. Used outside the context of the professional therapist's extensive preparation, these techniques could prove ineffective or, in some cases, harmful to one's development.

GAINING CONTROL

"Get away man! Nothin's goin' on that concerns you. It's no big deal, so just get them to let me outta here! I don't need you or this damn place!"

Emotions were running high as this high school junior confronted the school counselor while waiting to see the principal. For a quick moment, the school counselor thought of letting the boy have his way and dumping him. After all, there were plenty of kids who actually did want his help, so why should he take this abuse from a kid that is a pain in the neck anyhow? It was just a fleeting thought. The school counselor knew that this kid needed him badly and that by using patience and therapeutic skills he had a good chance to make real progress with the boy.

Every therapist likes the client who comes with a clear problem, respect for the therapist, a thoughtful approach, good verbal skills, and is ready to take responsibility for making things better. Those are not likely to be the presenting characteristics of the young people encountered in these situations. Both bullies and victims more commonly blame others, disbelieve that anything can be done, demand that someone else fix things their way, and are ready to give up any personal responsibility for making things better.

This less than perfect situation is no time to jump in and try to create a quick therapeutic fix. The first task of the therapist must be to improve the conditions that will allow for effective therapy at a later time. Actions for gaining control of the situation focus attention on getting the most emotionally charged situations and responsibilities settled in a timely manner and by the people responsible for them.

Be calm but firm in recognition of the seriousness of the situation.

Training and experience told the school counselor in the example not to give in to the emotions stirred by the student's angry response. These emotions probably would have led to a thought of "give the boy a piece of your mind," which only would have hurt the potential for future work. Remaining calm, not letting the boy push emotional buttons, and not making light of any aspect of the situation was the appropriate action.

Remaining calm when someone is angry and verbally or physically threatening is no easy matter. It takes every degree of will power, knowledge, and experience to maintain a personal yet professional position when fight or flight are the only reactions those around you are experiencing. Deep breaths, waiting a fraction of a second before you speak, remembering the emotional state that people are experiencing, and harboring no expectations that logic and reason will immediately prevail are basic tools for keeping yourself in control.

One of the most difficult things to accept is that the therapeutically brilliant things we might have on the tip of our tongues will not be heard if you say them at this confrontation point. What could be a great statement, "Do you recognize your role in all of this?" will only be useful when logic, reason, and an ability to look back on a situation are in control. Attempting to provide great insights, which only will be discounted at time of high negative emotions, will diminish their value at a later time when they might be more useful.

Anything you can do to calm things down and help the standard administrative and judicial processes for dealing with these conflicts take its course will be a positive step. Keeping your reputation for being caring, open, understanding, and nonjudgmental intact while also showing confidence in the system are the two main objectives of these initial interactions.

Keep therapeutic actions separate from disciplinary actions.

Therapy and discipline are related to each other in a healthy environment, but they should not be done by the same people. It can only hurt the eventual therapeutic relationship if this school counselor is seen as able and willing to influence what happens to people in disciplinary actions. Someone else in the model system, probably the principal or a disciplinary team, should decide whether individuals are sent home, suspended, or given detention or assignments.

Even with a clear set of rules upon which to make judgments, common situations like this one are seldom straightforward and simple. Parents, students, and probably teachers will have differing views and probably all be lobbying for different considerations in the decisions. Whatever decisions are made will be seen as fair and objective by some and unfair and prejudiced by others. That type of baggage automatically accompanies the role of administrator. It should be accepted by the administrator but avoided by the therapist whenever possible to give the therapy relationship the best chance for success.

No one can avoid making judgments on people altogether, but those who conduct therapy must keep as much distance from making official disciplinary decisions as possible. This is not as easy as it might sound. Knowledgeable and unbiased professionals often recognize that, in specific situations, things could be more productive if they were done differently than those responsible would normally do. The tendency is to shape discipline oneself in order to create the best circumstances for the client's therapy; however, rules and consequences are designed not only for therapy but also to enforce standards of the community. Therapists must not put themselves in positions where they use their influence to change standard consequences for some clients and not for others. Once they make this jump, clients and others will begin trying to sway therapists to act more as decision-makers and less as therapists.

Readers might interpret this section to say therapists should not advocate for their clients. Nothing could be further from the truth. Therapist advocacy should seek to change inadequacies in the system and not ask the system to change. A model system is provided throughout this book, not because it is perfect, but because it is imperfect. It is presented so that no one person will have personal control of all that happens. Such a system should be applied with consistency in order for people to believe in it. No system will direct people to do always the absolute best thing, but a good system will at least lead everyone in mutually agreed upon directions. Effective advocacy for clients is accomplished when members of the system can be convinced that a change in direction is needed, not for one person, but for many.

Develop productive helping relationships not focused on fault.

Therapy in these cases must not focus on deciding who was right, who was wrong, and whether punishments were correct. That is the job of others, and therapists must not allow clients to drag them into the debate as they will try to do. Discussing these issues to gain an understanding of the client's thoughts and feelings is certainly appropriate, but trying to reach conclusions together is not. *The focus should be on making things better rather than placing blame.*

Developing a supportive and future-focused therapeutic relationship is the early therapeutic goal so that healing, improving conditions, and strengthening oneself are given the most attention. A sample statement that combines the student's need to be heard about right and wrong issues but that also focuses attention on future actions might be, "This situation really burns you up because you feel like the whole problem is being dumped on you unfairly. If nothing else, I guess we need to see what kind of things you could do to create a better situation."

The statement above will not fix any injustice or alleviate anger and frustration. It may even raise the student's frustration because of his or her desire for an adult to agree with him and to fix things for him. The statement had the limited purpose of simply giving attention to the student's frustration while also showing that the conversation needs to move forward towards affecting the future. This combination of recognizing the client's problem and directing therapy forward places necessary emphasis on the idea that *problems are viewed through the past while their solutions are to be found in the future.*

EVALUATING THE PROBLEM

"I haven't got anything to say really. I don't know why people are so upset. Jean is just a crazy person and she drives everyone nuts."

Don't expect to find bullies and victims in therapy who are ready to accept personal responsibility for the problems. Both will probably begin by blaming someone other than themselves. Two primary exceptions can be found to this pattern and neither is very healthy. Some students will be ready to take full responsibility but only as a ploy to get you and the system off their back. No responsibility for actions is actually being accepted. It is just that the right words are being used. They want to avoid talking about or acting on the problems as much as possible. Their hope is that you will excuse them if they just confess to everything.

A second form of unhealthy exception is demonstrated by those individuals who accept responsibility because they have a low self-concept and believe this is just another of their failures. This is usually a victim who believes that the wrongs experienced at the hands of others are just the way things have to be. A victim is likely to be compliant, isolated, and depressed and feels little to no control of the situation.

The evaluation stage of therapy with bullies and victims starts with an exploration of the widest variety of possible causes rather than one person or one issue being fully responsible. Potential responsibilities of the other person and one's own possible responsibilities must both be open for discussion. Emphasis must be given to the idea that this exploration is not designed to place blame but instead to identify all the things that might be changed to improve the future.

Begin with individual attention.

Always see clients one at a time at first. Bullying and harassment cases, in particular, emphasize a significant power differential between the perpetrator and the victim. Initially seeing bullies and victims separately allows the therapist to eliminate the dynamics of this power differential from therapy until such time as the difference may not be so great. Relationship problems are overcome more easily when people can see each other as more similar than different and more equal than unequal.

Another reason for beginning with individual sessions is that each person needs individual attention given to his or her unique problems first. The elements in conflicts include both unique individual problems and other problems that only arise when two people come together in certain circumstances. It is not possible to completely treat a bully-victim conflict without confronting the individuals' needs or the needs of the relationship. The starting place should be the individual ones because making individuals feel more secure and healthy creates potential for dealing with the joint relationship problems.

Talk with the bully first.

To whatever degree possible, attempt to see the bully before you see the victim. One of the most troublesome issues to handle is explaining how you know and what you know about the problem. This is not a volunteer therapy situation, where the only issues to be discussed are the ones the client brings. In bully-victim cases, you and probably many others will recognize a problem, and the participants will not have much opportunity to deny it. As a result, the bully in particular will be looking for someone as a scapegoat for the hassles. Whether directly stated or not, the bully's question will be "Who told?", and his or her desire will be to get whoever it was.

Bullies will be expecting and probably hoping to blame the victims for telling. This is the perfect scapegoat. Bullies have proven already that they can overpower the victim, and a blaming and get-even attitude can be used to justify their continued hostility.

The therapist is in a much better position to protect the victim from continuing hostility when the bully can be told honestly that the therapist's information came from anywhere other than the victim. The therapist's information about the problem is not used to place blame but simply to understand the situation. A close evaluation of the accuracy or origin of each point is not necessary because the information is used only as a starting place to begin conversations with each of the participants.

Attend to needs not directly related to bully-victim interactions.

Bullies and victims may have needs separate from bully-victim interactions. In therapy, these separate issues must be given attention early in the process, as they often affect later stages. A common example is problems at home having a negative impact on relationships at school. Each student should have personal needs attended to by the therapist both because it is a good thing for the individual and also because it is generally a positive factor in healing bully-victim problems.

Therapists can become overly focused on overcoming the obviously harmful bully-victim situation. A great deal of pressure comes from adults and students alike to see that things improve quickly; however, therapists must be strong in tending to the individual needs of clients as well as the bully-victim relationship problems. The problems are related, and both must be given attention continuously in order for the greatest progress to continue.

Search for the common understandings of the bully and the victim.

Talking to bullies, victims, and bystanders will provide many widely varied stories of what occurred and why. The differences can appear so extreme and overwhelming that the therapist will have difficulty maintaining hope that anything but keeping people apart will be possible. Sometimes permanent separation is the only option, but usually more commonalties of understandings can be found between bully and victim so that progress on their relationship is a real possibility.

Common understandings and goals are sought in order to begin serious work on answering the question, "How can working cooperatively on the issues benefit both of us?" We know that countries, tribes, and families who have been enemies for decades can make peace. The change comes when they can identify common problems and needs and can realize that working together is the option with more realistic benefits for everyone. The reasons for developing better relationships are no different for youth and adults who have been in conflict. Therapeutic exploration needs to focus on those issues, needs, and goals that could better be reached by working together than by being in continual conflict.

Staying out of trouble probably is the most frequently used common goal for bringing bullies and victims together. Even those students who might use their bully or victim role to seek attention really only want the attention and not the trouble. Bringing too much trouble on themselves only gets them ostracized in ways that reduce the attention they desire. They may not say this directly, but it becomes obvious because, given time to calm down, they seldom want out. What they want is a significant amount of attention from individuals or groups and also to be allowed to stay in their groups.

Common understandings and goals are the critical content for bringing bullies and their victims together. As they begin to recognize similarities in the other individual, they realize that the concept of getting along is not a dream in some crazy adult's head. Helping students find and explore those similarities is a major part of the therapist's work with these students.

ACTIVE INTERVENTIONS

"Okay, so Joe has his own problems and maybe some of them are not too different from problems I've got. But he always knows how to say things that really hurt me and I can't stop him. I hate it, and there's nothing I can do about it."

Increased understanding is great, but alone it is never the solution. Unless understandings can be turned into actions, they are just ideas, not realities. The boy in the example above is letting the therapist know that, although he has learned a lot and it sounds pretty good, he still doesn't see how the information is going to make his life better. This is the beginning of a new and important stage for the therapist-student relationship. The proof of success here will no longer be understanding. Progress now must be judged on accomplishments and improved conditions in the relationship.

The action phase comes after a solid working relationship is formed and both student and therapist have a more consistent picture of the problem's dimensions. The picture will continue to become more accurate as additional information and insights are realized, but obtaining common ground on the basic picture is enough to begin serious work in the action phase. Exploring and experimenting with actions that can be taken outside the therapeutic relationship is essential for real-world progress to be achieved. The actions provided below by no means substitute for using the orderly process described in Chapters 4, 5, and 6 or the basic therapeutic techniques used throughout a professional practice. These actions are ones that need special attention in the process for this particular group of clients.

Move from individual therapy to joint meetings of people in conflict.

The place to begin work with individuals who have been in conflict situations is with them as individuals. Their pain, suffering, and anger are things they hold inside and that need to be given attention before other steps are taken; however, these individuals were in conflict with other people and not just within themselves. Part of a total healing and growth process eventually needs to include those with whom they have had or are having conflicts.

The problem for the therapist is making ongoing decisions of whether, when, where, and how to move from individual therapy to joint meetings between bullies and victims. These are difficult decisions with significant positive or negative implications for the therapy relationship and the development of everyone involved. Success strengthens all participants and increases confidence in the system, but failure has the opposite effect.

Bullies, victims, and bystanders who see no change in how things are working reaffirm their anxieties and the use of their old defense mechanisms. It becomes easy to conclude that the best thing to do is to hold on to the old ways of interacting. People know that lashing out at those you know can be overpowered; hiding from conflict and using passive-aggressive behaviors never fully achieve the desired results. On the other hand, they also remember that "If I don't have other ways of getting by that I can see work, at least these poor ones get me through the day."

The move from individual to joint meetings, if it becomes possible, creates a more holistic approach to problems related to conflict. Joint issues of conflict can be approached and joint solutions can be developed; however, outcomes of more stable and satisfactory environments are probably not the greatest benefit of successful joint meetings. The benefit of successful joint meetings that creates the greatest long-term growth is the recognition that conflicts once believed to be unresolvable can be resolved by using specific procedures and skills. Awareness of one's access to individual skills and systematic ways for effectively dealing with joint problems of conflict not only alleviates current problems but also can be transferred to deal with similarly difficult issues in other areas of one's life.

The potential future benefit of skills and systematic procedures learned through successful joint meetings makes it imperative to employ these procedures when conditions are right. Using these meetings at only appropriate times and with adequate preparation and follow-up are critical factors. Preparation and follow-up, in particular, should specifically include times when skills and systems developed to deal with joint conflicts are introduced, employed, and reviewed. The continuing value of these lessons must not be lost in the euphoria of successfully negotiating through difficult times.

Make decisions to have joint meetings based on specific criteria.

The decision to move from individual therapy sessions to joint meetings should be based on specific conditions being present. It is equally important that these specific conditions be emphasized in joint meetings in direct and obvious ways. Joint meetings should be viewed as times and places to accomplish highly specific things that became readily apparent from individual sessions. The function of joint meetings is to continue the positive progress established in individual therapy with participants.

Therapists should be confident that certain criteria are met prior to deciding to bring conflict participants together:

(a) Participants realize that there have been power differentials in their relationship and these will not be allowed in joint meetings. Participants will treat each other as equals and, therefore, are equally responsible for creating a better environment.
(b) Participants have explored and have understanding of the beliefs, feelings, and situations of the other individuals involved as well as their own.
(c) Participants must recognize that the others involved have similarities in goals and needs that can be better met by joint interactions than separate individual meetings.
(d) Participants both desire a more satisfactory relationship.
(e) Participants will be able to state clearly and specifically their desired differences in their relationship. The therapist must recognize that the changes desired are mostly compatible and that the compatibility is understood by participants prior to joint meetings.

(f) Participants understand and agree to honest participation in the purposes, format, and follow-up for the joint meetings.

(g) Participants briefly practice their role in the joint meetings during prior individual meetings with the therapist.

Avoid making the move from individual to joint therapy too early.

Deciding prematurely to move to joint meetings promotes situations where the same interpersonal dynamics that created problems previously will remain in place. Moving too early usually means that a power differential and a lack of willingness to change the situation in mutually beneficial ways will continue. These conditions make any helpful progress unlikely and create the probability that the meetings will fail. Failure in joint meetings has negative implications for the participants who lose hope, the therapist who loses reputation, and everyone else who loses confidence in the system's ability to work.

Premature joint meetings tend to take one of three forms, none of which is positive. In the first form, the therapist reacts to the reticence of participants to get involved by lecturing both parties. The lecture will stress the damaging implications of the problem, how people ought to treat each other, and the need for better ways of interacting. Only the less powerful person is likely to be impressed by the lecture because he or she is the one most likely to seek the therapist's approval. The more powerful person realizes that the use of the lecture means little will happen to change things.

A second form of reaction to premature meetings is that the individuals can stake out and attempt to hold their original grounds. They probably either will say nothing more than restating their case or will add arguments to prove who is right and who is wrong. Arguing is the primary focus and hardening of the problem positions is the result. Everyone leaves frustrated and less hopeful for common solutions than before.

A third form of reaction involves intelligent and socially aware individuals who may realize that saying what the therapist wants to hear will get them out of the office and out of trouble quickly. They are not interested in solutions but only to go on about their business and be relieved of the pressure to change. Responses tend to be smiles and simply saying all the right things quickly. Therapists sometimes can be tricked by such seeming support, but the result is that nothing has changed. The bullying likely will continue, although probably in less public ways but with similar if not worse negative consequences.

Hold joint meetings that are well thought out and orderly.

Joint meetings should never be arranged under the presumption of the therapist that "Once I get them together, I'll just see what happens." Better therapy groups are those where the subjects, directions, and process are very open and flexible. These joint bully-victim meetings usually cannot be molded to fit that open model. They need the organization and structure laid out in Chapter 6 that consists of specific introductions, order of interactions, and statements of closure.

Early joint meetings, in particular, should be planned to be relatively brief (15 to 30 minutes) and tightly structured. The early goals are to clarify and confirm common goals, means for working on goals jointly, and means of evaluating follow-through. The more progress between and at follow-up meetings, the more flexibility and student directedness can become the driving forces of the joint meetings.

Conduct joint meetings in a manner that leads to participants' follow-up activities.

Joint meetings serve little purpose and can be detrimental if they do not lead to follow-up activities that are carried out successfully. Students should go to the joint meetings knowing that these meetings are designed to lead to follow-up actions by the students. Also, they should have thought through and discussed potential actions in the context of the question, "What kinds of things would you be willing to commit to doing if she agreed to something that met one of your needs?"

Therapists can determine potential areas for positive follow-up actions after holding individual discussions with both participants. Active listening and reflection will confirm that some desirous actions are currently out of the question whereas others of possibly more limited value are achievable. The potential to carry out joint actions successfully is more important than the size of the strides taken. Small steps with outstanding chances of success are always a preferred path for early joint sessions. More risky steps can be taken after participants have built a basis of success that will not crumble due to difficulties and failures.

Use reverse role-playing to promote empathy development.

Perhaps the most consistent theme in helping bullies and victims to improve their relationships is the need for them to gain more empathy for the other person. Self-exploration is necessary and important, but in these situations the relationship of self to another individual is also a critical dimension for success. Dealing with a relationship is not something one does alone, and the more accurately all participants understand each other, the greater will be the potential for developing mutually supportive ways of behaving.

The objective of reverse role-playing is for individuals to see actions, try out behaviors, and develop better understanding for other people and their relationships to them. Frequently suggested as a learning technique for use in awareness building groups, it is also an effective tool for individual therapy. Reverse role-playing is particularly valuable in those situations where questions of how others think or feel are important to progress. Some samples of these types of questions are provided below:

What would happen if . . . ?
What would it be like if . . . ?
How do you think she would react if . . . ?
How would other people feel if . . . ?
What would he do if I . . . ?

A therapist choosing to use reverse role-playing in these situations might say, "Well, it would be nice to know how Jean would react if you did that, but she's not here. Let's do a little role-playing here and see if we can imagine what would happen. You react to me as you think Jean would. I'll react as I think you would. You've seen and thought enough about her that you can guess how she would react. Try to get in touch with how she would feel and you be her. I'll start."

This scenario includes a problem that would benefit from a real life exploration of both individuals' feelings and behaviors and potential different reactions. The therapist can guide the role-play by being flexible enough both to challenge student ideas and to confirm their ability to understand and take reasonable actions. A major benefit of this technique is to get worrisome ideas and anxieties out in the open through acting out life situations rather than just thinking about them.

When possible, use positive incentive systems and behavioral contracts.

Commitment to improvement and support of success is a key ingredient to progress in any area including this one. Solidifying that commitment and assuring the support for successes often can be done through the initiation of positive incentive systems and behavioral contracts. These traditional therapeutic mechanisms fit well in many situations where bullies and victims are being treated either as individuals or in joint work.

People who have recognized a need to improve their situation or, at least, to reduce the negative consequences for themselves are particularly appropriate for these techniques. They often realize the need to change but cannot do so without the establishment of more concrete goals and rewards to keep them going in the early stages.

Self-monitoring of incentives and contracts can be very useful for many bullies and victims. The therapist in these situations often wants to create a situation where participants recognize needs to improve, select ways to do it, and are encouraged for their success. The more self-selection of goals and actions that is possible, the more emphasis should be on self-monitoring. Self-monitoring provides the additional benefits of directly supporting personal responsibility and a more trusting relationship with therapists, peers, and other adults. Taking this type of increased personal responsibility for one's actions is a long-term goal of all therapy.

Chapter **10**

ACTIONS FOR BULLIES, VICTIMS, BYSTANDERS, AND PARENTS

OVERVIEW

How many times have you sat in front of a child or parent who believes in you and only wants you to tell him or her what to do to make things better? That seems to be the situation virtually every time and, each time it happens, you feel frustrated and inadequate. Generally, you want to take their situation into your own hands and fix it as a plumber would fix a water leak. Take control, tell them what to do, relieve them of the responsibilities that trouble them, and make it all better. These are the ways you may like to teach and do therapy, but dealing with human beings is never that direct, no matter how obvious the problem seems to be.

No easy answers exist to give frustrated, angry, worried, and distraught students and parents; however, actions can be taken and goals sought that will improve the situation in the long run if not immediately every time. The ideas for victims, bullies, bystanders, and parents presented in this chapter will not work for everyone, every time, and in every situation. Who implements them, how they do it, and under what conditions will each alter the overall results.

Professionals cannot promise that the ideas that follow will make things better immediately, but they can promise that these actions are sound, reasonable, and that they have helped many others. These actions are ones that would benefit everyone to some degree.

Individuals involved in bullying, violence, and harassment generally do not employ these concepts as consistently or as effectively as most people. The reasons are many. The person who knows only comfort and safety will not learn the same self-protective behaviors as someone forced to live in a fear-inducing environment. Small, uncoordinated children will learn different behaviors than large, coordinated children. Self-confident parents will convey different messages than those who feel inadequate. Cultural or racial minorities will see and react to life differently than those who are in the majority. Whatever the reason, it is clear that people find their own unique ways to get through life. The professional's job is to help them recognize and continue the ideas and behaviors that serve them well, eliminate those that are not productive, and add those that will make life better.

The ideas presented in this chapter will be more effective as one portion of a larger program of administration, education, and counseling. Used in isolation, they are likely to have positive consequences, but they also may prove ineffective or even harmful without the support of individuals and groups who believe in them. Assertive behaviors, for example, are positive things for children and adults to learn and practice; however, learning to use them takes practice and early attempts will be awkward or even inappropriate. Whether people will be either understanding, instructive, helpful, and respectful or disappointed, angry, rejecting, and degrading during these early stages will have a major influence on future progress.

Any of the activities used should take into account unique circumstances, have explanations and practice preceding their use, and evaluation and revision sessions following their use. Assuring that this process takes place is the task of professionals even more than giving out the helpful pieces of advise, which almost anyone could do. Teachers, therapists, administrators, and many well-educated parents can provide that assistance.

IDEAS FOR VICTIMS

A human instinct toward loved ones or friends is to be protective. This is particularly true for those who have been victimized. We want to soothe the wounds and do what we can to protect them from further harm. These motivations are basic and generally necessary for self-preservation and preservation of those we hold dear. These are valuable reactions for those who would help victims get out of immediate trouble; however, should these protective reactions continue to be the only ways that problems are handled, the victim will not become better able to handle future difficult situations personally. Victims must receive support and protection, but they also must be taught techniques for facing problem situations on their own.

Continuous protection of victims and teachings limited to avoidance reactions can produce an individual who only knows how to run away from problems or seek someone else to solve them. Victims also must develop more self-assertive approaches that inspire confidence in their ability to acquire and maintain control of one's own life. A balance between knowing when and how to retreat and when and how to go forward is essential when dealing with conflict. Too much regular emphasis on either side will produce problems in dealing with conflict.

The following ideas are for those victims seeking ways to limit or eliminate their victimization through their own behaviors. Punishing bullies and making others do things better generally cannot be accomplished by victims and will not be provided in this section. These are responsibilities for others to enact.

Employing the suggested ideas often will have a positive effect on how victims are treated, but they do more than that. They will help victims see themselves in the more positive light that accompanies taking responsibility and credit for personally productive behaviors. Increased self-esteem and a belief that controlling one's own future are the most important benefits that can be acquired by personally taking positive actions.

Avoid giving the bully an emotional payoff.

People find satisfaction in making something work out the way they planned it. Whether the action was meaningful, right, or wrong is often less important than whether they could feel good about its success. Bullies can find a similar satisfaction in making a person react in the way they want. The more intensely the victim reacts in a way the bully wants, the greater the pleasure. When victims can reduce the level of their reactions, they become much less desirable targets.

A bully can walk down the hall at school punching three smaller boys on the arm. One boy shows more pain, fear, and pleads for the bully not to do it again. Another shows fear but also threatens in an unconvincing way. The third boy flinches, shows little expression, and says, "Hi."

All three boys are less physically powerful than the bully and, therefore, could become victims. The minimal emotional reaction from the last boy provided the bully with the smallest emotional payoff and therefore makes him the least likely of the three to become a victim. The boy who showed the most traditional fear and pain probably provides the most satisfaction to the bully and makes him the most likely future victim. The bully realizes that he probably can get the same high emotion, yet totally nonthreatening behavior consistently. The boy who showed anger and ineffectually threatened the bully is a likely victim candidate. Because both boys know he probably cannot back up his threat, the demonstration of anger offers the bully another excuse to bully him further.

No one can be sure that the scenarios suggested in the above example actually would happen. Many other variables influence what happens, although these outcomes would be the most common. When the emotional reaction of the victim is of the type and level expected, however, the bully will reap the emotional payoff. Victims who can find ways to rob the bully's emotional payoff will take the pleasure out of the bully's behaviors and decrease the likelihood that these behaviors will continue over time.

Be physically and verbally assertive (not aggressive).

Bullies are not looking for significant challenges when they pick victims. They are seeking people who shy away from standing up for themselves. Bullies do not want to get physically, socially, or verbally bloodied each time they force their will on another person. They want easily manipulated targets. Those who show little confidence in their ability to stand up for themselves offer the best probability of an easy target. This type of person can be treated as a toy to be played with at the bully's discretion.

Regular victims of bullies generally do not believe they have the skills or ability to stand up for themselves effectively in the situations where they are bullied. They communicate this lack of confidence through behaviors and the words or lack of words they use. Other people who may be no more adequate to stand up to a bully, but show their inability less obviously, seldom are selected as victims. The difference is that those not chosen will appear to be more self-confident because of the more assertive words and behaviors they use.

Assertive behaviors and words are how people convey confidence that they are good people with rights that they cannot be required to give up. They may choose to give up those rights when the occasional need arises, but they will not give them up continuously. Those less frequently selected as victims may give in to a bully, but they also convey that this was by their choice and they will not choose to do so consistently. Regular victims, on the other hand, convey that the bully is choosing for them to give in and that they cannot stop the bully now or in the future.

Assertive words and behaviors are those that convey confident messages that one's ideas and status are defensible without demeaning the other person. Standing up straight rather than slumping, making eye contact rather than looking at the floor, and standing with shoulders squared to the other person rather than turning away are simple postural actions that convey confidence without demeaning the other person.

Hostile and harsh comments and threatening behaviors are not self-supportive but communicate aggression and disrespect instead. Such aggressive responses are most likely to provoke any person, particularly a bully. "You're a jerk," "Shut up," and "I'll get you if you do that again" offer direct challenges to bullies. Upon hearing such comments, bullies will quickly consider, "Can this person back up these insults?" If the answer is "No," then the bullies will be encouraged to go further with their harassment, because now they feel noble about defending their honor. Avoiding aggressive and threatening comments and behaviors is just as important as learning assertive ones.

Staring, pointing, putting up fists, or striking out are aggressive behaviors that are likely to raise the level of conflict rather than reduce it. Just as aggressive words do, this type of action communicates a challenge rather than self-confidence. These actions may work if the bully believes such challenges are harmful to him or her, but often this is not the case and the gestures may do more harm than good.

Do something unexpected.

Bullies want to know that, in a certain place, with a certain person, at a certain time, they can threaten and harass someone with predictable results. They know that doing these things to the wrong person, in the wrong place, at the wrong time, could produce problems for themselves, which is not an objective of bullying. Predictability of the victim's response is necessary for a bully to continue harassing a person. Victims make continued bullying less likely by making their reactions less predictable.

A common place for bullying is in the cafeteria where a bully might make a person move from one place to another for no reason other than the desire to exert influence. Most often a victim will move the first time to avoid a hassle and hope it only occurs once. Many times this works. If the bullying continues, it becomes apparent that simple avoidance of the hassle is not working. The bully can see this as a perfect situation. Moving a victim from seat to seat is easy because the victim gives in the same way every time and no one else gets involved.

The victim needs to change the pattern in this example so that the bully will become more concerned about the possible negative outcomes. For example, the victim might simply not move one day. Now the bully has to decide whether using physical force or louder threats would attract too much negative and undesired attention from authorities.

Victims in this situation might begin talking loudly to a friend or make an assertive response in a voice loud enough to attract attention, "Every day you tell me to move. Today I'm not moving!" Either of these examples might or might not have immediately positive reactions. They even could spur bullies to assert themselves more in the immediate situation; however, the victim's inconsistent and attention-attracting behaviors make that person a poor choice for a victim over the long run, because it continues to be unclear what will happen next.

Practice necessary behaviors.

Victims think about hundreds of ways to react differently next time. They think about behaviors that are subtle, ones that are more direct, and others that are violent. Part of the reason victims lose effectiveness in other aspects of their lives is that they spend so much time ruminating on what else they could do to the bully. Their problem is not their lack of ideas on what else they could do but their lack of action.

Adults and peers need to help victims practice new behaviors in safe environments. Every victim has thought, "Next time I'll just tell those bullies that I'm not putting up with it any more!" Usually they do not do it because the idea cannot be seen in reality. A thoughtful counselor, teacher, or parent could role-play this scenario with the victim and then talk about several critical questions. How did it feel? What effect might it have? Could we change it to make it better? What might we try next? The answers certainly will not all be positive and comforting. Doubts will arise about how things might work that could never be answered completely until they are tried in an actual situation. The value of this practice is that ideas can be tested, dropped if they are really bad, used if they are good, and changed to make them better.

Practice should start in the safest possible environment. For example, begin with a parent or counselor, where *embarrassment* probably will be the major hurdle to overcome. The more threatening *fear of rejection* because of what someone might think or how successful the attempt turns out will be less of an issue with a parent or counselor than with peers.

Just because victims have tried new behaviors in the safest environment does not mean they are necessarily ready to use them with bullies. Taking intermediate steps such as trying similar behaviors out with peers can move understanding and competency to higher levels through practice without directly facing the most difficult situation immediately. The assertive behaviors that victims learn can help them with many relationships, not just those with bullies. Practicing them on others can have the additional positive impact of improving relationships in general.

"You cannot put it off forever." Sooner or later in the critical situation, a good idea must be used or it will lose its potential value. Victims will have great fear that their words or action will backfire and make things worse. Sometimes they are right. The way to overcome fears, activate ideas, and increase the possibilities of the new actions working is to provide increasingly realistic opportunities for practice. The last step of using the new actions with one's tormentors still will raise anxieties, but they will be accompanied by additional self-confidence from planning, practicing, evaluating, and redesigning the actions. Victims' tasks are never easy, but practice will make them easier and more likely to be successful.

Strengthen continuing friendships and make new ones.

Bullying requires that victims be isolated in some way. This isolation could be physical, as when one is cornered in an isolated area with no one around. It also can be a social-emotional isolation where people are around, but they will not get involved. A victim cannot be bullied over time if people around are present to intervene. Unfortunately, reactions of most victims is to isolate themselves out of a desire to avoid public humiliation. *Reversing the common pattern of increasing victim isolation is an effective way to decrease the potential of remaining a victim. Strengthening old friendships and developing new ones are among the best methods for reversing the isolation trend.*

A parent called the former school counselor from 2,000 miles away to say that her son was being bullied this year by another boy who previously had been a friend. It became so bad that she removed her son from school and was teaching him in the safety of their home. She wanted to know what she could do to help the situation and whether or not the counselor considered withdrawing him from school as a good idea. In spite of a variety of complications within the situation, the counselor later assured the concerned mother that taking the boy away from friends and peers at school to protect him was not a good idea in this case. Being isolated at home was making it increasingly difficult for him to develop friendships that could help protect him from being bullied. The family needed to create more, not fewer, opportunities to increase friendships that would carry over into school where the problems occurred.

Victims must work as hard as possible to strengthen their friendships and increase the number of friends they have. They often are selected as victims partly because they have few friends or friends who are not willing to stand beside them in difficult times. Bullies do not want to challenge a crowd. They want one victim at a time with no possibility of others becoming involved. Developing friendships that will make such support likely increases safety for victims.

Having friends is often as important to avoiding being bullied as the quality of those friendships. Good friends who are not there when you need them are not much help. Youth should seek ways to be with their friends at the times they are generally attacked by bullies. The concept is simply that being in a crowd makes a person a less desirable target. Finding ways to be with groups of friends will increase security for the same reasons that adults know to walk as a group, rather than alone, in a troubled neighborhood. There is safety in numbers.

Seek support when necessary.

Victims need to know that they are not in this alone. They feel singled out and in many ways that is exactly true and is the way that bullies want it. Youth naturally learn that the first step in handling their problems is to do it themselves. It is a more difficult task to learn exactly when outside help is needed and how to use it appropriately.

Every kindergarten teacher knows the struggle children experience in learning when to tell on someone and when to handle it on their own. Some learn never to tell, and they often do not get the help they really need. Others learn to "tell" an adult about every little thing that someone else may have done wrong and take no responsibility for dealing with their own situations. It is finding the proper balance between these two extremes that successful existence as an individual in a community requires. It is not a simple balance to achieve.

Victims will tend, as the kindergarten children, to be at one extreme or the other regarding when, where, and how to seek help. Telling all the time reduces their credibility, but not telling at all cheats them from using the adult support that is rightly available to them. The challenge for well-meaning adults and peers is to help victims see the impact of both extremes and to develop more appropriately balanced ways of responding.

Taking self-responsibility for actions is always more productive in the long run than allowing others to do things for you. No student should be encouraged to just let the teacher handle it as the only solution. At times, an authority figure should handle the situation and people should be encouraged to seek that authority figure at those times. Even then, victims should look within themselves for better ways of interacting that could help avoid such situations in the future. Allowing authorities to handle a situation and taking no self-responsibility for future similar situations increases the chances that a similar situation will occur again.

When is the appropriate time to seek help? The answer depends on the type of help needed. Any time a person is uncomfortable with a situation is a good time to seek help in evaluating the situation and looking for productive ways of responding. Seeking guidance from a professional or peer should require no hesitation. This type of support is beneficial when it assists the individual in understanding the situation and planning new ways to respond. Everyone should be encouraged to seek ideas and actions that further personal understanding and skill development in order to increase individual responsibility for behaviors and subsequent results.

Seeking someone to intervene on behalf of a victim is appropriate in two key situations. When there is a real possibility of significant physical or emotional harm, adult intervention should be sought immediately. "Ms. Jones, Mary has threatened to beat me up the minute I walk out this door. I'm afraid and need your help." Fear is high, and the possibility of real harm is immediate. These are good reasons to seek help and good reasons to give it.

A second situation for seeking adult intervention is when the situation continues without progress, even though the student has worked with others to develop new reactions. "Ms. Jones, I know we've talked about this before and you have seen me doing the different positive things we talked about. But Bill is still knocking my pencils off my desk, calling me names, and threatening me on the playground. I don't know what else to do. He still will not let me play with the other kids."

This boy has taken the initiative to try new ways of dealing with Bill and has even done so with the help of an adult. An adult is legitimately needed, not to fix the situation, but to intervene in a way that will allow the victim to benefit from new behaviors being tried.

Children need help learning when and where to ask for adult help. Making the best use of adult guidance and intervention where necessary is important for anyone and particularly those who find themselves in victim situations. Encouraging self-responsibility for dealing with problems along with recognition of when to seek supportive assistance is essential. A balanced combination of the two produces independent and self-confident individuals who also recognize that they are not in this alone.

IDEAS FOR BULLIES

Bullies get relatively little sympathy from adults in comparison to victims. Once they are identified as having broken the written or unwritten rules of social behavior, causing hurt to another, punishment rather than sympathy is the common means of dealing with them. Our legalistic society places great weight on judging right versus wrong and then taking punitive actions (i.e., toward the guilty) or supportive actions (i.e., toward the victims) based primarily on that judgment. This model seems to have moved our nation in positive directions quite effectively, if not perfectly.

Our criminal justice system advocates the concept of rehabilitation as well as punishment for offenders, but punishment gets by far the most emphasis, perhaps brought about the nature of the system or that carrying out punishment is easier than is rehabilitation. We can put people in prison or suspend them from school "as the rules direct" much more easily than we can change a person's thinking and behaviors.

Changing the thinking and behaviors of bullies requires more than the necessary follow-through on punishments. Most people perceive the rules and mores of society as serving them and the punishments as for disruptive individuals. Bullies tend not to recognize that these rules and mores support them also. Instead, they see the rules and mores along with their associated punishments as roadblocks to their own needs. The challenge of working with bullies is to help them recognize the personal value of following the rules and mores of their school and peer society.

Bullies need to be aware of the negative consequences associated with bullying behaviors and also the benefits of conducting themselves differently. Awareness needs to extend beyond cognitive knowledge to a personalized acceptance of changing their thinking and behaviors in order to create a better existence for the bully as well as for others. This is no easy task. Success depends on helping bullies develop in several ways:

1. recognize the legal, social, and personal consequences of bullying;
2. identify and seek support from those who care about you;
3. increase the ability to empathize with victims and bystanders;
4. gain a more accurate and thorough self-concept; and
5. improve social problem-solving and anger management skills.

The model for creating a system of dealing with bullying and victimization is designed to create situations where these things are more likely to be learned. The following sections provide some specific concepts and actions that should be emphasized within that system.

Recognize the legal, social, and personal consequences of bullying.

Rules and mores provide people with guidelines for how to get along. They set up the accepted, behavioral limits so that members can recognize more easily where, when, how, and with whom they can fulfill their own needs without degrading others. Societal tools used to teach its members about these are the formal and informal consequences. Therefore, part of any rehabilitation program must be the consistent implementation of the pre-set consequences and the bullies' understanding of these consequences.

Written documents should lay out clearly and succinctly the official rules, consequences, and the basic reasons for the rules. Materials of this type will reduce what can become interminable and mostly nonhelpful discussions over what the rules really are. With this accomplished, discussions can move more quickly to their value to people in general and their personal implications for bullies who violate them.

The mores of a group are generally unwritten rules, which makes a clear understanding of them more difficult. These include discussions about what people need in order to feel safe, to protect themselves, and what to do informally as a group to keep people in line. Bullies are able to recognize the concepts because they generally are adept at setting up their own limited set of mores about how people should behave in their presence, including the consequences for not obeying. However, bullies' ideas and techniques normally will focus on coercing those less powerful to meet the bullies' needs. The logical argument for this position might be represented in a statement such as, "So if we all use your model, then adults who are stronger than children should be allowed to make children do anything they want?"

Bullies want to have unlimited power over others, but they do not want others to have it over them. The need for societal mores and rules can be impressed on bullies by using their own unreasonable words and ideas to demonstrate the problems that would be created for them if others used the same model.

A common statement by bullies being forced to see a counselor is, "I don't have any problems. I'm doing fine. It is the other kid that's got the problem." They are quick to deny any of their own difficulties, which makes sense, because they have a self-concept that can accept very little weakness or failure. Well-meaning people often try to point out the psychological or social problems, but these efforts generally fail. They simply can be denied under the presumption that "I know me better than you do." It may or may not be true, but it is impossible to refute successfully.

A better way to convince bullies of their problem is to accept their denial of personal problems and attend to problems that cannot be denied. Assuming that punishments have been handed out and that the bully doesn't like those punishments, the discussion of problems can begin with ways to avoid such punishments in the future. This is not as profitable as a direct approach to their personal problems but is much better than arguing over whether or not they have such problems. The discussion of how to avoid future punishments, for example, will raise issues of changing behaviors and understanding others so that their problematic reactions can be avoided. Both of these are quality areas for discussion and can lead to more personalized discussions later.

Identify and seek support from those who care about you.

Bullies often suffer from feeling that only those who agree with them are friends. Those who disagree must be enemies. Helping bullies recognize that adults and peers can care very much about them, while not necessarily agreeing with them or their actions, is an important positive growth step.

Seldom do bullies look outside of a small circle of victims and friends for confirmation. The confidence they have in their abilities is limited to a small number of actions that they employ again and again with the same people. They fear risking new behaviors with other people or in diverse situations for fear of showing their perceived inadequacies. This overprotectiveness results in a limited self-perception. The old behaviors and relationships may not be great but, if they ignore all other possibilities, they don't seem that bad.

Helping bullies recognize that more adults and peers really do care about them than they now believe is an important goal. Verbally opening up just a little more or trying a new behavior with a parent, counselor, teacher, or peer that will reinforce their better aspects can be a major confidence builder for bullies. This type of support is not available to them in their immediate circle of peers.

Those who encourage bullies to seek support from new people must be ready to put aside the student's history and to be supportive rather than doubting. Sharing perceived weakness with someone new is a big gamble from the bully's point of view, who will approach the task with great awkwardness, tentativeness, and wariness. Any perceived slight, regardless of how small or unintentional, will likely send the bully immediately back to the closed circle of ideas and friends that support bullying behaviors.

Increase the ability to empathize with victims and others.

Bullies tend to see their victims primarily as objects rather than as human beings like themselves. This provides the permission to treat victims poorly with reasoning and labeling such as the following:

"They don't act the way they should."
"They need this treatment."
"They don't count."
"They shouldn't get in my way."

Each example emphasizes what the victim should be or do, but not one of the examples seeks any understanding. Not attempting to empathize is common and causes all decisions to be based on presumptions about the other person rather than on actual understanding.

Bullies who tutor or mentor students much younger than themselves often give up many of their bullying ways while in the situation. These younger students provide little threat to the bullies' need for power. In fact, they desire and appreciate assistance, which, in turn, lowers the guard of bullies. As bullies relax, they often also explore more about the younger child's life, fears, needs, and hopes than they ever do with similar age peers. This results in developing closer feelings to the younger students, accompanied by fewer bullying behaviors. This is just what we would expect of anyone who spends non-defensive time trying to understand another person. The vast majority of bullies are not unalterably hurtful to others, but they need to see more connectedness between themselves and those they choose to abuse.

We need to employ ways of encouraging bullies to explore the daily existence, thoughts, feelings, hopes, dreams, and fears of their victims and other people. The more they can do this, the more commonality they will feel and the less potential for abusive actions.

Many examples for encouraging empathy have been provided in the model chapters and elsewhere. A review of several categories of these examples includes the following:

- provide videos and speakers who can give high quality personalized examples of the problem and consequences,
- read books that demonstrate the thinking and feelings of people who are abused and also of their abusers,
- ask questions and use reverse role-playing that encourage bullies to examine the victims side,
- have open discussions in small groups or in classes where many people's feelings and perceptions can be given focus, and
- bring bullies and victims together when the conditions are appropriate.

Gain a more accurate and thorough self-concept.

All people have doubts about their own qualities and acceptability. The variations in people are not whether they have these doubts but how realistic the doubts are and what actions the doubts cause. Actions that cause self-doubts to be viewed openly and realistically put people in a position to overcome them appropriately. Actions that repress viewing and discussing allow doubts to create an inaccurate self-concept resulting in ineffective behaviors.

The insecurities, fears, and difficulties in reaching out to others experienced by bullies almost never find direct, open, and realistic expression because bullies are so uncomfortable with them. Their means of overriding self-doubts is to use their power over weaker individuals in an attempt to disprove self-doubts without facing them directly. Asking them to stop bullying others for logical, reality-based reasons will have little effect because their reasons for acting this way are not based on a realistic or logical picture of themselves or how they interrelate with others.

Helping bullies obtain a more accurate picture of themselves is essential if they are to change such behaviors as opposed to just finding ways not to get caught. Many productive self-concept development methods, books, and programs are available on the market. The PIC model presented in this book is designed to emphasize this growth in several ways. Each of the following concepts recommended in the PIC method can lead to a more accurate and thorough self-concept:

- participating in open group discussions of previously tabu topics,
- carrying through on the realistic consequences of unacceptable actions,
- increasing accurate understanding of others' situations and feelings,
- providing opportunities for self-disclosure with a safe and caring counselor, and
- promoting the practice of new behaviors with individuals and groups.

A more realistic self-portrait should develop from these self-concept-promoting actions. This more accurate picture will allow bullies to make more logical and reality-based decisions on how to run their lives and relationships.

Improve social problem-solving and anger management skills.

The variety of techniques used for dealing with their frustrations and social interactions are very limited for bullies. They have become dependent on a few techniques for achieving only a few acceptable conclusions. Demanding or acquiescing are their primary problem-solving models and they recognize little middle ground.

Overpowering others and being overpowered are a bully's basic tactics. Winning or losing is the only outcome. The social consequences are invariably negative for bullies who see only black and white options. The help they can use is in developing more and better options.

Bullies need help learning new social problem-solving and anger management skills in addition to recognizing more acceptable outcome options. These additional skills and outcomes will provide the direction and means necessary to gain more frequent and satisfying social relationships. Some critical areas for skill development include the following:

- negotiation skills,
- win-win outcomes,
- give-and-take relating,

- listening skills,
- conflict management,
- anger management techniques, and
- relaxation techniques.

IDEAS FOR BYSTANDERS

It is the victims first and bullies a distant second that will be seen as need-ing assistance. Those individuals who have been observers of the problems will get relatively little attention because they are not seen as needy enough when only limited time and energy are available. Many will see this group as being in no need at all. Unfortunately, this group is affected by bullying and victim-ization even when they are not directly involved. Their confused feelings and concerns also need recognition and attention if they are to achieve maximum development toward making quality future decisions in difficult situations.

Most interventions for bystanders will be group interventions. Their prob-lems generally are group-related, and their situations will have many similari-ties to the majority of others in the group. Discovering the commonalty of feel-ings and concerns can be empowering as it creates a unity of purpose and rec-ognition of available support. Producing these conditions is not only important for the social and psychological well-being of the individuals involved but also for creating the type of environment to intervene in the abuse of people.

Recognize and give permission to act on your feelings and discomfort.

Bystanders tend to feel afraid, embarrassed, and inadequate about their non-response or ineffective response to the abuses they observe. They want things to be different and they desire to help; however, they are afraid of being phys-ically, emotionally, or socially hurt if they attempt active involvement. Their positive motivations probably have prompted them to intervene in the past but with little effect and possibly even incurring the bully's wrath. They look around to see what others do and often observe little or no new ideas. They stop trying and consequently feel bad for their decision.

The negative pattern is common, resulting in individuals with feelings of inadequacy. Those who find peer groups with whom they can discuss negative feelings will do better than those who keep the feelings to themselves. Once it is realized that "these bad feelings are not only mine," people feel not as odd and become more willing to continue talking about the situations. Those who keep things to themselves will continue to feel like "I am uniquely inadequate" and will be less likely to discuss openly the situations for their personal feelings.

The first step in reversing the pattern of bystander embarrassment, inadequacy, and fear is to help them recognize their feelings and the fact that they are not unique. The many discussions of group awareness-building activities suggested throughout this book are designed to encourage this first step. This lays the groundwork for bystanders to get off the sidelines by giving them informal permission to recognize openly what is going on and to get involved as a group rather than in isolation. It tells them that support is available in the form of the many others in similar situations and with similar feelings.

Decide on specific actions to take.

There are better and worse actions for bystanders to take, but any action that helps in any way will benefit everyone. The worst way to promote future effective action-taking is to take no action. Even ineffective or inappropriate actions can be revised and thereby lead to better designed actions in the future. We can learn much from our mistakes but little from our inactions. The question, what would have happened if . . . ?, can be answered only when something has been tried.

Bystander feelings of inadequacy tend to originate from inaction more so than wrong actions. Reversing this trend is critical if they are to improve bystanders' feelings about themselves and their ability to affect their environment. Discussions that begin to create a recognition of the problems and the bystanders' feelings surrounding them must progress to decisions on taking specific actions in order to create positive change.

Provide immediate and/or follow-up support for victims.

Bystanders can become involved by helping victims either through direct intervention or personal support. It may be possible to change the problematic situation for the victim by direct intervention if bystanders have enough power, skill, or influence. The larger the numbers of bystanders available and the more united they are in their approach, the greater will be the possibility for direct intervention being successful. This is a direct approach but certainly has a potential for high threat and risk depending on the situation and the people involved. Students should give considerable discussion to the possible direct means of intervention, potential consequences, and ways to make the best out of a situation where things go wrong.

A less direct, but also less risky, alternative is to find ways outside the immediate conflict situation to be available, understanding, and supportive of victims. Individuals often can provide this form of support better than groups because of a greater opportunity for privacy in this embarrassing situation. The individual approach is easier to employ either when unity among bystanders is low or when the bystander was not present at the conflict situation.

Students may have initial difficulty in recognizing ways of being ready to give individual support to victims. This is often a result of both the bystander's anxiety and the victim's embarrassment. The resulting feelings of inadequacy push each towards the option of hiding from others. These feelings need to be given recognition so that some of the following examples of giving support to victims can emerge:

- spend time with victims,
- get physically and personally closer to victims rather than keeping your distance,
- talk with victims about casual things,
- invite victims to be involved in a variety of group activities,
- be encouraging of victim efforts and accomplishments,
- talk about serious things and problems when the victim wants,
- express your desire to find additional ways to help, and
- give support regularly (i.e., once doesn't do it).

Help bullies change in ways that are positive for themselves and others.

Bystanders will have a wide variety of conflicting feelings about bullies including the common ones of fear and dislike along with the less expected feelings of liking the bully in some situations. This confusion of feelings about bullies is common, is reality based, and can be a valuable tool for helping improve the situation. They provide the opportunity to treat bullies not as pariahs to be damned and avoided but as human beings who can be encouraged to give energies to their positive qualities.

Bullying is not a good thing, and concerned bystanders must denounce it; however, they need to focus their attention on the bullying behavior and not the person who is the bully. "What you did to that girl stinks!" is a valuable denunciation of the action. Statements such as "That was terrible! You are a jerk!" are a personal attack that could make things worse.

Denunciations of an action can be followed by feelings of liking and concern such as "That's not like you." This option makes no sense after a personal attack. Personal attacks tend to bring on additional attacks, which only makes the situation worse. Students can be more effective when they learn to discuss the problem behavior with bullies rather than demean them as bad people.

Some probably will see a particular bully as just a bad person. If enough different bystanders gather together, however, they will be able to identify positive qualities in the bully. The bully's positive aspects need support and attention as much as the negative aspects need condemnation. Bystanders can offer that support in ways much less potentially volatile than condemnation and intervention. This makes these efforts potentially useful by everyone and not just the most confident and able of bystanders.

Seek help in appropriate ways and situations.

Bystanders often believe they are on their own in a situation they cannot handle. They want to do something but do not have the influence or authority to do what is needed. The answer to this real dilemma is that "Everyone needs help from time to time, and everyone has the right to ask for it when they need it." Peers, professionals, authorities, and parents all have their place as providers of help. Bystanders need to know when and how to ask for assistance.

The right time to ask for help is not whenever I'm anxious or only when a disaster has occurred. Somewhere between those two extremes are appropriate places to seek assistance. Seeking assistance too early reduces the opportunity to learn the extent of your abilities. People who ask for help too frequently and for too many things never learn of their full potential for dealing with difficult situations. They will suffer from this loss when they eventually need to deal with a difficult situation and cannot find someone else to take care of it for them. Bystanders need to be encouraged to face their anxieties and concerns by trying to do something on their own as often as possible. Someone will not always be there to fix things. Requests for help should be sought when the things they have tried do not work or when they have been unsuccessful in the past.

Avoiding disaster is an excellent reason to seek authority figures for help. Asking for assistance prior to a disastrous situation occurring allows for milder preventive measures than the severe measures needed to correct a major conflict in progress. Using bystanders' own experiences and observations, they can recognize how the level of tension rises, words get louder, pushing gets harder, and threats become more direct as a crisis point approaches. Probably one or more people has tried to intervene in some way with no success. Learning to recognize the progression of a conflict situation will help bystanders gain confidence in their ability to decide when is the right time to ask for help.

Well written and agreed upon school rules provide additional guidance on when, where, and how to seek the intervention of authorities. These rules should let students know when actions are appropriate to be reported and when not.

Acquiring personal support and understanding for one's own feelings and concerns is much less complex than seeking intervention support. We all need other people to help us sort out our feelings and emotional reactions to the lives we live. Keeping these things totally to oneself is harmful and causes both immediate and future problems. Every person needs friends and supporters who will help deal with fears and anxieties. Peers are often the first choice, but many times they either are not enough or are too close to the situation to be objective. Counselors are trained to be that helpful individual for "regular people with regular problems" and not just for those "people in trouble with serious problems." Parents, teachers, pastors, and other adults should be identified as additional sources of support for young people.

IDEAS FOR PARENTS

Parents provide more direct and indirect guidance to their children than anyone. The type of parental relationship and the style of one's home life are the earliest influences and provide the most permanent effects on a young child's life. Who parents are, what they know, and how they interact with children, the school, and the community cannot be left out of any quality plan for reducing violence. Their understanding and support of a program and its actions are essential in gaining the best results.

Parental influences are strongest when models at home, school, and play each communicate and demonstrate the same values and behaviors. Unfortunately, it seldom works that consistently. Different parents are not educated to raise children in the same ways or have similar expectations for their children's immediate or long-term behaviors. They learn how to be parents primarily from experiences with their own parents who were, likewise, not educated in any common model. The result is that all parents cannot be expected to treat their children in the same ways or view children's behaviors similarly.

All parents want good things for their children, but they may have very different ways of how to show it. These differences must be taken into account whenever professionals seek parental support for assisting their children or someone else's. It is beyond the scope of this book to deal with all the complexities of families, parents, and how to work with them. The ideas provided for parents are general ones that all focus on developing more commonality of direction and behaviors among parents, schools, and community interactions. The focus is on creating a more consistent world for young people with less decisions to make regarding which model to follow.

Model the behaviors you encourage in your children.

Consider a community where assertiveness, dependability, concern for others, sharing, fairness, equality of treatment, kindness, independence, cooperation, and competition were taught to all youth. Probably no one would argue with these qualities used in balance with each other. But what if in the same community, adults never practiced these teachings which their children were being taught? Would children follow the community's teaching or the models of the adults? There is no question that consistent modeling from those we look up to has more influence than how we tell people to act.

Well taught, good ideas become ingrained behaviors when youth see those whom they admire modeling those concepts in the real world. When adults do not model what they teach, those ideas are seen as words and not realities. Children learn more from the actions of the adults in their lives than from the words they are told. Parents who become convinced that the behaviors they want from their children at school must be continuously modeled by themselves take a major step towards changing a child's behavior.

A good starting place for parents to begin changing their children's behaviors is to identify the new behaviors desired. Perhaps more negotiating behaviors would be desired for a bully rather than the demanding and overpowering behaviors normally displayed. The bully's parents, who could be assisted to look at their own behaviors, likely would find that there are places where they could practice negotiating behaviors more often themselves. For example, very often parents will find that, although they emphasize negotiating for their children, they primarily use demanding behaviors in dealing with them. If these parents can begin to use more negotiating behaviors with their child, school personnel, and others, change for the child will be much more likely than simply saying "You do it differently or else."

Changing adult behaviors to match what they would have their children do is no easy task. Adult behaviors have developed over many years and altering them will never be easy, but the desire to help their children achieve a better existence is strong for parents and can be the push needed to help adults change.

Children who see their parents changing old behaviors for a better way often are impressed as much with their commitment to the struggle as with the new behavior itself. Many times when both parents and children are seeking to change old behaviors together, new and stronger bonds are formed in addition to developing better ways of get along. The task is not easy, but the benefits of even small successes can be great.

Modify enmeshed or disengaged families.

Many aspects of family interactions and style of living will have an effect on how children behave both within and outside the family. A common factor often related to children who become bullies or victims is the degree to which the family leans on each other for support and pleasure. Providing support is an important socializing and guidance role that families have the potential to play better than any other individual or group. Problems often develop for the children of families who provide either too few opportunities for such support or too many.

Families who provide inadequate support and pleasures for each other (i.e., disengaged families) are more likely to have children who seek that support elsewhere and often inappropriately. Bullies frequently come from more disengaged families where times of whole family play, discussions, negotiations, outings, problem solving, or even eating meals together are few to none. Everyone goes a separate way in extreme cases, and the children as well as the adults seek their sources of support elsewhere. For the children, this is likely to mean they will learn on the street from peers. The resultant extreme independence and reliance on immature individuals for guidance can lead to the learning of immature behaviors such as bullying to get one's way.

Encouraging families (often of bullies) to seek more quality time together is the basic source of growth for disengaged families. The more simply and easily that inclusive family activities can be incorporated into regular family life, the more likely they are to be accepted and used. The objective is to get the family started on some things that will make sense and can be easily accomplished with the belief that success and enjoyment of the activities will encourage their continuation and expansion. Just a sample of simple yet often overlooked ways of increasing the family's involvement with each other are listed here:

- check homework on a regular basis,
- provide a short time each day to let family members tell what they did during the day,
- turn the TV off for an hour two or three evenings a week to talk or play together,
- eat dinner together on a regular basis but not necessarily every evening,
- work on family projects,
- do at least one thing (virtually anything) together with time to talk each weekend, and/or
- go for a family walk.

Some families have the opposite problem from those that provide little consistent support for each other. These enmeshed families spend too much time together while they take care of virtually everyone's needs internally. Children from these enmeshed families have so many needs met so consistently within the family that they may not learn enough about how to support themselves or seek the support of others outside the family. They become overly dependent on their family for support and pleasure and suffer from inadequate independence and social development skills.

Youth who are regularly found to be victims at school often emerge from overly enmeshed families. They tend to have difficulty finding ways to stand up for themselves outside the family. Additionally, spending most of their socialization time at home, they have few good friends or do not know how to use those friends when they need help. They perceive few resources available to them outside their own family.

Encouraging enmeshed families (often those of victims) to do more things independent of each other is the focus of helping them grow. Progress is sought that provides ways for children and adults to spend time on outside friendships, have independent projects, and allow for times of privacy. These families do many good things for each other that should not be eliminated. The more healthy picture is one where a better balance can be obtained between family togetherness and family member independence.

Encourage consistency in discipline techniques.

A common feature of the families of bullies and victims is that discipline techniques are applied inconsistently at home. Health endangering disciplinary techniques or providing no discipline at all are commonly recognized as harmful to young people. Inconsistent use of the more moderate disciplinary techniques used by the vast majority of parents, however, also can cause problems.

Consider the example of inconsistent disciplining of a child who comes home late from school three days in a row. The child is sent to the bedroom and not allowed to have dinner the first day, ignored the second day, and taken out for ice cream the third day. What is the child to expect on the fourth day? No consequences have been taught that can be expected to come regularly with returning late from school; therefore, there is little reason to change the behavior. Discipline and attention are offered arbitrarily and, therefore, do not convey any well accepted messages.

Most families use some form of disciplinary techniques that can be modified to be applied more consistently. Probably most people have their own preferences for how people should discipline children; however, the preferences are not necessarily the same from one person to another. The objective in a particular situation need not be to change everything about a family's disciplinary actions. A more limited, but also more achievable initial objective would be to apply the family's current disciplinary techniques more consistently. Greater consistency in administering discipline will make the important messages behind the discipline more likely to be received and implemented.

Seek new information.

Whatever parents have known and done up to the point where their children are having problems has not turned out to be sufficient to stop the problems. Simply repeating what always has been done is not likely to change that trend. Parents need new information, ideas, and ways of interacting that they can add to their repertoire of positive actions.

Reading materials, parent organization meetings, and seminars on children's development, family interactions, and school policies are samples of the information that parents can access through their school and community library. Visits to the school counselor and teacher will add information about additional resources. These contacts also allow parents to find out more about how the school works, the problems they face, and the ways their child interacts with others.

Acquiring this new information will not necessarily make things look brighter for parents. They may find things about themselves, their child, other children and parents, the school, or the community that may not fit their picture of how things work. The more one learns about the realities and the possibilities of a situation, however, the greater the opportunity and motivation one will have to do something about it.

Knowledgeable parental involvement is a critical factor in successfully changing bullying, harassment, and violent behavior. The more parents learn, the greater productive involvement they are able to offer. When that involvement can be channeled into support for common goals, everyone will benefit.

Deal with others involved.

Helping one's own children through difficult times is an obvious responsibility that everyone expects of parents. It is less clear how far away from home this obligation extends. What are parents' roles when it comes to the other individuals, groups, and organizations involved with their children's troubles? How should parents deal with the school, other children, and other parents? The answers to these questions can vary greatly depending on the type of situation, its seriousness, and the nature of the individuals involved. Flexibility is required around a few consistent principles.

Parents need to be concerned about the safety of their children and be ready to express that concern. Children should not be protected from all difficult situations. They need practice in dealing with such situations in order to develop the coping skills necessary for adult life. Deciding which school situations are too dangerous and which ones are reasonable challenges is difficult for parents, but this difficulty does not relieve them of their responsibility. Parents have the right and responsibility to make sure the challenges their children face have adequate safety nets to protect them from unreasonably dangerous situations. Parents must place themselves in situations where they can learn as much as possible and speak out knowledgeably on behalf of their children.

Parents need to understand the problems of their children from a variety of viewpoints. It is most common for parents to look at a problem through their own eyes, which usually see only one side of the situation. To get a view that will allow for the most reasonable means to solutions, it is necessary to understand the views of others involved. The most effective actions are generally those that can be supported by the most people. Learning how teachers, other parents, other students, neighbors, and other family members view the situation will increase the parent's ability to select actions that have the greatest potential for success. Success at this task requires more listening than talking, more going to others than waiting for them, and more acceptance of views than demanding of acquiescence. These tasks are not easy to accomplish when emotions are running high, but perseverance will bring dividends.

Parents need to recognize that their children's lives are not their own and that who the child will be as an adult is still in the process of being formed.

Adults have lived long enough to know much about the kind of lives they choose to live. Our children still are learning about the lives they want to live. They need practice and experiences with different ways of life so that they can later choose what is best for them.

Experiencing people of different beliefs, cultures, and social groups in a diverse school setting creates conflicts along with the information needed for healthy childhood development. Children will experiment with ways of relating in school that are very different from what is taught at home. Parents must recognize that experimentation with ideas, people, and actions along with the challenges it brings, is not something to fear. This experimentation is a valuable part of the human development process. Guidance, values, and beliefs are conveyed and supported by good parents so that children can learn them and then compare them to others they encounter. It is through this learning and comparing that an individual develops similarities to his or her parents as well as those things that make the person an unique human being.

REFERENCES

Bandura, A. (1973). *Aggression: A social learning analysis.* Englewood Cliffs, NJ: Prentice-Hall.

Bastian, L., & Taylor, B. (1991). *National crime victimization survey report.* Washington, DC: United State Bureau of Justice Statistics.

Besag, V. E. (1989). *Bullies and victims in schools.* Bristol, PA: Open University Press.

Carlsson-Paige, N., & Levin, D. E. (1988, January). Young children and war play. *Educational Leadership,* 80–84.

Center for the Study of Social Policy and Annie E. Casey Foundation. (1991). *Kids count data book.* Washington, DC: Author.

Cole, R. J. (1977). *The bullied child in school.* Unpublished manuscript dissertation, Sheffield, England: University of Sheffield.

Dodge, K. A., Murphy, R. R., & Buchsbaum, K. (1984). The assessment of intention-cue detection skills in children: Implications for developmental psychopathology. *Child Development, 55,* 163–173.

Dodge, K. A., & Newman, J. P. (1981). Biased decision making processes in aggressive boys. *Journal of Abnormal Psychology, 90,* 375–379.

Drass, D. (1992). *Dreams under fire.* Los Angeles: Franciscan Communications.

Edelman, M. W. (1994). This is not who we are. In *The Progress of Nations: 1994 UNICEF.* New York: UNICEF House.

Edmondson, D. (1988, April). Bullies. *Parents,* 100–106.

Elliott, M. (1991). *Bullying: A practical guide for schools.* London: Longman.

Eron, L. D., Huesmann, L. R., Dubow, E., Romanoff, R., & Yarmel, P. W. (1987). Aggression and its correlates over 22 years. In D. H. Crowell, I. M. Evans, & C. R. O'Donnell (Eds.), *Childhood aggression and violence* (pp. 249–262). New York: Plenum Press.

Fattah, E. A. (1989). Victims and victimology: The facts and the rhetoric. *International Review of Victimology, 1*(1), 43–66.

Federal Bureau of Investigation. (1992). *Uniform crime reports for the United States, 1992.* Washington, DC: Federal Bureau of Investigation, U.S. Department of Justice.

Fingerhut, L. A., & Kleinman, J. C. (1990). International and interstate comparisons of homicide among young males. *Journal of the American Medical Association, 263*(24), 3292–3295.

Floyd, N. M. (1987, Winter). Terrorism in the schools. *School Safety, 22,* 22–25.

Frankl, V. E. (1984). *Man's search for meaning: Revised and updated.* New York: Washington Square Press.

Gilmartin, B. G. (1987). Peer group antecedents of severe love-shyness in males. *Journal of Personality, 55*(3), 467–489.

Goffman, E. (1968). *Stigma: Notes on the management of spoiled identity.* Harmondsworth: Pelican.

Greenbaum, S. (1989). *Set straight on bullies.* Malibu, CA: National School Safety Center.

Gutscher, C. (1993, Fall). Violence in schools: Death threat for reform? *America's Agenda,* p. 10.

Hartup, W. W. (1979). Peer relations and the growth of social competence. In M. W. Kent & J.E. Rolf (Eds.), *Social competence in children* (pp. 150–170).

Hanover, NH: The University of Vermont and University Press of New England.

Hazler, R., Hoover, J., & Oliver, R. (1991). Student perceptions of victimization in schools. *Journal of Humanistic Education and Development, 29*(4).

Hazler, R., Hoover, J., & Oliver, R. (1992). What kids say about bullying. *The Executive Educator, 14*(11), 20–22.

Himelein, M. J., Vogel, R. E., & Wachowiak, D. G. (1994). Nonconsensual sexual experiences in precollege women: Prevalence and risk factors. *Journal of Counseling and Development, 72*(4), 411–415.

Hoover, J., & Hazler, R. (1991). Bullies and victims. *Elementary School Guidance and Counseling, 25*(3), 212–219.

Hoover, J., Oliver, R., & Hazler, R. (1992). Bullying: Perceptions of adolescent victims in the midwestern USA. *School Psychology International, 13*(1), 5–16.

Hunt, R. D. (1993). Neurobiological patterns of aggression. *Journal of Emotional and Behavioral Problems, 2*(1), 14–19.

Lagerspetz, K. M., Bjorquist, K., Berts, M., & King, E. (1982). Group aggression among school children in three schools. *Scandinavian Journal of Psychology, 23,* 45–52.

Learning Publications Inc. (1988). Shocking violence in schools. *School Intervention Report, 7*(1), 1–2.

Lochman, J. E. (1985). Effects of different treatment lengths in cognitive behavioral interventions with aggressive boys. *Child Psychiatry and Human Development, 16*(1), 45–56.

Mendler, A. N. (1992). *How to achieve discipline with dignity in the classroom.* Bloomington, IN: National Education Service.

Miers, D. (1990). Positivist victimology: A critique. Part 2: Critical victimology. *International Review of Victimology, 1*(3), 219–230.

Mitchel, J., & O'Morre, M. (1988). In *Report of the European Teachers' Seminar on Bullying in Schools.* Strasbourg, Germany: Council for Cultural Cooperation.

Morgan, J., & Zedner, L. (1993). Researching child victims: Some methodological difficulties. *International Review of Victimology, 2*(4), 295–308.

National Education Goals Panel. (1993). *The national education goals report— Volume 1: The national report.* Washington DC: U.S. Government Printing Office.

National Institute of Education. (1978). *Violent schools—Safe schools* (Volume I). Washington DC: U.S. Department of Health, Eduction and Welfare.

Oliver, R., Hoover, J., & Hazler, R. (1994). The perceived role of bullying in small-town midwestern schools. *Journal of Counseling and Development, 72*(4), 416–419.

Oliver, R., Oaks, I. N., & Hoover, J. H. (1994). Family issues and interventions in bully and victim relationships. *The School Counselor, 41*(3), 199–202.

Olweus, D. (1978). *Aggression in the schools: Bullies and whipping boys.* Washington, DC: Hemisphere.

Olweus, D. (1994). *Bullying at school: What we know and what we can do.* Oxford, England: Blackwell Publishers.

Peck, M. S. (1983). *People of the lie: The hope for healing human evil.* New York: Simon & Schuster.

Roberts, M. (1988, February). Schoolyard menace. *Psychology Today, 53*–56.

Robinson, E. H., Rotter, J. C., Fey, M. A., & Vogel, K. R. (1992). *Helping children cope with fears and stress.* Ann Arbor, MI: ERIC Counseling and Personnel Services Clearinghouse.

Roland, E., & Munthe, E. (Eds.). (1989). *Bullying: An international perspective.* London: David Fulton.

Seligman, M. E. P., & Peterson, C. (1986). A learned helplessness perspective on childhood depression: Theory and research. In M. Rutter, C. E. Izard, & P. B. Read (Eds.), *Depression in young people* (pp. 223–250). New York: Guilford.

Shapiro, B. Z. (1967). Dissolution of friendship ties in groups of children. *Dissertation Abstracts, 27*(10-A), 35-17 to 35-18.

Sharpe, S., & Smith, P. K. (Eds.). (1994). *Teaching bullying in your schools: A practical handbook for teachers.* London: Routledge.

Smith, P. K. (1991). The silent nightmare: Bullying and victimisation in school peer groups. *The Psychologist: Bulletin of the British Psychological Society, 4,* 243–248.

Stephens, R. D., Greenbaum, S., & Garrison, R. W. (1988). *School bullying and victimization: NSSC resource paper.* Malibu, CA: National School Safety Center.

Stephenson, P., & Smith, D. (1989). Bullying in the junior school. In D. P. Tatum & D. A. Lane (Eds.), *Bullying in schools* (pp. 45–57). Stoke-on-Trent, England: Tretham Books.

Toch, T. (1993, November 8). Violence in the schools. *U.S. News & World Report,* 31–37.

Trawick-Smith, J. (1988). "Let's say you're the baby, OK?" Play leadership and following behavior of young children. *Young Children, 43*(5), 51–59.

Walker, H. M. (1993). Anti-social behavior in school. *Journal of Emotional and Behavioral Problems, 2*(1), 20–24.

Youngs, G. A., Rathge, R., Mullis, R., & Mullis, A. (1992). Adolescent stress and self-esteem. In G. R. Walz & J. C. Bleuer (Eds.), *Volume I: Student self-esteem—A vital element of school success.* Ann Arbor, MI: ERIC Counseling and Personnel Services Clearinghouse.

INDEX

ABOUT THE AUTHOR

Richard Hazler, Ph.D., is a Professor of Counselor Education at Ohio University in Athens, Ohio, where he lives with his wife, Kitty. They have two grown daughters, Shannon and Erin. His interest in bullies and victims began as a sixth-grade school teacher, and his direct involvement grew through his work as a school counselor. Over the years he has developed a wide variety of programs for at-risk students, general populations, and the gifted for grade schools, high schools, and universities. In addition to his public school background, Richard has worked as a therapist in universities, the U.S. Army, a prison, and private practice. Firsthand experience, later research studies, publications, and presentations have established him as consultant for schools and the media including television shows such as LEEZA, Life Choices, ABC 20/20, and NBC Dateline.

Richard is the editor of the "Student Focus" column in *Counseling Today* and has held numerous leadership positions in a variety of professional organizations. He has published numerous professional articles, and two of his recently co-authored books for therapists are *The Emerging Professional Counselor: Student Dreams to Professional Realities* (1994) and *Stress Busting Through Personal Empowerment* (1994).